AUTHORITY, POWER AND POLICY
IN THE USSR

AUTHORITY, POWER AND POLICY IN THE USSR

Essays dedicated to Leonard Schapiro

Edited by
T. H. RIGBY, ARCHIE BROWN AND
PETER REDDAWAY

First edition 1980
Reprinted (with alterations) 1983

Published by
THE MACMILLAN PRESS LTD
London and Basingstoke
Companies and representatives
throughout the world

Printed in Hong Kong

British Library Cataloguing in Publication Data

Authority, power and policy in the USSR
  1. Russia – Politics and government – 1917–
  – Addresses, essays, lectures
  I. Schapiro, Leonard
  II. Rigby, Thomas Henry
  III. Brown, Archie   IV. Reddaway, Peter
  320.9′47′084   JN6526 1917

  ISBN 0–333–25702–2 (hardcover)
  ISBN 0–333–34672–6 (paperback)

Contents

Preface to the 1983 Reprint

We are happy that demand for this work has been such as to lead our publisher to reprint in paperback as well as hardcover. The book appears to have been found useful by students as well as by specialists and it is good that it will now be more readily accessible.

The main body of the text remains unaltered, for it has not been necessary to bring it up to date. The combination of broad historical perspectives and more theoretical approaches adopted by the editors and contributors means that the book retains whatever relevance it had on first publication. By way, however, of updating Chapter 8, it is worth mentioning the deaths of two of the leading figures in Brezhnev's Politburo – in December 1980 of A. N. Kosygin (who from October of that year had ceased to be Chairman of the Council of Ministers) and in January 1982 of M. A. Suslov – and as an important development relating to Chapter 9, the removal from Moscow and exile to the city of Gorky in January 1980 of Academician A. D. Sakharov.

1982   T.H.R.
                                                                    A.H.B.
                                                                    P.B.R.

Preface

The idea of this book originated in the minds of several former students of Leonard Schapiro who wished to pay tribute to him on his seventieth birthday, and in so doing to make their own modest contributions to knowledge of a subject he has done much to illuminate. We have not entirely escaped the problems to which such ventures are prone.

Such has been Professor Schapiro's continued vigour as a scholar that the editors of this volume awoke rather late in the day to the fact that he was indeed approaching the landmark of three score years and ten. A late start, taken in conjunction with delays imposed by other commitments already undertaken, has meant that the book is being published closer to his seventy-second birthday than to his seventieth.

Our second problem was the wide gap between what is these days a viable length for a *Festschrift* and the very long list of potential eager contributors to a volume in honour of Leonard Schapiro. His friends – and warm admirers of his scholarship – are to be found in many universities throughout the world. To have invited even a small proportion of these authors to write a chapter would have made the volume impossibly large, while at the same time imposing a highly invidious task of selection upon the editors.

We felt obliged, therefore, to invite contributions only from those who had been students or colleagues of Leonard Schapiro at the London School of Economics and Political Science. Even then, considerations of length prevented us from asking all those whom we would have wished to invite, and there were a few scholars who were unable to accept our invitation because of pressure of other work. In view, however, of Professor Schapiro's distinguished and devoted service to the London School of Economics over the past quarter of a century, the 'LSE connection' is perhaps not an inappropriate one on which to base this *Festschrift*.

As should be clear from the writings of the authors of this volume (both here and elsewhere), Leonard Schapiro's students do not form a particular school of thought. The present authors, who include those who share neither Leonard's views on politics nor his views on political science, are nevertheless united in their admiration for his achievements as a scholar and teacher. (It is perhaps a special tribute to anyone in academic life when people of substantially different political and methodological predispositions recognise the great value of his work.) If anything else unites the contributors, it is a respect for, and aspiration to emulate, Leonard Schapiro's combination of meticulous scholarship with an interest in large and basic questions about the workings and nature of the Soviet political system and interpretation of its history.

From one common dilemma of *Festschrift* editors, we resolved to be free. Leonard Schapiro's own scholarship has ranged well beyond Soviet politics and history to (most notably) nineteenth-century Russian literature and social and political thought. A collection of articles which ranged so widely, without the intellectual unity which can be imposed by a single author, would have been a miscellany rather than a coherent book. Our aim from the outset, therefore, has been to produce a book which would make its own distinctive contribution to an understanding of Soviet politics, concentrating on the central themes of authority, power and policy which have figured prominently in Leonard Schapiro's own work.

The one chapter in a different *genre* from the others is the first – in which T. H. Rigby writes a brief assessment and appreciation of Schapiro's contribution to scholarship. A fuller account would have to speak of his influence as a teacher, particularly through his lectures and seminars at the LSE, of his role as guest lecturer and conference participant in many countries, as well as of his services to numerous academic institutions. Any such account, moreover, could be no more than a progress report, since Leonard Schapiro remains an active and highly productive scholar. Yet it is not too early to express gratitude for his services to scholarship and enlightenment, and for the personal gifts of his teaching, help and friendship. This is what we seek to do, in the most appropriate way we can think of, in this book.

1979   T. H. R.
                                                              A. H. B.
                                                              P. B. R.

Notes on the Contributors

ARCHIE BROWN, born in Annan, Scotland, in 1938, is a Fellow of St Antony's College, Oxford, and Lecturer in Soviet Institutions at the University of Oxford. After taking the B.Sc.(Econ.), specialising in Government, at the London School of Economics and Political Science from 1959 to 1962, he spent the next two years studying – under Leonard Schapiro's supervision – Russian political and social thought in the second half of the eighteenth century (in particular, the thought of S. E. Desnitsky). From 1964 to 1971, when he moved to Oxford, he was Lecturer in Politics at Glasgow University. He has been Visiting Professor of Political Science at Yale University and at the University of Connecticut and he gave the 1980 Henry L. Stimson Lectures at Yale. Mr Brown is the author of *Soviet Politics and Political Science* (1974) and *Political Change within Communist Systems* (forthcoming) and editor of and contributor to *The Soviet Union since the Fall of Khrushchev* (with Michael Kaser, 1975; 2nd edn, 1978), *Political Culture and Political Change in Communist States* (with Jack Gray, 1977; 2nd edn, 1979), *Soviet Policy for the 1980s* (with Michael Kaser, 1982) and *The Cambridge Encyclopedia of Russia and the Soviet Union* (with John Fennell, Michael Kaser and H. T. Willetts, 1982).

GRAEME GILL, who was born in Melbourne, Australia, in 1947, is Lecturer in Government at the University of Sydney. After studying at Monash University (where he took BA and MA degrees) from 1966 to 1973, he completed under Leonard Schapiro's supervision at the LSE in 1975 a doctorate on the role of the peasants in the Russian Revolution. From 1976 he was Tutor and from 1978 Lecturer in Political Science at the University of Tasmania before taking up his present appointment at Sydney. Dr Gill is the author of *Peasants and Government in the Russian Revolution* (1979).

NEIL HARDING was born in Pontypridd, Glamorgan, in 1942. He

graduated in Politics from University College, Swansea, in 1963, and from 1963 to 1965 studied Russian political thought, especially that of Mikhail Bakunin, under Leonard Schapiro's supervision at the LSE. Mr Harding has been Lecturer since 1965 and Senior Lecturer since 1980 in Politics and Russian Studies at University College, Swansea. During the 1981–2 academic year he was a Senior Associate Member of St Antony's College, Oxford. Mr Harding is the author of *Lenin's Political Thought* (vol. 1, 1977; vol. 2, 1981) and (with Richard Taylor) of *Marxism in Russia: Key Documents* (1983) and the editor of *The State in Socialist Society* (1983). For his study of *Lenin's Political Thought*, he was awarded the Isaac Deutscher Memorial Prize for 1981–2.

A. KEMP-WELCH was born in Morpeth, Northumberland, in 1949. He studied at the LSE from 1967 to 1975, taking the B.Sc.(Econ.) and then a Ph.D. in the Department of Government. His doctoral thesis on 'The Union of Soviet Writers, 1932–36' was written under the supervision of Peter Reddaway and Leonard Schapiro. From 1975 until 1979 Dr Kemp-Welch was a Research Fellow at St Antony's College, Oxford, and since 1979 he has been Lecturer in Politics at the University of Nottingham. He is the translator into English of the Polish text of the negotiations between workers and government at Gdansk 1980 and editor of a forthcoming volume incorporating that translation. He is also the author of *Stalin and the Literary Intelligentsia* (forthcoming).

ALEC NOVE was born in Petrograd in 1915 but educated in England. He was a student at the LSE and took the B.Sc.(Econ.) in 1936. From 1947 to 1958 he was in the Civil Service (mainly at the Board of Trade) and from 1958 to 1963 he was Reader in Russian Social and Economic Studies at the University of London (and a colleague of Leonard Schapiro at the LSE). From 1963 until 1979 he was Director of the Institute of Soviet and East European Studies at Glasgow University and from 1963 until 1982 Professor of Economics at Glasgow. He has been a senior visiting scholar at, among other institutions, the Russian Institute of Columbia University, New York; St Antony's College, Oxford; and the University of Paris. Professor Nove was awarded an honorary doctorate by the University of Giessen in 1977 and elected a Fellow of the British Academy in 1978. His publications include *The Soviet Economy* (1961; 3rd edn, 1969), *Was Stalin Really Necessary?* (1964),

The Soviet Middle East (with J. A. Newth, 1965), *An Economic History of the USSR* (1969), *Socialist Economics* (co-editor with D. M. Nuti, 1972), *Efficiency Criteria for Nationalised Industries* (1973), *Stalinism and After* (1975), *The Soviet Economic System* (1977) and *Political Economy and Soviet Socialism* (1979).

PETER REDDAWAY, who was born in Cambridge in 1939, is Senior Lecturer in Political Science at the LSE. After studying as an undergraduate at Cambridge University, he pursued graduate studies at Harvard and Moscow Universities and at the LSE, where from 1964 to 1965 he studied the politics of post-Stalin literature under Leonard Schapiro's supervision. Since 1965 he has taught at the LSE. Mr Reddaway is the editor or author of the following books: *Lenin: the Man, the Theorist, the Leader: a Reappraisal* (co-editor with Leonard Schapiro, 1967), *Soviet Short Stories*, vol. II (1968), *Uncensored Russia: the Human Rights Movement in the Soviet Union* (1972) and *Russia's Political Hospitals: The Abuse of Psychiatry in the Soviet Union* (with Sidney Bloch, 1977).

T. H. RIGBY, born in Melbourne in 1925, is Professorial Fellow in Political Science at the Research School of Social Sciences of the Australian National University. After wartime service in the Australian Army, he studied political science and Russian at the University of Melbourne, followed by postgraduate research in Soviet politics at the LSE (Ph.D. 1954). In 1956–7, as a Research Officer at the LSE, he assisted Leonard Schapiro in research for his book, *The Communist Party of the Soviet Union*. Dr Rigby subsequently worked in the Research Department of the UK Foreign Office and later in the UK Embassy in Moscow before becoming a Senior Lecturer and Associate Professor of Russian at the Australian National University. He took up his present position in 1964, and has been a senior visiting scholar in several different countries. Dr Rigby is the author of *Communist Party Membership in the USSR 1917–1967* (1968) and *Lenin's Government: Sovnarkom 1917–1922* (1979), and editor of and contributor to *Stalin* (1966), *The Disintegrating Monolith: Pluralist Trends in the Communist World* (with J. D. B. Miller, 1965) and *Political Legitimation in Communist States* (with Ferenc Fehér, 1982).

RICHARD TAYLOR was born in London in 1946. As an undergraduate, he studied modern languages at Cambridge University from 1964 to 1967 and, as a graduate student, the politics of the Soviet cinema – under the supervision of Leonard Schapiro – at the LSE from 1968 to 1970. Since 1971 he has been Lecturer in Politics and Russian Studies at University College, Swansea. Dr Taylor is the author of *The Politics of the Soviet Cinema, 1917–1929* (1979), *Film Propaganda: Soviet Russia and Nazi Germany* (1979) and *Marxism in Russia: Key Documents* (with Neil Harding, 1983).

1 Leonard Schapiro as Student of Soviet Politics

T. H. Rigby

Leonard Bertram Schapiro was born in Glasgow on 22 April 1908. His family was of Russian-Jewish background, and Leonard himself spent much of his childhood in Riga and St Petersburg-Petrograd. It is London, however, where he has made his life. After studying at St Paul's School and University College, London, he was called to the bar at Gray's Inn in 1932, practising on the London and Western circuits. This first career was interrupted by war service, initially in the Monitoring Service of the BBC and then on the General Staff at the War Office, where his knowledge of languages, particularly of Russian, proved a valuable asset. This experience deepened his interest in Russia, and in the nature and origins of the Soviet political and social order, which he began to study systematically after the war while resuming his practice as a barrister. Publications started appearing, beginning with a series of closely researched and thoughtful articles in the field of international law,[1] a subject on which he also lectured part-time at the London School of Economics and Political Science, followed in the early 1950s by his first essays on aspects of the Soviet political system proper, one on the trade unions[2] and one on the Communist Party between the Eighteenth and Nineteenth Congresses.[3] In 1955 his book *The Origins of the Communist Autocracy* appeared, 'the story of how a group of determined men seized power for themselves in Russia in 1917, and kept others from sharing it; and the consequences which ensued both for themselves and for their political rivals when it became evident that they enjoyed but little popular support'.[4] Schapiro's close concern with the interconnection of power, authority and policy, which serves as the subject of this book, is already apparent in this formulation. In the same year he accepted an invitation to join the full-time teaching staff of the London School of Economics as Lecturer and from 1963 as Professor of Political Science with special reference to Russia, a chair he held until his retirement in 1975. It was an unusual path to a chair in political science, perhaps somewhat reminiscent of Voznesensky's 'parabolic trajectory', and one which gave him a distinct blend of knowledge and commitments which goes far to explain both the style and content of his work as a student of modern Russia, a matter to which we shall return.

Schapiro's writings reflect three main lines of enquiry, in which he figures respectively as political historian, political scientist and theorist, and historian of ideas. They all show, however, an inner unity of vision and concept, and different lines often intersect in the same work. Apart from *The Origin of the Communist Autocracy*, Schapiro's outstanding contribution on the political history of the USSR is his *The Communist Party of the Soviet Union*, which came out in 1960 and appeared in a revised and updated edition in 1970,[5] remaining the fullest and most influential treatment of its subject in a Western language. These two larger studies are flanked by numerous essays, both of a more general character[6] and on such special topics as the development of army–party relations,[7] the Jews in pre- and post-revolutionary Russia,[8] and Soviet historiography.[9]

As a political scientist Schapiro is a methodological conservative, whose mode and language of analysis owe much to his wide reading in history, law and normative political theory, while taking little from the mainstream political science of recent decades, much of which he would perhaps see as a misguided attempt to import from the natural sciences a type of conceptual rigour and *zakonomermost'* offering little for understanding the affairs of men. It is ironical that a strong movement has emerged seeking to dissolve the study of Soviet politics more or less completely in this mainstream, at just the time when doubts about its assumptions and achievements have been growing on its home ground. In this matter Schapiro may perhaps be seen as having enjoyed what Trotsky termed 'the privilege of backwardness'. Be this as it may, he has shown what superb results can still be attained through the traditional virtues of careful and exhaustive study of the facts, precision of thought and language, objectivity of analysis which by no means excludes the exercise of moral judgement, and the marriage of common sense with *Verstehen* in the Weberian sense. These virtues may be seen to good advantage both in his excellent introductory textbook, *The Government and Politics of the Soviet Union*,[10] and in his articles on particular aspects of the regime and its policies, such as the government machine,[11] the legal system,[12] the party,[13] and Soviet relations with other states and communist parties.[14] In his essays in broader interpretative analysis, they join forces with his deep study of classical and nineteenth-century political theory to produce challenging statements, particularly on the validity and uses of the concept of 'totalitarianism'.[15]

All Schapiro's work since *The Origin of the Communist Autocracy* can be seen as an exploration in time of the significance of the events described there, on the one hand examining their consequences for the evolving Soviet system and on the other tracing their roots in the Russia of the past. Since Schapiro was convinced that what the Bolsheviks made of the Russia they appropriated was determined not just by its objective conditions but largely by the ideas in their heads, tracing these roots meant first and foremost delving into the political and ideological soil of late Imperial Russia. Of particular interest here is his *Rationalism and Nationalism in Russian Nineteenth-Century Political Thought*, based on a series of lectures he gave at Yale in 1965.[16] The central dilemma for Russia, as Schapiro sees it, was that, while the autocracy was the dominant source of her backwardness, the *tabula rasa* solution of sweeping away the autocracy and substituting something entirely new could not fail to prove illusory, leading to the revival of autocracy in a new form, as was borne out by Russia's experience after 1917. What hope there was for an escape from this dilemma lay in a liberal-conservative strategy of improvement and institution-building within the framework of the old order, a hope which acquired some basis with the reforms of the 1860s and the later creation of quasi-parliamentary institutions, but which was frittered away by the naive radicalism and impracticality of liberal politicians and finally dashed by the premature suicide of the old order. Against this background the personality of Lenin acquires special importance as the connecting link between the old autocracy and the new, and it is not surprising that Schapiro has devoted much attention, both in his books and in separate articles, to elucidating the motives and actions of 'this strange and troubled genius'.[17]

Schapiro, I believe, would reject endeavours to build a value-free science of human action not only as theoretically mistaken but also as morally irresponsible, a point on which he shares common ground with many who would regard themselves as his political opponents. To repress or conceal one's values and opinions is as unbecoming to the scholar as to allow them to cloud his judgement or to act as a substitute for evidence and argument. Schapiro is not a coldly clinical analyst of modern Russia, but a man involved through his family background and youthful experiences in the events and problems he seeks to comprehend, cherishing the generous, humane and liberal sentiments which enabled part of the old intelligentsia to contribute so much to enriching and liberating the human spirit,[18] and abhorring the brutal and arbitrary authoritarianism and arid dogmatism which the old political order communicated to its ultimate destroyers and its present heirs. And yet how English, too, are the qualities, convictions and standards infusing Schapiro's work: the suspicion of vague abstractions, the distrust of panaceas, the respect for hard facts, common sense and practical judgement, the high store set on tolerance, fairness and diversity, the insistence on law as a necessary if not sufficient condition of justice and as protection against the twin evils of arbitrariness and anarchy, the abhorrence of irresponsible power.

While Schapiro would reject assumptions that the Soviet Union (or any other country) must of 'historical necessity' evolve or undergo revolutionary transformation in any particular direction, no more would he expect the system to remain immutably fixed. Nor, unlike some other analysts of Soviet affairs, would he reject the significance of 'in-system' and piecemeal change, since 'reform of the political system can only be achieved within the limits of existing institutions, otherwise the reform will prove illusory, because the old institutional framework will survive through all the vicissitudes of apparent change'.[19] Moreover, although in terms of freedom and justice only modest comfort may be drawn from the policies and practices of the Khrushchev and Brezhnev regimes, at least there is progress from the rampant horrors of the Stalin tyranny. Indeed, as Schapiro speculated in the admittedly more sanguine atmosphere before the Czechoslovak reform movement was crushed, 'if the Soviet Union should eventually succeed in reconciling Leninism with the political realities of human society, there will (as has happened before with extreme doctrines) be nothing left of Leninism but the name'.[20]

The balance of change since the deposing of Khrushchev has been drawn in different ways. Many, including Schapiro, impressed by such developments as the increased repression of active dissent, the partial 'rehabilitation' of Stalin, and the extreme rigidity of political structures and personnel, are inclined to view the period as one of grey, if not black, reaction. Others, pointing to evidence for wider and more genuine consultation of expert and interested opinion in policy-making, greater diversity of officially tolerated expression on less sensitive issues, the narrowing of inequalities in real income, and other positive changes, see overall improvement, rather than a falling-back, as compared with the Khruschev period.[21] What most would probably accept is that while piecemeal change is inevitable, and indeed demonstrable, its immediate manifestations are contradictory and its long-term cumulative effects incalculable.

Fairly general agreement would also be forthcoming for the proposition that while the structure and distribution of power, the terms in which authority is claimed and exercised, and the perception and choice of policy alternatives all represent in some degree autonomous spheres of change, what happens in each of them also exercises powerful constraints on what can happen in the others. Certainly an intense awareness of this has always informed Leonard Schapiro's writings on Soviet politics, both in elucidating the past and in evaluating current developments and the possibilities they hold for the future. Along with a sophisticated appreciation of the interconnectedness of authority, power and policy, moreover, his works are permeated by a passionate concern with the implications for the human spirit of the outcomes of their interaction. The interweaving of these two strands of perception, the one intellectual and the other moral, is perhaps the key to both the distinctiveness and the importance of Schapiro's work. Of the many splendid examples which could serve to illustrate this, the reader's attention is particularly drawn to Schapiro's epilogue to the second edition of his *The Communist Party of the Soviet Union*, for no better introduction could be found to the present work than this brief essay.

NOTES

1. 'The Soviet Concept of International Law', *Year Book of World Affairs*, vol. ii (London, 1948) pp. 272–310; 'Soviet Participation in International Institutions', ibid., vol. iii (London, 1949) pp. 205–40; 'The Post-War Treaties of the Soviet Union', ibid., vol. iv (London, 1950) pp. 130–50; 'The Limits of Russian Territorial Waters in the Baltic', *British Year Book of International Law, 1950* (London, 1951) pp. 439–48; 'Repatriation of Deserters', *British Year Book of International Law, 1952* (London, 1953) pp. 310–24;

'European Court of Human Rights', *University of Western Australia Annual Law Review*, II (1951–3) 65–79. Leonard Schapiro is author of all the items referred to in the notes to this chapter, except that in note 21. These notes are intended to serve as a fairly comprehensive, although not exhaustive, bibliography of his writings on Russia and the USSR. They omit, in particular, his prefaces to several books, some of his briefer occasional articles and his many reviews, some of which, perhaps especially those published in the *New York Review of Books*, constitute substantial and original essays.

2. 'Il movimento sindicale nell 'Unione Sovietica', *Sindicalismo*, I, no. 4–6 (Oct–Dec 1951) 32–50.

3. 'Developments in the Soviet Communist Party between 1939 and 1952', *Year Book of World Affairs*, vol. VII (London, 1953) pp. 125–48.

4. *The Origin of the Communist Autocracy: Political Opposition in the Soviet State. First Phase: 1917–1922* (London, 1955; 2nd edn, 1977). The passage cited is the opening sentence of the Preface to the 1st edn.

5. *The Communist Party of the Soviet Union* (New York and London, 1960; 2nd edn, revised and enlarged, New York and London, 1970).

6. 'The Basis and Development of the Soviet Polity', in Milorad M. Drachkovich (ed.), *Fifty Years of Communism in Russia* (University Park, Pa, and London, 1968) pp. 48–74. See also 'Out of the Dustbin of History', *Problems of Communism*, XVI, no. 6 (Nov–Dec 1967) 86–91; 'Communism', *Encyclopaedia Britannica*, 15th edn, vol. IV (1974) pp. 1020–7.

7. 'The Birth of the Red Army', in B. H. Liddell Hart (ed.), *The Soviet Army* (London, 1956) pp. 24–32; 'The Great Purge', ibid., pp. 65–72. See also 'The Political Background of the Russo-German War', ibid., pp. 93–9.

8. 'The Role of the Jews in the Russian Revolutionary Movement', *Slavonic and East European Review*, XL, no. 94 (1961) 148–67; 'The Russian Background of the Anglo-American Jewish Emigration', in The Jewish Historical Society of England, *Transactions*, XX (1964) 215–31; Introduction to Lionel Kochan (ed.), *The Jews in Soviet Russia since 1917* (London, 1970) pp. 1–13.

9. 'A New History – A New Mythology', *Problems of Communism*, IX, no. 1 (Jan–Feb 1960) 58–61; 'Continuity and Change in the New History of the CPSU', in John Keep (ed.), *Contemporary History in the Soviet Mirror* (London, 1964) pp. 69–82; 'The Conflict between Tsar and Society', *Government and Opposition*, I, no. 2 (1966) 271–8.

10. *The Government and Politics of the Soviet Union* (London and New York, 1965; 6th edn, 1977). See also Schapiro's useful outline, 'The Structure of the Soviet State, Government and Politics', in Robert Auty and Dimitri Obolensky (eds), *An Introduction to Russian History* (Cambridge, 1976) pp. 331–59.

11. 'Soviet Government Today' (with S. V. Utechin), *Political Quarterly*, XXXII, no. 2 (1961) 124–38.

12. 'Judicial Practice and Legal Reform', *Soviet Survey*, no. 29 (July–Sep 1959) 54–60; 'Prospects for the Rule of Law', *Problems of Communism*, XIV, no. 2 (Mar–Apr 1965) 2–7.

13. *The USSR and the Future: An Analysis of the New Program of the CPSU* (New York and London, 1963) (Schapiro was editor and author of the Introduction, pp. xi–xix, and the chapter entitled 'The New Rules of the CPSU', pp. 179–96); 'The Party's New Rules', *Problems of Communism*, XI, no. 1 (Jan–Feb 1962) 28–35; 'The Twenty-Third Congress of the CPSU', *Survey*, no. 60 (July 1966) 72–

84; 'Keynote-Compromise', *Problems of Communism*, xx, no. 4 (July–Aug 1970) pp. 2–8; 'The General Department of the CC of the CPSU', *Survey*, xxi, no. 3 (Summer 1975) 53–65; 'The International Department of the CPSU: Key to Soviet Policy', *International Journal* (Toronto), xlii, no. 1 (1976–7) 41–55; 'The Party and the State', *Survey*, no. 38 (Oct 1961) pp. 111–16; 'The Soviet Politburo: How Strong is Brezhnev?', *Lugano Review*, no. 1 (1975) 4–6; see also note 3.

14. 'Two Pillars of Communism: A Study of Russo-Chinese Relations', *Round Table*, li, no. 202 (Mar 1961) 144–53; 'The Chinese Ally from the Soviet Point of View', in Kurt London (ed.), *Unity and Contradiction: Major Aspects of Sino-Soviet Relations* (New York, 1962) pp. 353–74; 'The Sino-Soviet Dispute and the Twenty-Second Congress', *India Quarterly*, xviii, no. 1 (1962) 3–9; Foreword to Guenther Nollan, *International Communism and World Revolution: History and Methods* (London, 1961); *The Soviet Union and the World Communist Movement* (Canberra: Australian National University, 1968). Here also may be mentioned three special reports of the Institute for the Study of Conflict, London, of which Schapiro was a member of a panel of authors: *The Peacetime Strategy of the Soviet Union* (Feb–Mar 1973); *European Security and the Soviet Problem* (Jan 1972); and *The Strategic Intentions of the Soviet Union: Fallacies in Western Assessment* (Mar 1978).

15. *Totalitarianism* (London, 1972); 'The Nature of Total Power', *Political Quarterly*, xxix, no. 5, (1958) 105–13; 'Reflections on the Changing Role of the Party in the Totalitarian Polity', *Studies in Comparative Communism*, ii, no. 2 (Apr 1969) 1–13; 'The Roles of the Monolithic Party under the Totalitarian Leader' (with Lewis), in John Wilson Lewis (ed.), *Party Leadership and Revolutionary Power in China* (Cambridge, 1970) pp. 114–48; 'Totalitarianism in Foreign Policy', in Kurt London (ed.), *The Soviet Impact on World Politics* (New York, 1974) pp. 3–21; 'Totalitarianism', in *Marxism, Communism and Western Society* (Freiburg), viii (1973) pp. 188–201. Other broadly interpretative papers include: 'The Party and the State', *Survey*, no. 38 (Oct 1961) 111–16; 'Collective Lack of Leadership', *Survey*, no. 70–1 (Winter–Spring 1969) 193–9; 'Has Russia Changed?', *Foreign Affairs*, xxxviii, no. 3, Apr 1960, pp. 391–401; *Political Change in the Soviet Union since Stalin's Death* (Paris: Centre de Recherches sur L'URSS et les Pays de l'Est, 1965); Introduction and 'Putting the Lid on Leninism: Opposition and Dissent in the Communist One-Party States', in Leonard Schapiro (ed.), *Political Opposition in One-Party States* (London, 1972) pp. 1–14, 33–57; 'The Effects of Detente on the Quality of Life in the Soviet Union', in Robert Conquest *et al.*, *Defending America* (New York, 1977) pp. 217–30.

16. *Rationalism and Nationalism in Russian Nineteenth-Century Political Thought* (New Haven, Conn., and London, 1967). Other writings on the history of Russian political thought include: 'The Pre-Revolutionary Intelligentsia and the Legal Order', in Richard Pipes (ed.), *The Russian Intelligentsia* (New York, 1961) pp. 19–31; 'The *Vekhi* Group and the Mystique of Revolution', *Slavonic and East European Review*, xxxiv, no. 1 (1955–6) 56–76; 'Marxism behind the Iron Curtain', in Henry L. Plaine (ed.), *Darwin, Marx and Wagner: A Symposium* (Columbus, Ohio, 1962) pp. 117–38; 'Plechanov als Politiker', *Forschungen zur Osteuropaeischer Geschichte*, vol. ix (Berlin, 1961); Introduction to R. N. Carew Hunt, *The Theory and Practice of Communism* (Harmondsworth, 1963); and 'The

Political Thought of the First Provisional Government', in Richard Pipes (ed.), *Revolutionary Russia* (Cambridge, Mass., 1968) pp. 97–113. See also 'Some Afterthoughts on Solzhenitsyn', *Russian Review*, XXXIII, no. 4 (Oct 1974) 416–21; and 'Changing Patterns in the Theory of Revolution and Insurgency', *Royal United Service Institute Journal*, CXV, no. 659 (Sep 1970) 3–12.

17. Leonard Schapiro and Peter Reddaway (eds), *Lenin: The Man, the Theorist, the Leader: A Reappraisal* (London, 1967) p. 19. See also 'Lenin's Contribution to Politics', *Political Quarterly*, XXXV, no. 1, (1964) 9–22; and 'Lenin's Heritage', *Encounter*, XXXV, no. 1 (July 1970) 57–9.

18. If the value which Schapiro places on the qualities and legacy of the old liberal intelligentsia is implicit in many of his writings, his translation of Turgenev's novella *Spring Torrents*, with his critical essay on it (London, 1972), together with his *Turgenev: His Life and Times* (London, 1978), may be seen as his most concrete and touching tributes to them.

19. *Rationalism and Nationalism in Russian Nineteenth-Century Political Thought*, p. 168.

20. *Lenin: The Man, the Theorist, the Leader*, p. 12.

21. Such views have been most effectively argued by Jerry F. Hough in his *The Soviet Union and Social Science Theory* (Cambridge, Mass., and London, 1977), Part 1.

2 A Conceptual Approach to Authority, Power and Policy in the Soviet Union

T. H. Rigby

Force is an element in any political system and its crucial role both in establishing and maintaining the Soviet regime scarcely needs demonstrating. However, in most systems the compliance of the population with the demands of their rulers depends not only on the threat or actuality of coercion, but also on a measure, at least, of belief in the 'legitimacy' of such demands, and I would claim that the Soviet Union is no exception to this. In other words we are dealing here with a system of *authority*, and not just of power.

Let me make it clearer what is being asserted here. It is certainly not argued that compliance would be assured if it were not backed by coercion, let alone that the Soviet rulers could count on gaining election in a free vote. This, however, would perhaps need to be said of most structures of political authority throughout history. The concept of 'legitimacy' is simple in principle but notoriously slippery in application.[1] In any social setting people's actions are governed not only by what is expedient but also by what is right and proper. Sometimes the expedient and the proper are seen as conflicting, and a choice is made between them; more often they are interwoven, and it is typically very difficult to know how far a person acts as he does because there are advantages in doing so, or costs in not doing so, or because he believes it right to. However, the fact that the strength and nature of 'belief' in social norms as a factor in determining adherence to them cannot easily be defined or measured is not usually taken as grounds for rejecting the importance of the normative dimension to social behaviour.

'Legitimacy' is a central element in the normative system of a

9

political order. A system is 'legitimate' insofar as the compliance of the ruled with the demands of their rulers is governed by a belief that the grounds on which these demands are issued are valid. Such beliefs may not be universal in the society, they may vary in character and intensity from group to group, from individual to individual, and from case to case, and they may prove very brittle even when they seem rock-hard: it is not only in Imperial China that rulers have suddenly lost the 'mandate of heaven'. The grounds of legitimacy are similarly diverse: traditional rules of succession, election by a majority or according to some other accepted formula, demonstration of heroic or superhuman powers, etc. Moreover, two or more principles of legitimacy may be at work in the same political system, perhaps in different 'mixes', depending on the social group or field of action concerned.

When we consider a political order as a system of *authority* we usually have in mind a particular pattern of legitimacy combined with a particular structure of power, the two being as closely intertwined as norm and expediency tend to be on all levels of social behaviour. The obstacles to precise description and measurement attendant on this last fact, and on the complexities sketched in the previous paragraph, have made authority a rather unfashionable subject of political study in a period when political science has been dominated by an urge to the analytical rigour and quantitative verification proper to certain of the natural sciences. In the study of communist systems this has been compounded by a certain reluctance on the part of Western scholars to concede any basis of legitimacy to these regimes, or if they do, to reduce it to an over-rationalised notion of 'ideology'. There is some excuse for this. The overt claims to legitimacy by these regimes are indeed couched mainly in terms of Marxist–Leninist doctrines in which, so some Eastern European intellectuals tell us, no one believes, and least of all the rulers themselves. In fact, the sources of legitimation are much broader and more complex than this, a matter we shall return to later. So far as belief in the 'ideology' is concerned, there is admittedly little prospect that arguments about this could be resolved on the basis of evidence whose objectivity and conclusive-ness will command general assent. My own view is that, so far as the Soviet Union is concerned, it would be as misleading to assume a universal cynicism or indifference towards the official legitimating values and world-view as to take avowals of them at face value, but that they probably acquire much of their force by association with other sources of legitimacy.[2] It would be by no means unique to the Soviet system of authority if there turned out to be considerable discrepancy between the pattern of legitimating values in terms of which power is claimed and exercised and those in terms of which compliance is in fact granted.

How, then, are we to characterise the Soviet political order as a system of authority? If we check it against Max Weber's classical typology of rational – legal, traditional and charismatic authority,[3] we find it displays (in different 'mixes' at different times) elements of all three, but without really being 'caught' by any of them. This, of course, would scarcely surprise Weber, who expected his 'ideal types' to appear rarely, if ever, in pure form, and in his discussion of actual social structures sketched out all sorts of sub-types as well as transitional and mixed types of authority. Nevertheless, I will argue that in characterising the authority system of the USSR it will be necessary not only to combine his categories in a distinctive pattern, but also to introduce analytical distinctions that he fails to make.

Although modes of legitimation form the starting-point of Weber's characterisation of authority-types, he holds that these are associated with distinctive modes of administration and kinds of administrative staffs, and these figure large in his analysis. Despite certain theoretical and empirical difficulties which need not detain us at this point,[4] the notion of *congruence* between the grounds on which the rulers claim the right to command, the structures through which their commands are transmitted, and the way the persons staffing these structures are qualified, recruited, rewarded and relate to the rulers, is one of obvious importance when we come to study particular authority systems. With this in mind, let us look a little more closely at how Weber's typology fits the Soviet case.

Rational grounds, 'resting on a belief in the "legality" of patterns of normative rules and the right of those elevated to authority under such rules to issue commands',[5] are very prominent in the validity claimed by Soviet leaders for their exercise of power. The political system is said to be derived from a scientific world-view, the derivation being argued in rational terms. The structure and powers of particular institutions are prescribed in formal documents (the constitutions of the USSR and the constituent republics, the CPSU rules, etc.) and their decisions are clothed in legal forms (laws, regulations, administrative orders, resolutions of party bodies). Nor is all this a *mere* façade, since both the character of institutions and their substantive activities do *partly* correspond with the legal forms. Moreover, the machinery through which the rulers' commands are implemented appears to conform closely with Weber's characterisation of a 'bureaucratic administrative staff', a central feature, in his view, of the 'pure type' of rational-legal authority: for it consists of a hierarchy of offices – each with a prescribed competence, staffed by appointive, salaried, career officials who have no property in their office or the facilities it presides over, and who occupy it at the will of their superiors. Indeed, the collective omnicompetence of such bureaucratic hierarchies in Soviet society, all of them dependent on the supreme political authorities, have been seen by some analysts as rendering it the bureaucratic system *par excellence*.[6]

And yet there are serious difficulties in characterising the Soviet regime as a system of rational–legal authority. Some of these, relating to the nature of Soviet bureaucracy, we shall take up later. Let us here just note some of the more obvious problems. The Soviet Constitution, even in its latest variant, is a notoriously misleading and incomplete guide to the distribution of power in the system. The Soviets, formally sovereign, play in fact an entirely dependent and largely cosmetic role. The same applies to the 'supreme' bodies of the party, its congresses and conferences, and in somewhat lesser degree its central, republican and local committees. Federal forms clothe an extremely centralised power-structure. Most important of all, the role of party officials in the work of government, though referred to in a vague and general formula in article six of the Constitution, is nowhere spelt out in concrete, formal terms indicating just where the powers of party bodies end and those of government bodies begin. This core aspect of the Soviet system, the party–state relationship, is regulated, as it always has been, by discretion and not by law.

There is another whole dimension to this: the Soviet regime, as Leonard Schapiro has frequently reminded us, has never been prepared to limit itself within the rules which it itself prescribes. Most notoriously does this apply in the administration of the criminal law, especially in cases seen as having political implications: the extra-legal licence permitted the police and the 'guidance' of judges by party instructions. Though the 'dictatorship of the proletariat', described as 'power unlimited by any laws', is no longer an officially-claimed attribute of the system, and the scale of arbitrary police repression was drastically curtailed after Stalin's death, the regime remains prepared to employ extra-legal measures to combat political non-conformity, as Peter Reddaway reminds us in this volume. Moreover, if there are times when it is ready to punish where no punishment is due, there are others when it prefers to abstain from punishment where the law has, in fact, been violated. In the economy this is often seen as being so widespread as to be essential to its effective operation, since managers are constantly being placed in situations where their tasks cannot be achieved while observing all the laws, regulations and instructions to which they are subject.[7]

However we classify the Soviet authority system, surely we cannot call it 'traditional'. After all, the regime is forever proclaiming and celebrating its origins in a revolution to overthrow the whole existing order and its destiny to totally transform social reality on the way to 'communism'. Yet even here qualifications are called for. Formal doctrines notwithstanding, fostering an attachment to traditional symbols (the Kremlin, Russian national heroes, etc.) is a prominent element in the process of political socialisation, and efforts are made to canalise the attitudes so formed to foster an identity with the existing political order and leadership. In the thirties and forties this was even taken to the point of promoting the images of dominating Russian rulers of bygone times as a sort of 'calk' of the figure of Stalin. For large circles of party and government officials, and police and army officers, identification with the historical Russian state and nation appears to provide an important source of loyalty to the regime, while among ordinary Russians, however cynically they may themselves sometimes regard their leaders and their policies, one frequently encounters hostile reaction to foreign criticism as a slur on what, after all, is *nashe* – 'ours'.

On a different level, it has often been pointed out how quickly the revolutionary Bolshevik regime took on the authoritarian–bureaucratic features of its Imperial predecessor, and recent studies of Russian 'political culture' have brought out important continuities in this on both the élite and mass levels.[8] The origins of some segments of the government machine go back more than a century and a half to the ministries established under Speransky, or even longer to Peter the Great's *kollegii*. There are many indications of behavioural as well as structural continuities; hence the proclivity of Soviet feuilletonists to invoke the satires of Gogol and Saltykov-Shchedrin when lampooning the pathologies of contemporary bureaucracy. Thus traditional elements of both an objective and a subjective character do play *some* part in the Soviet authority system.

There will be less hesitation in identifying charismatic elements in the authority system. Granted nothing could have been further from the intention of the modest and matter-of-fact Lenin than to claim personal authority on the basis of *charisma*, defined by Weber as 'a certain quality of an individual personality by virtue of which he is set apart from ordinary men and treated as endowed with supernatural, superhuman, or at least specifically exceptional powers or qualities'.[9] And yet there is no doubt that the men he gathered around him, who formed the core of his Bolshevik movement, and helped him to establish the Soviet state, were bound together by something more than a cool rational conviction in the correctness of his theories and policies; for many, perhaps nearly all in the inner circles of the party, there was also the shared experience of having 'fallen under his spell' and a shared belief in his exceptional powers and qualities.[10] They were, in fact, not just 'members', as in a formal organisation, but 'followers', as in a charismatic movement. The great authority that Lenin exercised within the infant Soviet regime cannot be explained merely in terms of his formal office as Chairman of the Council of People's Commissars (in fact, the powers attaching to this office under Lenin were as much a function of Lenin's personal authority as the reverse) nor of his membership of such party bodies as the Central Committee and Politburo.

If the personal charisma of Lenin was thus an element in the initial Soviet authority structure, the latter also rested in large part on the special hold which the party, as an organisation, had over its members and which also smacked of charisma.[11] Adherence to this revolutionary Marxist movement had the emotional impact of 'enlightenment' or 'revelation', and of commitment to an authority which possessed the secrets of history and the means to the salvation of humanity. In this context the 'Word' was the word of Marx, and Lenin was for some its fallible interpreter, for others its 'prophet', for others again its embodiment.

The transformation of Lenin's revolutionary movement into a ruling party set in train processes which Weber characterises as 'the routinisation of charisma'. The followers, who have formerly lived 'in a community of faith and enthusiasm, on gifts, "booty", or sporadic acquisition', become office-holders, and 'in the long run "make their living" out of their "calling" in a material sense as well.

Indeed, this must be the case if the movement is not to disintegrate. Hence, the routinisation of charisma also takes the form of the appropriation of powers of control and of economic advantages by the followers or disciples, and of regulation of the recruitment of these groups.'[12] At the same time, 'the "laity" becomes differentiated from the "clergy"',[13] i.e. the rank-and-file party membership from the professional party officials.

After the death of Lenin, both these charismatic elements in the regime's authority, heretofore completely genuine and uncontrived, became objects of deliberate propaganda and manipulation. Now that party membership no longer meant a life of sacrifice and deprivation but rather the path to power, social recognition and relative comfort, intense personal conviction in its revelatory and saving grace was progressively transformed into a contrived, conventional litany. On the other hand, with direct personal experience of the living Lenin no longer possible, schools and kindergartens, the media, the arts and public ceremonies were harnessed in the effort to maintain and to implant in new generations a sense of reverence and discipleship towards the founder of the party and the state. Though waxing and waning, these two strands of quasi-synthetic charisma have remained important ingredients of the Soviet authority system ever since.[14]

Meanwhile, however, other leaders emerged who sought to appropriate and weave them into a pattern of individual authority of their own, increasingly stamped with a partly or wholly contrived charisma linked with their actual or alleged personal qualities and achievements. The egregious case is, of course, Stalin's, which Graeme Gill examines in this volume. There were abortive efforts to establish Malenkov's personal claim to the 'apostolic succession' to Lenin and Stalin in 1953 (the fake photograph with Stalin and Mao, the appellation – harking back to Lenin – of 'head of the Soviet Government', etc.). The later 'personality cult' of Khrushchev, who had denounced his predecessor Stalin and 'cults' in general, was necessarily something different: his image was that of the dynamic but shrewd and earthy populist leader who commanded authority by his exceptional capacity to spot the right answers to great practical problems and to pursue them with unparalleled boldness and energy. With Brezhnev we are back to the 'apostolic succession', notwithstanding the false pope Khrushchev and the erring one Stalin. His claim, like Stalin's in the late 1920s, is that he it is who leads along 'Lenin's path', and a renewed intensification of the Lenin cult accompanied (and partly preceded) the burgeoning projection of his own image, through media publicity, the acquisition of ever-new honours and titles, the publication of his speeches and memoirs and of books celebrating his life and exploits, and so on. Of special significance, in providing an unprecedented channel of *personal* authority, is the practice of incorporating into the resolutions of party and other meetings held around the country in the wake of Central Committee plenums, of passages obligating the bodies concerned to be guided not only by the formal decisions of the plenum but also by the 'conclusions and directions' (*vyvody i ustanovki*) uttered by Brezhnev in his plenum speech.

The fact that the personal dominance asserted by these leaders has not flowed more or less automatically, as in a 'pure' rational–legal system, from the occupancy of some particular office, like the Prime Ministership in Britain, the Presidency in the United States, or the Chancellorship in Germany, is also suggestive of a charismatic system. Formal positions have, of course, been vital as means to and channels of personal authority, but there is none in the Soviet Union that suffices to impart it: except for Lenin, leaders have had to work and fight for it *after* appointment to high office. As Archie Brown shows in Chapter 8, the pattern of supreme power has taken many forms, from the extremes of oligarchy to the extremes of tyranny, and there has been no consistent pattern of posts occupied by those dominant leaders who have emerged.

In this context it is also worth noting the role of personal bonds of patronage and clientage in the Soviet bureaucracies. Patron–client groupings, which appear to be endemic at all levels, introduce a non-'rational–legal', quasi-charismatic element into politico-administrative career-making in the USSR.

As Weber pointed out, charismatic features or vestiges are not uncommon in systems of a predominantly rational–legal type. Such systems frequently evolve from processes of 'routinisation' following revolutionary changes induced by a charismatic movement,[15] and they may preserve charismatic or quasi-charismatic elements at the summit.[16] By the same token, no actual rational–legal system is entirely free of traditional elements, and in particular the important role of symbols associated with the nation-state and its historical past, which we have referred to in the Soviet case (and to which, incidentally, Weber gives little attention), is shared by all modern polities. Could we, then, regard the Soviet system as a variant of the rational–legal type, modified by the persistence of charismatic and traditional features?

Unfortunately, this attractively simple solution is not very convincing, for the major deviations of the system from the rational–legal ideal type, some of which we have already noted, can be accounted for only in part by the intrusion of charismatic and traditional elements. To appreciate this more fully, it will be necessary to turn now to a question only briefly touched on so far, namely the character of Soviet 'bureaucracy' and its relation to some broader characteristics of Soviet society.

Despite the enormous influence of Weber's ideal type of bureaucracy, most researchers have found it necessary to modify it when studying actual administrative or managerial organisations. One source of difficulties is Weber's stress on the technical knowledge and training of officials, which, as Talcott Parsons was one of the first to point out, is essential only to certain roles within a bureaucracy, while for many (including many senior) officials technical competence is either entirely irrelevant or of secondary importance for the exercise of their 'powers'.[17] This distinction between the official as the possessor of specialised knowledge and the official as bearer of decision-making responsibilities is one we shall come back to, but for our immediate purpose another overlapping distinction is of more crucial importance, namely that between the official as implementor of rules and the official as achiever of some specific task or goal. This may be illustrated by comparing the policeman directing traffic with the policeman tracking down and apprehending a criminal. As this case indicates, both rule-applying and task-achieving roles may be aspects of the same official job, but typically one or the other predominates, not only for the individual official but also for the organisation he works in. Thus a customs or taxation department or a pensions service is essentially a rule-applying agency, while a publishing house, an industrial plant or an airline is essentially a task-achieving agency. In the former the rules are central and applying them to particular cases is ideally an automatic (if sometimes complex) job minimising the exercise of judgment and initiative. In the latter rules are peripheral and the particular task (producing the brochure, getting the plane from A to B), for which judgement and initiative may be crucial, is central.

Armies perhaps bring out best of all the relationship between rule and task in a task-achieving organisation. No army can function without internal rules of procedure and discipline, but in action these will not guide the officer in his vital decisions, which call for judgement and initiative and on the aptness of which the fulfilment of his task and its contribution to the overall goal – victory – will depend. Much the same applies in a large industrial organisation. Again the rules play a facilitating role, and good management is not a matter of applying them but of exercising judgement and initiative in the execution of production tasks.

Although Weber saw that bureaucracies in modern society operated in large-scale private organisations, parties and armies as well as the state, he held that the application of rules to particular cases was a central feature of bureaucracy in general,[18] a view that calls for modification in the light of our distinction between rule-applying and task-achieving bureaucracies. At the same time his belief that a system of rational–legal authority is peculiarly appropriate to modern capitalism and that rule-applying bureaucracies are typical of the state administration in capitalist societies[19] seems valid. The main reason is that under capitalism the coordination of economic and a wide range of other activities is achieved largely through the market, and the central role of the state is to provide, administer and enforce a stable framework of law and regulations for market forces to operate effectively. Such a system will maximise 'formal' rationality, and this is the kind of rationality Weber has in mind in his model of 'rational–legal authority'. It will not, however, guarantee 'substantive rationality', i.e. consequences of economic and other activities perceived in terms of prevalent values as being the proper ends of such activities. The tension between formal and substantive rationality may lead the state to undermine the former by regulative and redistributive interference with the market as well as the provision of educational, health, transport, power and other services outside the market framework.

As Weber predicted, socialism (or at least 'actually existing socialism') requires 'a still higher level of formal bureaucratization than capitalism'.[20] What he did not foresee was that, while agencies of the rule-applying kind continue to be required, these are strongly overshadowed by others of a predominantly task-achieving kind. For on the one hand, the state (partly disguised as 'voluntary' or 'cooperative' organisations) takes over and runs nearly all spheres of social action; on the other, the market is reduced to a minor role in the overall coordination of social action, which is now handled *administratively*, through the bureaucracies of the state and the state-party. Whereas under capitalism social action is determined only partly by commands issued within 'imperatively-coordinated groups' (*Herrschaftsverbände*) and the state is only one (albeit the most important) among a great number and variety of such *Herrschaftsverbände*, under 'actually existing socialism' command becomes the overwhelmingly predominant determinant of social action, and all groups are linked together into a single *Herrschaftsverband*, such that there is a direct chain of command from the supreme political authorities to those operatively responsible in every sphere of social activity.

In such a 'mono-organisational society', as I have termed it elsewhere,[21] the regime is primarily concerned not with regulating activities, but with *directing* them. The main business of government is not to improve the framework of rules within which autonomously motivated individuals and groups can best operate, but to determine the social activity of individuals and groups by setting their *tasks*. By the same token, the prime criterion for judging the worth of most officials is not their success in achieving compliance with the rules but their success in fulfilling their tasks. Rule-violations may even be tacitly condoned in the interests of task-fulfilment. As we saw above, this is one of the obstacles to viewing the Soviet regime as a rational–legal order. There *is* a rationality here, but it is a substantive rationality rather than the formal rationality essential to rational–legal authority. Action is 'rational' insofar as it is appropriate to achieving tasks contributing to some overall goal.

Weber did not have a name for systems ordered in this way, and I propose calling them 'goal-rational systems'.[22] It scarcely needs adding that such a label does not necessarily imply that the goal is realistic or the means (the bureaucratic machinery and the tasks set them) well adapted to its attainment, any more than the concept of a rational–legal order necessarily implies that the laws are good ones or effectively enforced.

In the Soviet Union the supreme legitimating value is the goal of 'communism', a concept whose contours are sufficiently vague, like those of justice, order, democracy, the national good, honour, righteousness, etc., which figure in other authority systems, to allow the leadership wide flexibility of action in seeking it, but which differs from these in that it is not seen as an existing quality of the socio-political order but as something to be worked and fought for in the future, like victory in a war (in modern war the armed forces and even the whole society of a country become a single goal-rational system.) Its necessity and inevitability are justified by incessant 'exposure' of the exploitative, inefficient, predatory and 'doomed' character of the 'capitalism' it is claimed to transcend. The goal is constantly proclaimed in media programmes, school lessons, speeches, books, ceremonies, banners and posters at work places and in the streets, is displayed as the *raison d'être* of the socio-political order in the basic legitimating documents, the Constitution of the USSR and the Communist Party Rules, and is daily invoked as justification of the regime's demands on their citizens on the job and off it.

It is up to the leadership to translate the overall goal into intermediate and partial goals, like five-year economic plans, indoctrination programmes, etc., and of party and government agencies to break these down into concrete immediate tasks for all work groups throughout the country. In this context, it is not surprising that the word 'task' (*zadanie*) is constantly on the lips of leaders and propagandists, for it is the primary defining concept for approved social action; not only is work in the economic field described and evaluated in terms of officially prescribed tasks, so too is the activity of writers, judges, deputies to soviets and party members. The military parallels are obvious, and it is the goal-rationality of the authority system and not just the organisational traditions of Bolshevism that explain the prominence of military language: people and resources are 'mobilised' in 'campaigns', and factories, farms, schools, theatres, and all other institutions are engaged in a 'struggle' for 'victory' on their various 'fronts'. Exemplary performers in any field are 'heroes'.

It is hardly surprising that in such a system political leadership emerges not from a rule-bound process of competition to control the rule-making and rule-applying machinery, but from success in a career of task-achieving assignments, and that legislative bodies should not exercise a genuine rule-making and executive-constraining role, but be utterly dependent, both as to their membership and their activities, on the task-assigning leadership. The constitutional forms and rituals which suggest otherwise serve a cosmetic and 'mobilisational' role transparent to all but the politically infantile; while these form a significant component of the system's legitimating doctrines and symbolism, the *actual* power-relationships which they embellish are accorded full legitimacy through such formulas as 'the leading and directing role of the party', 'democratic centralism', etc.

The traditional elements in the legitimation and operation of the system, which we noted earlier, may be seen generally as departures from the pure type of goal-rational order. They spring from deeply entrenched attitudes and predispositions, which the leadership tolerates and indeed actively fosters, either because they share them or because they perceive their value in reinforcing their regime's authority and effectiveness. At the same time, however, they seek to integrate national pride and loyalty with their goal-legitimated authority by crediting the historical Russian nation with the exceptional qualities which enabled it to pioneer the 'socialist' revolution and transmit it to the other nations of the old Empire and later beyond her borders. The leadership, in defending and advancing the cause of socialism, also – and in part *thereby* – embodies the will, integrity and interests of the historical Russian state and nation.

Those elements that we have identified as 'charismatic' appear to be more closely consonant with the goal-rational order. The very adoption of such a goal presupposes an original prophetic vision and a dedicated 'movement' (the 'party') committed to its realisation. It also implies a *path* to its realisation and *leaders* capable of perceiving that path and shepherding the party and the masses along it. The regime will gain in authority to the extent that people are gripped by this vision and believe in the exceptional qualities of their leaders in conducting them towards it; performance of their tasks will be enhanced if they so believe and will depend on their at least *acting* as if they do. The party, as 'the leading and directing force of Soviet society' becomes the guardian of the vision and must act as a 'disciplined vanguard' leading the people along the path marked out by its leaders for its realisation.

What can be said about power in such a system? Most obviously, it betokens the strict centralisation of political power and its untrammelled extension into all fields of social activity. Autonomous or countervailing centres of power cannot be tolerated, for they would challenge the very principle on which the authority of the regime rests. In this sense it can be defined by that much-abused term 'totalitarian'. Ironically, as Schapiro has pointed-ed out,[23] such a power structure was prefigured, not by Marx, but by some of the utopians whom he sought to transcend; and the common element is plain: the absolutisation of the Goal and the relativisation of all other values.

To speak of power as 'totalitarian' in this sense does not mean, however, that it is totally concentrated at one point. The *distribution* of power in the Soviet system is marked by a number of features congruent with the goal-rational order of authority: it is practically monopolised by officials, and those responsible for task-achieving activities are in general more powerful than those responsible for rule-applying activities; it is arranged hierarchically, but there are many hierarchies with different amounts and kinds of power; the most powerful hierarchy is the one bearing primary responsibility for coordinating the others and vetting their performance, namely the party apparatus at central, republic, regional, city and district levels, whose top officials, their 'first secretaries', exercise something like 'prefectural' or gubernatorial powers and status in their respective areas;[24] at the summit the weak authority of formal rules encourages considerable flux in the degree of concentration of power and its distribution among different positions and collective bodies; nevertheless the requirements of effective task-achievement favour the emergence of a dominant leader who may then exploit the charismatic potentialities in the authority-system to build a position of exceptional personal power.

This far-from-simple pattern of power is further complicated by the power correlates of the 'informal organisation' which flourishes in Soviet bureaucracies no less than in large organisations elsewhere, reflecting 'the spontaneous efforts of individuals and subgroups to control the conditions of their existence'.[25] Officials exploit the resources afforded by their positions to build informal patterns of obligation and dependency which reinforce or circumvent formal power relationships, so seeking to enhance their security, rewards or opportunities. The clientelist groupings referred to earlier are perhaps the most important manifestation of informal organisation in the sphere of power. Yet another complication deserves mention: the power associated with technical knowledge. This cannot be defined away simply by pointing out that the bearers of technical knowledge occupy advisory 'staff' positions and that decision-making powers are monopolised by their 'line' colleagues – the ministers, factory directors, party secretaries and so on – as extensive research on the power relations of line and staff in large-scale Western organisations makes clear. To make matters even more involved, technical inputs may sometimes enter the system through its informal organisation. I have referred to the role of informal organisation and technical knowledge as 'complications', for I believe that they modify the 'map' of the distribution of power sketched in the previous paragraph without, however, negating it.

Although this account would probably gain fairly general endorsement from most of those enjoying some familiarity with the Soviet system, it is both incomplete and subject to question on grounds of definition and evidence. An adequate discussion of these matters would require a separate essay (at least) in itself. Nonetheless some aspects of them must be briefly considered.

This 'map' implies a concept of power in terms of the exercise of will and conscious choice by favourably placed individuals. However, if my earlier analysis of the authority-system is valid, it is clear that the power exercised by individuals is highly dependent on the political and social structures and the legitimating values which form the context of their action. To say that such and such happens because certain individuals have made certain decisions is therefore to tell only half the story. It is unnecessary to take the Althusserian view that the real units of political action are social structures of which individuals are merely the agents[26] in order to maintain that an analysis of the distribution of power in Soviet society needs to take account not only of what the incumbents of certain positions do, but also the bias and constraints on what they do imposed by institutional and ideological factors. These factors define not only who is to share in power and who not, but in what ways and on what issues power may and may not be exercised. They are as important as much for what they define *out* of the political process as for what they define *in*. It follows from this that a narrowly behaviouralist approach to identifying and estimating power in terms of who prevails in conflicts over specific issues[27] will not do. Methodologically, by the way, this is just as well for the Sovietologist, since data on the history of particular decisions is extremely difficult to come by. In recent years students of American politics, too, have not only argued [28] but demonstrated[29] both the inadequacies of what I have called the 'narrow behaviourialist' approach (or 'pluralist' approach – a misleading label in the present context) to power, and the importance of 'non-decisions' and the institutional and ideological influences lying behind them.

It will help to throw this dimension of the Soviet power system into clearer relief if we compare it briefly with the equivalent in the industrialised countries of the West, with their still predominantly capitalist economy and predominantly rational–legal order of authority. Here outcomes ('decisions' is too limiting a term) in all spheres of social activity result largely from the interaction, part competitive and conflictual, part cooperative and associational, of large numbers of autonomous groups and individuals, and *some* of this interaction, yielding *some* of the most important outcomes, is channelled into a public political process operating through institutions specially set aside for the purpose. Thus power operates in and is largely defined by a *market*, a state of affairs which, its defenders would argue, has led to a wider dispersal of power and a wider *access* to power by groups wishing to convert their concerns into 'issues' and seek favourable outcomes of them, than any other system that has yet existed. And yet, as already indicated, considerable evidence has been amassed by the critics of this system that the structure and weight of institutions, the 'rules of the game', the effects of education and socialisation generally, the influence of the media and prevalent beliefs all conspire to 'bias' the system, giving certain groups disproportionate power over what concerns become 'issues' and over the processes leading to their resolution. While a pluralist model of power in this kind of system may still be valid (I believe it is, though this question is not essential to my argument), such a model must certainly be substantially modified to take account of this bias.

Now the most obvious feature of the Soviet system is that those directing the bureaucracies through which the society functions enjoy a monopoly of legitimate control over the processes of education and socialisation, over the structure and operation of institutions, over the media and all other public influences on belief, this monopoly being backed by enormous organisational and coercive resources. Their capacity to define issues and to determine how they will be resolved is therefore extraordinary. The very notion of a competitive *market* process, in which groups and individuals seek autonomously to advance their concerns, is ruled out by the doctrine that the true (objective) interests of all are in harmony and are best advanced by unselfish efforts to achieve the tasks perceived by the party leadership as leading to the final goal of communism. Comparing the level of 'bias' here with that found in contemporary capitalist democracies, surely we must acknowledge differences in quantity which amount to a difference in kind. Consider, for instance, that such basic concerns as those of workers to have unions that would press to improve their wages and conditions, of intellectuals for a reduction in censorship controls, of Christians, Muslims and Jews to practise their religion without gross impairment of their educational and career opportunities, of the non-Russian nationalities to enjoy greater autonomy, or of under-privileged groups to seek a greater share of economic resources, are excluded from all legitimate access to power under this system. Ferenc Fehér has very aptly characterised the system in this aspect as one of 'the dictatorship over needs'.[30] The examples just given illustrate the limitations of the 'narrowly behaviourialist' approach to power referred to earlier. Since these matters simply do not come on to the political agenda to issue in *decisions*, no exercise of power regarding them would be acknowledged under this approach. True, in recent years the dissent movement has provided ample evidence of a sense of grievance surrounding such matters, as Peter Reddaway relates in this volume, but our criteria for the recognition of power will need to be less restrictive, more like those of the American critics of 'pluralism' or of such 'radical' English writers as Steven Lukes[31] if we are to maintain, as common sense would surely suggest, that the 'non-decisions' on these matters represent an exercise of power *over* those concerned with them.

That the Soviet power system lacks a 'market' dimension expressed through a public competitive political process does not mean that it is free of competition for and conflict over its uses. Politics there is, but for the most part concealed from public view, and pursued within and between the various offices and depart-ments of party and government.[32] To the extent that the contenders in this 'bureaucratic crypto-politics' can be seen as affording 'virtual representation' to various interests and concerns in the society at large it may be defined in Jerry Hough's terms as 'institutional pluralism'[33] – provided the limitations of this concept are borne in mind. These limitations may perhaps best be appreciated by recalling that 'bureaucratic crypto-politics' are found in the government machine of the capitalist democracies as well, and then trying to imagine what it would mean for 'pluralism' and the structure of power generally if this were the *only* politics operating in these countries, if the whole public competitive political process were absent, and the spokesmen of all official and voluntary organisations, all communications media and all 'representative bodies' presented a unanimous front of support for the current policies of the government.

Although this is the first explicit reference to policy, much that I could say about it is already implicit in my analysis of authority and power, and it would be tedious to spell it out in detail. Nevertheless, a few points must be specified. Policy is understood in this book as the action flowing directly from a set of related authoritative decisions and 'non-decisions' in some specific area of social activity. While the burgeoning literature on public policy in Western countries over the last decade has failed to produce an agreed definition of policy, it is usually employed in much the sense proposed here. What is more, the picture of the policy process that emerges from this literature on (mainly) American and Western European government displays some important features familiar to students of the USSR:[34] policy-making *is* typically a *process* often going on in a number of arenas, rather than being reducible to a specific 'decision'; unintended consequences are more likely than not; both policy formation and implementation are heavily conditioned by organisational structure and 'ideological' assumptions; both are also conditioned by the interests and commitments of individual officials, organisations and external groups.

There are, however, two important and related differences, which have already emerged in the discussion of power. *One* arena which is typically of great if not decisive importance in Western policy-formation, namely the public political arena, is almost empty in the Soviet case. And the confrontation of ends, typical of the former, though not really absent from the latter, is as a rule deeply concealed and disguised, and the debate is about *means*. In the former, policy-making has rather the character of a rough spectator sport, with much mutual abuse between the umpire, players and their supporters; in the latter, it is a *task* like any other.

Some qualifications are in order.[35] The public political arena is not entirely empty. Discussions and criticism about the technical aspects of policy and the effectiveness of implementation may by implication convey doubts or proposals about the proper ends of policy and the measures for achieving them. They may also serve as 'cover' for making claims on resources. Apart from influencing the climate of opinion in which policy is made, such discussion and criticism may occasionally play a major part in directing attention to a matter and so turning it into an 'issue' requiring resolution: the campaign against the pollution of Lake Baikal is an outstanding if exceptional example.[36] Occasionally there are controlled public discussions on proposed measures which afford unusual opportunities for the concerns of affected groups to be voiced.[37] Such public manifestations may be only the tiny visible tip of the policy iceberg, giving little idea of the vast shape concealed in the bureaucratic depths: but at least they tell us there *is* an iceberg, and give us some, albeit unreliable, information as to its movements. There is a further aspect: civil disturbance as a means of seeking policy changes to redress grievances, despite the harsh suppression it attracts, has been not unknown in the post-Stalin USSR, though all known cases have been confined to particular cities or districts. However, violence influences politics more by its potential than its actual use; if this applies to the role played by the repressive machinery of the state in securing the compliance of the population, the same may also apply in reverse. The occasional desperate outbursts in the Soviet Union itself and the more massive workers' riots in Poland are a reminder to the Soviet leadership that there are limits beyond which it may be unsafe to push the masses, and thereby a probable influence on policy. The same may apply to some of the movements of 'dissent' discussed below by Reddaway. Such aspects should not be ignored, but they should be seen, I would urge, as *qualifications*. If they were to become the dominant influences on policy-making, this could only mean that the system was under-going radical change – as in Czechoslovakia in 1968.

This chapter has sought to outline a set of related concepts for understanding authority, power and policy in the USSR. It has been based on a particular view of the empirical reality of Soviet society and politics, but this view has not been presented in detail and empirical aspects have been used illustratively rather than being explored and argued systematically. They are therefore contestable on both theoretical and empirical grounds. Even, however, if the arguments presented here are rejected in whole or in part, they will have served their purpose if they sensitise readers to some of the larger questions raised by the matters discussed in this book.

Two important matters have been neglected. One is the social aspects of the distribution of power in the USSR. Is there a 'ruling élite' and if so what are its boundaries? Can one speak of 'classes' in the Soviet Union with varying access to power, and if so what is the objective basis of class differentiation? The other matter is change over time. Changes in the international environment have had obvious effects on policy, and perhaps they have exercised more subtle influences on the power and authority structure as well. I have mentioned changes in the shape of power and authority at the top, but not their effects on the policy process and on the role and importance of different instruments of power and administration (party, government, police, etc.). The personalities and opinions of dominant leaders have also affected both the policy process and concrete policies. Finally, there are the cumulative effects of such long-term social changes as urbanisation, industrialisation, and educational and technological advance on the subject-matter of policy, the complexity of policy-making, the resources available for making and implementing policy, the social distribution of access to power, and the efficacy of different legitimating values.

NOTES

1. For a useful recent review of some alternative understandings of political legitimacy, see Uriel Rosenthal, *Political Order: Rewards, Punishments and Political Stability* (Alphen, 1978) ch. 7. The usefulness of the concept is far from universally accepted. For an analysis of compliance which makes no use of it (though allowing for 'normative grounds' of compliance), see Amitai Etzioni, *A Comparative Analysis of Complex Organizations: On Power, Involvement and their Correlates* (Glencoe, Ill., 1961). A penetrating discussion of political legitimation in the USSR and Eastern Europe, from an analytical standpoint different from that adopted here, will be found in Richard Löwenthal's essay 'The Ruling Party in a Mature Society', in Mark Field (ed.), *The Social Consequences of Modernization in Communist Societies* (Baltimore, 1976).
2. Cf. Rudolf Bahro, *The Alternative in Eastern Europe*, trs. David Fernbach (London, 1978), pp. 237–9; Archie Brown, 'Eastern Europe: 1968, 1978, 1998', *Daedalus*, winter 1979, pp. 151–74.
3. Weber's term *legitime Herrschaft* is variously rendered by his translators. His most extensive and systematic discussion of the concept is to be found in his *Wirtschaft und Gesellschaft* (Tübingen, 1922) pt 1, which is available to the English reader as Max Weber, *The Theory of Social and Economic Organization*, trs. A. M. Henderson and Talcott Parsons, ed. with an Introduction by Talcott Parsons (New York, 1947). References in the present chapter are to this edition. Weber returned to it in Part 3 of the same work, the relevant section of which has been translated by Edward Shils and Max Rheinstein (eds), *Max Weber on Law in Economy and Society* (Cambridge, Mass., 1954). Henderson and Parsons usually translate *Herrschaft* as 'imperative control', but where reference is to *legitime Herrschaft* they prefer 'authority'. H. H. Gerth and C. Wright Mills in *From Max Weber: Essays in Sociology* (London, 1947) use 'authority' for Weber's *Herrschaft*, with or without the limiting adjective. Shils and Rheinstein, however, consistently translate *Herrschaft* as 'domination', as does Reinhard Bendix, in his most valuable expository work *Max Weber: An Intellectual Portrait* (Garden City, NY, 1960).
4. See T. H. Rigby, 'Weber's Typology of Authority: A Difficulty and Some Suggestions', *Australian and New Zealand Journal of Sociology*, ii, no. 1 (1966) 2–15.
5. Weber, *Theory of Social and Economic Organization*, p. 328.

6. See especially Alfred G. Meyer, *The Soviet Political System: An Interpretation* (New York, 1965).

7. See Joseph S. Berliner, *Factory and Manager in the USSR* (Cambridge, Mass., 1957) esp. ch. 18.

8. See Stephen White, 'The USSR: Patterns of Autocracy and Industrialism', in Archie Brown and Jack Gray (eds), *Political Culture and Political Change in Communist States* (London, 1977) pp. 25–65.

9. Weber, *Theory of Social and Economic Organization*, p. 358.

10. See T. H. Rigby, *Lenin's Government: Sovnarkom 1917–1922* (Cambridge, 1979) pp. 110–12. The fact that Trotsky had never been part of this community of Lenin's followers probably contributed significantly to his isolation within the party leadership in the 1920s.

11. While in Weber's analysis of basic authority-types the discussion of charismatic authority is focused on the charisma of particular leaders, elsewhere he also discusses movements or institutions embodying charisma. See esp. Weber, *Wirtschaft und Gesellschaft*, vol. II, ch. 11. Cf. Bendix, *Max Weber*, ch. 10.

12. Weber, *Theory of Economic and Social Organization*, p. 367.

13. Ibid., p. 369.

14. 'Synthetic' is used in the sense of contrived, manufactured from elements which are in part at least artificial. Indeed, it is hard to see how a belief in the charismatic qualities of the dead Lenin and of the party he founded could be spread to the mass membership of the party and to the population at large without such contriving, and in this respect the experience of the Soviet regime is no different from that of other large movements, states, churches, etc., which claim a charismatic legitimation, except in the means at its disposal to instil the required beliefs and attitudes. 'Synthetic' is not intended to mean false, i.e. that the purported charismatic qualities do not actually exist; the force of charismatic legitimation rests on a belief in such qualities whether they exist or not. In fact, a 'synthetic' charisma may or may not rest on actual qualities of its bearer, and in this respect there are obvious difference of degree (at least) between the original charisma of Lenin and the early Bolshevik movement on the one hand, and later Soviet leaders on the other.

15. Weber, *Theory of Economic and Social Organization*, pp. 369, 383, 389.

16. Ibid., pp. 332–3.

17. See Parsons's introductory essay, ibid., p. 59. Indeed, as studies of the administration of such organisations as hospitals and law firms have shown, the greater the centrality of professional knowledge in carrying out the functions of organisations, the more their patterns of authority, power and decision-making are liable to deviate from the Weberian and other hierarchical models of bureaucracy. Weber's insistence on the importance of formal professional training reflected, of course, the bureaucratic traditions of his native Germany, where, in contrast with the Chinese or English preference for the liberally educated amateur, officials were expected to possess qualifications in appropriate specialised aspects of the law.

18. Ibid., p. 330.

19. Ibid., p. 338.

20. Ibid., p. 339.

21. See T. H. Rigby, 'Politics in the Mono-Organizational Society', in Andrew Janos (ed.), *Authoritarian Politics in Communist Europe* (Berkeley, Calif., 1976)

pp. 31–80; and 'Stalinism and the Mono-Organizational Society', in Robert C. Tucker (ed.), *Stalinism: Essays in Historical Interpretation* (New York, 1977). The mode of social coordination referred to as 'the market' has been broken down by some authors into 'the market' and 'bargaining' or 'price' and 'bargaining'. This distinction is efficacious for some purposes, but it is more useful here to distinguish simply between the relationship of superior and subordinate actors operating through commands, and the relationship of autonomous actors operating through deals, the former aggregated into and structured by hierarchies, the latter aggregating into and structured by *markets*.

22. There is a degree of congruence between the distinction made here between rational–legal systems and goal-rational systems, and that made by Michael Oakeshott between states understood in terms of *societas* (or civil association) and states understood in terms of *universitas* (or corporate association). See his *On Human Conduct* (Oxford, 1975) pt 3. In the state as *universitas* 'there are managers, not rulers; role performers related to a common purpose, not *cives* or subjects; instrumental rules, not *lex*' (p. 264). Such a state is 'teleocratic'. One may also note the view of Ivan Szelenyi and George Konrad that the basic source of the power structure in 'state-socialist societies' is the assertion of *telos* over *techne*, and therewith of substantive over formal rationality. See their *Towards the Class Power of the Intelligentsia* (New York, 1979).

23. Schapiro, *Totalitarianism*, ch. 4.

24. See Jerry Hough, *The Soviet Prefects: The Local Party Organs in Industrial Decision-Making* (Cambridge, Mass., 1969). Cf. T. H. Rigby, 'The Soviet Regional Leadership: The Brezhnev Generation', *Slavic Review*, XXXVII, no. 1 (1978) 2–3.

25. Alvin W. Gouldner, 'Organizational Analysis', in Robert K. Merton, L. Broom and L. S. Cottrell (eds), *Sociology Today* (New York, 1958) p. 250.

26. For a strong statement of this view, see Nicos Poulantzas, 'The Problem of the Capitalist State', *New Left Review*, LVIII (1969) 67–78.

27. As exemplified in Robert A. Dahl, *Who Governs? Democracy and Power in an American City* (New Haven, Conn., and London, 1961), and defended in Nelson W. Polsby, *Community Power and Political Theory* (New Haven, Conn., and London, 1963).

28. See especially Peter Barach and Morton S. Baratz, 'The Two Faces of Power', *American Political Science Review*, LVI, no. 4 (1962) 947–52.

29. Notably by Matthew A. Crenson, *The Un-Politics of Air Pollution: A Study of Non-Decision-making in the Cities* (Baltimore and London, 1971).

30. Ferenc Fehér, 'The Dictatorship over Needs', *Telos*, no. 35 (1978) 31–42.

31. See Steven Lukes, *Power: A Radical View* (London, 1974). I have not explicitly argued here for what Lukes terms a 'three-dimensional view' of power, according to which 'A exercises power over B when A affects B in a manner contrary to B's interests' (p. 34) irrespective of whether B knows it is happening or recognises his interests. It would be an interesting exercise to explore the efficacy and implications of this view in considering the Soviet case, but this would lead us into a theoretical morass from which we would not quickly extricate ourselves.

32. T. H. Rigby, 'Crypto-politics', *Survey*, no. 50 (1964) 183–94.

33. Jerry F. Hough, *The Soviet Union and Social Science Theory* (Cambridge, Mass., and London, 1977) ch. 1.

34. Policy-making in the USSR has been the direct or indirect subject of a very considerable and varied literature, of which the following are a few examples: R. Conquest, *Power and Policy in the USSR: A Study of Soviet Dynastics* (London, 1961); Alexander Dallin and Alan F. Westin, *Politics in the Soviet Union: Seven Cases* (New York, 1966); Peter H. Juviler and Henry W. Morton, *Soviet Policy-Making: Studies of Communism in Transition* (New York, 1967); Robert J. Osborn, *Soviet Social Policies: Welfare, Equality and Community* (Homewood, Ill., 1970); H. Gordon Skilling and Franklyn Griffiths (eds), *Interest Groups in Soviet Politics* (Princeton, NJ, 1971); Paul Cocks, Robert V. Daniels and Nancy Whittier Heer, *The Dynamics of Soviet Politics* (Cambridge, Mass., and London, 1976), esp. pt 3; Richard B. Remnek (ed.), *Social Scientists and Policy-Making in the USSR* (London and New York, 1977); Theodore H. Friedgut, 'Interests and Groups in Soviet Policy-Making: The MTS Reforms', *Soviet Studies*, XXVIII, no. 4, (1976) 524–47; Hannes Adomeit and Robert Boardman, (eds), *Foreign Policy-Making in Communist States* (Farnborough, Hants, 1978). Since it is extraordinarily difficult to obtain much direct information about the policy-making *process*, our views on this must be based largely on inference, and a systematic review of the whole problem would greatly aid our thinking about it and assist further research.

35. A fuller account would also have to note developments in the capitalist democracies which could be seen as tending towards the Soviet model. Writers have pointed to the 'teleocratic' implications of such 'rational' techniques of 'decision-making' by Western governments as cost-benefit analysis, systems analysis, etc., and the tendency of these to reduce the role of the public political process in policy-making. See, for instance, G. M. Dillon, 'Policy and Dramaturgy: A Critique of Current Conceptions of Policy-making', *Policy and Politics*, v, no. 1 (1976) 47–62, and Peter Self, *Econocrats and the Policy Process* (London, New York, Melbourne, 1975).

36. See Donald R. Kelley, 'Environmental Policy-Making in the USSR: The Role of Industrial and Environmental Interest Groups', *Soviet Studies*, XXVIII, no. 4 (1976) 570–89.

37. See Joel J. Schwarz and William R. Keech, 'Group Influence and the Policy Process in the Soviet Union', *American Political Science Review*, LXII, no. 3 (1968) 840–51.

3 Authority, Power and the State, 1916–20

Neil Harding

In 1916 Bukharin produced a masterly article, 'Towards a Theory of the Imperialist State'.[1] In it he came to the conclusion that the modern bourgeois state had grown into a monstrous oppressive power, militarist in ethos, absolute in its pretensions, swallowing up all the vital forces of society and destroying all group and individual autonomy. In his nightmare vision the 'mailed fist', the 'iron heel' of the modern imperialist state impressed its ruthless stamp upon a cowed and servile society. The pattern of domination and subservience which the Marxist idea of the state encapsulated, had been brought to its perfected expression. The imperative for Marxists to concentrate all their attention on the destruction of this new Leviathan was, he believed, inescapable.

In 1920 Bukharin published his *Economics of the Transition Period*,[2] the fullest and most theoretically cogent Bolshevik vindication of the dictatorship of the proletariat. Bukharin now argued the case for the creation of a proletarian state power mightier by far than any state the world had witnessed. The wheel had turned full circle. Within the space of four years Bukharin had moved from the imperative to transcend all the old patterns of political and administrative authority to the specification of a necessary revolutionary progression in which the building of an omnipotent political and economic power was not merely vindicated but glorified. In 1916 Bukharin had rejected the conventional distinctions between Marxism and anarchism on the question of political power and authority. By 1920 he had produced a rescript for the political system of Stalinism, more thorough and convincing than any which Stalin or his henchmen ever produced. It is one of the more savage ironies of the

Russian Revolution that the omnipotent state that Bukharin lauded was to claim him as its most eminent victim.

Let us return now to Bukharin's analysis of the state in 1916. He proceeded from the deceptively simple and unimpeachably orthodox proposition that the state was a product and reflection of class differentiation within society. That proposition, he pointed out, was the starting point of Engels's *Origin of the Family, Private Property and the State*.[3] The state appeared, therefore, at a specific stage of social evolution when the productive forces, and the consequent division of labour within society, were sufficiently elaborated to give rise to distinct classes. The *raison d'être* of the state was to preserve, with the power of the army and the police, the relationship of domination and subordination which was intrinsic to the mode of production so long as the means of production remained the property of a particular, and constantly shrinking, social class.

The essential nature of class society was, in Bukharin's analysis, contained in overlapping patterns of domination and subordination. Thus capital was, in essence, not a specific level of development of the productive forces; its essential character was not to be observed in factories, machinery or railways but was to be sought in a particular relationship between groups of men. 'Capital', Bukharin asserted, with all of Marx's authority to lean on, 'is a social power.'[4] It essentially expressed the relationship between those who needed to hire wage-labour and those obliged to sell their wage-labour. It expressed a system of social relationships of domination and subordination. This system of social relationships was, of course, enshrined at the superstructural level, in the law. It was the apparent impartiality of the law which gave it its authority – its claim to be obeyed. In a similar way the liberal-bourgeois state claimed to be above classes. It was represented by its ideologists as merely the impartial arbiter of competing claims, with no particular ends of its own to pursue. So long as the apparent universality of the bourgeois state could be maintained, it was, Bukharin contended, the most powerful prop to bourgeois authority. The more widespread the illusory belief in the impartiality and universality of the bourgeois state, the more its authority was enhanced, the less it would be obliged to have recourse to the coercive agencies of power which it commanded.

The illusory neutrality of the bourgeois state could, however, in Bukharin's analysis, be used as a plausible account of its nature only as long as capitalism remained competitive. The more monopolistic capitalism became, the greater the class differentiation within society. The greater the class differentiation within society the more the state would be obliged to forsake its claim to authority in neutrality and universality and rely upon a positive interventionist role in managing the whole national economy and subordinating society to its aims by relying ever increasingly on naked coercive power. In proportion, therefore, as the bourgeois state attained its perfected final form as the imperialist state, its essential nature would be exposed. And just as capital was expressive of a particular form of authority and power so too was the state:

> In the same way that capital is not for Marx a thing, a means of production in and for itself (*in und für sich*) but a social relation, expressed in things, in just the same way the essence of the state consists above all not in its technical-administrative roles, but in that relationship of domination which is concealed behind it.[5]

In Bukharin's historical sociology the development of the productive forces under private ownership led to increasingly refined relations of domination and subservience within the productive process which were reflected in ever-increasing class differentiation and class antagonism within society which, in turn, obliged the state to intervene directly with ever-growing coercion to protect the economic, social and political domination of the ascendant class.

Bukharin had, in his *The World Economy of Imperialism*,[6] written in 1914, already begun to develop his ideas on the intimate connection between the development of finance capital and the changing form of the bourgeois state. In this he followed directly in the footsteps of Rudolf Hilferding who, in his *Finance Capital*[7] of 1910, had shown how the advent of monopoly capitalism had decisively altered the nature of the bourgeois state. In the epoch of the rise of capitalism the new entrepreneurs had viewed the interventionist policies of the feudal state, its pretensions to control prices, labour and foreign trade, as inimical to their own interests. Production and trade, they asserted at that time, could only prosper with the free play of market forces, which the intervention of the state could only disrupt. The complement of *laissez-faire* was, therefore, minimal government.[8]

By the turn of the nineteenth century, so Hilferding argued, the situation had undergone a qualitative change. Above all, the structure of capitalism had been quite transformed. The tendency for capital to become concentrated in fewer and fewer hands had reached its apogee. Four or five major banks now effectively disposed of the entire capital of major industrial countries. Trusts and cartels, under the impetus of the major banks, had established monopoly control over all the major sectors of the economy. The great magnates of finance capital now urgently needed a powerful state to establish high protective tariffs around the spheres of industry they controlled. They needed a powerful army and navy to expand the economic territory available to them for the export of superabundant capital which could find no profitable outlet in the metropolitan economy. Each expansion of economic territory necessarily involved an increase in the military might of the bourgeois state, for subject peoples would have to be forcibly deprived of their land and traditional modes of production as preconditions to their availability as wage-labourers and con-sumers. Each expansion of economic territory would, moreover, have to be protected against the predatory intentions of rival states. As the state grew in military might, as the bureaucratic apparatus needed to administer colonial regimes expanded, the level of taxation, levied predominantly on the working class, was bound to rise. Hilferding's conclusion was that in the era of finance capitalism the workers were subject to a triple impost – surplus value levied directly by the monopoly capitalist, artificially high monopoly prices for commodities sustained by the tariff walls of the imperialist state, and excessive taxation levied directly by the state to guarantee the economic territory so vital to monopoly capitalism. As a result of this triple impost the living conditions, the real wages of the working class, were bound to fall. Class conflict was bound to become more pronounced and the imperialist state would be forced to arm itself directly against its own workers. The illusory neutrality of the bourgeois state, relatively easy to sustain in the earlier period of competitive capitalism, would be swept aside. The pattern of domination and subordination which the state embodied would be made inescapably apparent. The state would, in order to secure the profits of the banks, cartels and trusts, have to intervene in the actual organisation of industry and the supervision of labour. The bourgeois state, in the epoch of finance capital, stood revealed not as an impartial arbiter of competing interests but as the armed guarantor of the particular interests of the financial barons.[9]

Bukharin pursued this argument further still. He maintained that in the years immediately preceding the war, and especially during the war itself, the process of the *étatisation* (*ogosudarstvlenie*) of society had been hugely accelerated. Increased international competition had replaced competition for the internal market and had resulted in the insistence, tirelessly canvassed by the imperialist state and its apologists, on the utmost internal unity in the face of foreign threat. The politics of liberalism which legitimised, within certain bounds, the clash of diverse interests, was replaced by the enforced unanimity of the embattled militarist state-capitalist trust in whose light individual rights, or the autonomy of social groups, were positively mischievous, if not actually subversive. The imperialist state swept in to submerge them.

> . . . the state absorbs into itself a whole series of bourgeois organisations.
>
> In this respect too, the war provided a huge stimulus. Philosophy and medicine, religion and ethics, chemistry and bacteriology – all were 'mobilised' and 'militarised' exactly in the same way as industry and finance.[10]

Nor was it merely 'bourgeois organisations' which the imperialist state was swallowing up. It was threatening to suborn, and was actually in the process of absorbing, the labour movement and the socialist parties as quasi-governmental agencies of its own power. Strikes had been prohibited, mobility of labour denied, workers had been tied as indentured men to their factories and their militant leaders had been imprisoned. The trade unions and labour parties had not only acquiesced but actually assisted in the tasks of mobilising the working class for the military front and for the production fronts. They had fallen willing prey to the predatory imperialist state, absorbing its mythology of the 'national interest' and even vindicating the *étatisation* of social and economic life as increments towards 'state socialism'.[11] The awful prospect now emerged of the extinction of the heroic, militant role of the working class, the suicide of its historical mission as the gravedigger of capitalism and inaugurator of a properly human existence. The labour movement and the socialist parties had meekly acquiesced in this process and were becoming the pliant labour departments of the imperialist state.

The liberal bourgeoisie, according to Bukharin's argument, had preserved their authority with minimal coercive force so long as the illusion of the class impartiality of the state and law could plausibly be maintained and was generally believed in. The interests of the finance-capitalist bourgeoisie, by contrast, demanded policies requiring a vast extension of the coercive power of the state and its direct intervention in managing the economy and the labour movement:

> Thus there arises the finished form of the contemporary imperialist robber state, an iron organisation, which envelops the living body of society with its tenacious, grasping claws. It is – The New Leviathan, beside which the fantasy of Thomas Hobbes seems but a child's plaything.[12]

The precarious authority of the imperialist state, in Bukharin's account, rested upon an identification of trade and imperialist policies with 'national interest'. So long as the workers marginally profited from the super-profits of imperialist exploitation this ideological justification of the growth of state power was little questioned. The imperialist bourgeoisie consequently had little need to use the coercive power at their command to sustain their domination within society. At the point when taxation began to eat into real wages, more especially when competing imperialist interests led to war and the need for massive sacrifice of life on the part of the workers to defend the super-profits of the imperialist bourgeoisie – at that point, Bukharin maintained, life itself would impress upon the minds of the proletariat the hollowness of the state's claim to represent the general interest. But the state's whole claim to authority derived from its pretension to represent the general interest. In proportion as this was disputed, it was obliged to intervene with naked force, and the more it did so the more the illusion of its class neutrality was exposed. The war, Bukharin believed, would finally reveal an essential character of the state as the guarantor of a system of social relations of domination and subordination. It would stand revealed as a vehicle of war within (against the proletariat) and war without (against competing state-capitalist trusts). The war, according to Bukharin, would finally sever the last chain which bound the workers to the national state. They would be forced to recognise that, in any computation, the pennies they had received from imperialist super-profits had now in truth become widows' mites.[13]

The imperative to destroy the imperialist state was therefore, in Bukharin's account, many-faceted. Unless it was destroyed, society would be reduced to a servile, atomised mass under the heel of the new barons of finance capital. Individual rights and the autonomy of groups would vanish and the movement for working-class emancipation absorbed as an adjunct of state power. Wars of ever-increasing dimensions would destroy productive forces, especially the most vital one – human labour power. Against this threatening barbarism, and against the prospect of a total state and a servile society, Bukharin raised the flag of revolt on which appeared Bakunin's device – smash the state!

Lenin was, at first, rather scandalised by Bukharin's bold conclusions:

> The distinction between the Marxists and the anarchists on the question of the state . . . has been defined *absolutely incorrectly*: if you are to deal with this subject, you must speak *not* in that way; you *must not* speak in that way.[14]

He was, nonetheless, clearly impressed with Bukharin's logic and his characterisation of the omnipotent power of the state-capitalist trust. Furthermore, Lenin must have appreciated the practical clout of Bukharin's theorising. He had, after all, graphically demonstrated the apostasy of all labour and socialist leaders who had flocked to the aid of their bourgeois states in their hour of greatest peril. He had shown how their meek subservience to the imperialist state was tantamount to the suicide of the historical goals of the proletariat. Bukharin had provided Lenin with another stick with which to beat the men who had reneged on their revolutionary responsibilities by pleading the concept of unripe time. Time, Bukharin argued, had run out. His own analysis of imperialism, bolstered by Lenin's *Imperialism, the Highest Stage of Capitalism*,[15] had demonstrated that the objective conditions for socialism on a world-wide scale had fully matured. His analysis of the state now impressed upon all the waverers, pacifists and revolutionary procrastinators the urgency for immediate action – either smash the imperialist state or be swallowed up by it.

The problems which now confronted Lenin were twofold. First, did the audacious project of smashing the state have any warrant in Marx's thought? Second, what forms of authority and power were to replace the old state form, and were the agencies through which they were to be exercised immediately available?

On the first problem it is curious, though perhaps symptomatic of Marxists of the day, that Bukharin relied almost exclusively on Engels for his analysis of the state. It did not take Lenin long to discover, in Marx's *The Eighteenth Brumaire of Louis Bonaparte*,[16] a convincing parallel between Bukharin's analysis of the imperialist state and the 'bureaucratic excrescence' of Louis Bonaparte's regime, 'this appalling parasitic growth, which enmeshes the body of French society like a net and chokes all its pores'.[17] In 1852, as Lenin noted, Marx had already come to the conclusion that 'All the revolutions perfected this machine instead of smashing it,'[18] and this, according to Lenin, was 'the chief and fundamental point in the Marxist theory of the state'.[19] In *The State and Revolution* Lenin concluded that world history was now undoubtedly leading on an incomparably larger scale than in 1852, to the 'concentration of all the forces' of the proletarian revolution on the 'destruction' of the state machine.[20] Lenin was quick to notice not merely Marx's account of the nascent form of the malaise Bukharin had diagnosed, but Marx's detailed prescription for its remedy. The form of administration, the Commune, that had been elaborated by the workmen of Paris upon the fall of Louis Bonaparte – that was the antidote to bureaucratic centralism and the omnipotence of the state. It was, as Marx observed, and Lenin insisted, 'the political form at last discovered under which to work out the economic emancipation of labour'.[21]

The Commune was, therefore, as Lenin tirelessly repeated from his *April Theses* until at least the spring of 1918, the popular agency through which the old patterns of bourgeois authority embodied in bourgeois state power were to be transcended. The Commune, according to both Marx and Lenin, immediately eliminated the coercive agencies of power, the separate bodies of armed men, police and army, which had always guaranteed the domination of particular classes in history. The policing and defensive functions they had hitherto arrogated to themselves were now to be vested in the entire population in arms. Power, as exercised by bodies of armed men separate and distinct from the population as a whole, was done away with at a stroke. Nor was it simply the coercive functions of the state which were to be eliminated, but all its administrative, economic, political and regulatory functions were to be reintegrated into the armed people. The people universally

armed and organised as a militia were to reabsorb all the powers
hitherto arrogated to the state and, insofar as they did so, the state
would cease to exist. In his articles from April 1917 to April 1918
Lenin repeatedly insisted that the project in hand was to eradicate
all the old patterns of power and authority, to eliminate the age-old
relationship of domination and subordination which had rent class
society. All the people, Lenin insisted, all without exception, must
be taught the art of government:

> to teach the people, down to the very bottom, the art of
> government not only in theory but in practice, by beginning to
> make immediate use everywhere of the experience of the masses.
> Democracy from below, democracy without an officialdom,
> without a police, without a standing army; voluntary social duty
> guaranteed by a *militia* formed from a universally armed people –
> this is a guarantee of freedom which no tsars, no swashbuckling
> generals, and no capitalists can take away.[22]

The authority of the soviet/commune form of administration
derived from its *genuine* universality. All were to participate in
deliberations on all aspects of public policy, all were to play their
part in implementing decisions. The division between legislative
and executive powers was to be done away with, for the Commune
was at once a legislative and executive body. It was Lenin's view
during this period that only by destroying the old state, only by
erasing the old relations of domination and subordination, and the
psychology that went with them, could Russia be saved. The
slide into economic ruin could only be arrested by unleashing the
initiative and enthusiasm of the mass – by relying upon the agencies
of popular economic self-administration thrown up by the
Revolution. The factory committees and the poor peasants'
committees were to be the agencies of economic regeneration. All
other possible expedients had been tried and failed. The administrative chaos into which Russia had fallen could not be
redeemed, in his view, by conventional governmental state forms;
only organs of direct democracy of the soviet/commune type could
galvanise the people at large into establishing a new legitimate
authority. By the same token Russia's desperate military-strategic
situation could not be relieved by relying upon a conscript army led
and directed by a privileged officer caste, but only by a universal
militia which would rouse not merely the people of Russia but the

people of the whole world to take up arms against imperialist barbarism.

The project to dissolve the state and to inaugurate mass self-administration was not, in Lenin's view, simply an article of faith enjoined upon Marxists by the experience of the Commune. It was the only way out of the economic, social, political and military crises which the imperialist war had produced. If imperialism and its consequences dictated the imperative to restructure the relationship of authority within society it had also, according to Lenin, itself developed the very mechanisms and organisational structures through which the people at large could universally participate in administering their own economic and social life. The process of growth of finance capital *was* the process whereby the big banks had monopolised the capital resources of the industrialised countries controlling all the inputs and outputs of the entire national economy. The big banks had therefore established, in Lenin's account, a ready-made structure of nation-wide accountancy and book-keeping – that essential pre-requisite for the administration of things.[23] Likewise the trusts and cartels had enormously simplified the task of the social appropriation of the industrial base. They had, to a large extent, overcome the anarchy of production, the disparity between production and consumption which had prevailed under competitive capitalism, by developing techniques for matching output with demand. They had therefore rationalised production, concentrating it in the largest, best-equipped plants which brought the socialisation of labour to its apogee.[24] Instead of having to take over a multiplicity of small units of production the people in arms had merely to lay hold of the ready-made mechanisms elaborated by the trusts and cartels in order to control the major sectors of industry. The banks, the trusts and cartels, the Post Office – these were the mechanisms which the development of finance capital had so simplified that they could be managed by any literate work-man.[25] This, Lenin declared, was the apparatus necessary to the commune/soviet form of administration precisely because it would not involve establishing a stratum of officials standing above the people, precisely because it was an apparatus which was concerned not with the domination of one group of men over others (as the state had been) but with the management of things by all men. The mobilising and organising agencies through which this apparatus could be made to realise the interests of the mass had, he maintained, been spontaneously created by the people themselves in the course of the development of the Russian Revolution from February 1917 onwards. The soviets of workers', soldiers' and peasants' deputies, the factory committees and committees of poor peasants, the Red Guard as embryo of a universal militia, the producers' and consumers' communes which had spring up, had covered every facet of Russian life with self-acting organs of popular power.

The initial vision of genuine direct democracy and genuine freedom was based on a class analysis which held, as its central axiom, that the poor peasants comprised the great majority of Russia's rural population and that their real interests were at one with those of the urban proletariat.[26] Through revolutionary practice, through organising themselves and learning to articulate and pursue their own interests, the peasants would rapidly ascend to revolutionary consciousness and an awareness of this community of interest. It was Lenin's belief, based upon projections from his class analysis, that unfettered revolutionary practice would rapidly reveal this real identity of interests uniting the vast majority of Russia's population. Universal self-activity and the reabsorption by the armed people, organised in a multiplicity of communal and soviet organisations of all the power and authority hitherto arrogated to the state, was both the goal of socialism and the only means appropriate to its realisation. Universal participation in all the decision-making processes of social life was the condition for decisions acquiring authoritative status. Universal participation in all the aspects of social and economic administration was the necessary condition to prevent the emergence of a caste of bureaucrats claiming exclusive jurisdiction. Universal participation in the policing and defensive functions of society was the necessary condition to prevent the emergence of separate bodies of armed men impressing the power of a particular group upon society.

The claim to power and the claim to authority of the Soviet regime derived, therefore, from its pretensions to universality. As in the ancient Athenian *polis* or Rousseau's city state, the only road to establishing a real community of interests lay through obliging all to play their part in deliberating upon and executing public policy. This project, in turn, clearly rested upon the view that there was a real community of interests shared by all but an insignificant number of citizens.

In Lenin's scheme, as in Rousseau's, it was not necessary to assume that this community of interest would immediately become apparent with the introduction of direct participatory democracy. It would, in Lenin's view, take time for the mass of the people to rid themselves of the self-seeking, particularistic attitudes which bourgeois society had ingrained into them. In theory Lenin's views were sound enough, but in the practical situation of Russia in early 1918 recurrent crises made the dimension of time the rock upon which his theoretical projections were to founder. By the spring of 1918 famine had bitten hard into the urban centres. Lenin recognised full well the causes of the famine. War and revolution had brought about a virtual collapse of industrial production and of the transportation system. Consequently trade between town and country in any large-scale organised way had ceased. The urban workers had nothing to offer the peasants in return for grain, and grain was therefore withheld. There could, in this situation, be no possibility of waiting until the peasants came to an awareness of their real long-term community of interest with the proletariat, since, before that occurred, the proletariat would have been starved to death or obliged to disperse and return to the countryside. In a situation where six peasants were starving one worker to death one does not, Lenin remarked, appraise the general interest by taking a vote among all seven.[27] Force would have to be used.

The organised power of the urban workers would compel the peasantry to disgorge its grain. The pre-eminent responsibility of the government to feed the towns was, in Lenin's view, the occasion and sufficient justification for it assuming the form of a dictatorship. But it was not merely the peasantry who were afflicted by self-seeking narrowness – sections of the working class also fell prey to these tendencies and they, too, would have to be coerced into accepting their real class interests articulated by the *avant-garde* of the class.[28]

The response of the Bolsheviks to the cycle of crises which they had to face in the first three years was to apply to society at large the organisational model of the army. Trotsky was far from being the only leading Bolshevik who believed that the grain crisis, the fuel crisis and the railway crisis, the general crisis of production, could only be solved by applying the same sort of mobilisation, centralised direction, discipline, subordination and accountability which had proved to be the republic's salvation in the civil war.[29] Initiative in all spheres had by 1920 become the preserve of the organs of state, it proceeded from the top down. The Council of People's Commissars

almost entirely displaced the role of the soviets, the Supreme
Economic Council had long won its battle with the factory
committees, and was on the verge of effectively absorbing the trade
unions, the regimental committees had lost out in their battle
against the re-establishment of a corps of professional officers.[30] The
result was that the theory of the commune state, the claim to
legitimacy in universality, was radically out of joint with prevailing
practice. It was, once again, Bukharin's audacious intellect which
attempted to bring the two together. He now provided the first, and
still the most theoretically cogent, vindication of the dictatorship of
the proletariat with an entirely new account of relations of power
and authority within society.

Bukharin's argument in *The Economics of the Transition Period*
represented a fundamental revision of Lenin's optimistic scheme of
1917. Lenin had, as we have seen, argued that the development of
the big banks, trusts and cartels had created ready-made and
simplified mechanisms which could be taken over by any literate
workers and employed to serve the ends of public need rather than
private greed. Lenin's recipe was, in short, smash the state but
utilise the administrative mechanisms created by finance capital to
secure universal participation in the administration of things. By
1920 Bukharin, chastened by the experience of the recurrent crises
and civil wars of the young republic, had come to the conclusion
that this project was inherently utopian. Just as revolutionaries
could not simply lay hold of the ready-made state machine and
wield it for their own purposes so 'one cannot entirely "seize
possession" of the old economic apparatus . . . the "revolutionary
decomposition of industry" is a historically inevitable stage which
no amount of lamentation can escape'.[31]
   All productive systems, according to Bukharin, had their costs.
Under capitalism, for example, competition resulted in periodic
and increasingly severe crises of over-production, bankruptcies,
amalgamations, recessions and the destruction of productive
forces.[32] To some extent state monopoly capitalism overcame this
anarchy of production within the national economy, but only at the
cost of replicating it on an international plane and devoting an ever-
larger share of resources to unproductive consumption, i.e. to the
army, navy and swollen state apparatus. It also exacerbated the
uneven development of capitalism, particularly by further depress-
ing agricultural production.[33]

All the devices which the finance capitalists resorted to in order to stabilise the system and to allow the process of production and reproduction to continue, merely served to increase its costs. The dominance of the banks, trusts and cartels, the growth of militarism, the Leviathan state absorbing society into itself, and finally, the inevitable outbreak of imperialist war: 'All these processes were completed under conditions of *vast annihilation of productive powers*. The rebuilding of the structure was accompanied by a decline of productive powers.'[34] It was of the nature of 'critical' epochs, in Bukharin's account, that they threw into doubt the very possibility of completing the cycle of production on the basis of the old relations of production.[35]

In Bukharin's view, therefore, the more desperately finance capitalism struggled to retain its mode of production and political power, the more its costs, in terms of productive forces destroyed or wastefully employed, would escalate. The socialist revolution, Bukharin now acknowledged, could not arrest this process: on the contrary it completed the disintegration of the old industrial base by exploding the patterns of authority that had been its cement. Before entering the land flowing with milk and honey the revolution would first have to travel through a ravaged land. For a social revolution was class war raised to its fiercest intensity in war and civil war. Its costs were enormous:

For in the revolution the shell of productive relations, i.e. the personal apparatus of labour is exploded, and this means, and *must* mean, a disturbance of the process of reproduction and consequently also a destruction of productive powers.

If that is so – and it is absolutely so – then it must be *a priori* evident that the proletarian revolution is inevitably accompanied by a strong decline of productive powers, for no revolution experiences such a broad and deep *break* in old relationships and their *rebuilding* in a new way. . . . The extent of the costs of proletarian revolution is determined by the depth of communist revolution.[36]

These costs, the costs of revolution and civil war, of eliminating the old patterns of authority in the productive process and in the superstructure, were extensive indeed in Bukharin's account. There was, in the first place, the actual physical annihilation of elements of production: factories, machines, livestock, railroads and

persons. In the second place there was the exhaustion, or discount-
ing, of all the scarce available elements of production – the
depreciation of machines through over-use and lack of servicing and
repairs, the exhaustion of the working class and the consequent
employment of 'surrogates' in the means of production and labour
powers (a larger percentage of women, of non-proletarian and half-
proletarian elements, etc.).[37] Thirdly, and most important, there
was the smashing of the old 'hierarchical system of labour' and 'the
dissolution of the cohesion between city and country'; this,
Bukharin maintained, 'is the *main cause* of the decline of productive powers in the transitional period'.[38] The peasants
having seized the lands of the landlords and the Crown were no
longer obliged to find cash to pay their rent and redemption
payments. The imperative to produce cash crops for sale on the
market – the imperative for the peasants to be commodity producers – no longer applied. '*Productive powers are not physically destroyed
here. . . . They exist in natura, but they exist outside of the process of social
reproduction.*'[39] There was, finally, 'the regrouping of productive
powers in terms of unproductive consumption. Under this belongs
above all the satisfaction of the needs of civil war and of socialist
class war.'[40] This, Bukharin noted, inevitably involved the exhaustion of the material forces of production, throwing into question the
next cycles of reproduction. The civil war also absorbed 'the best
human material, the administrators and organisers among the
workers'.[41]

At the end of the civil war the socialist revolution was, Bukharin
contended, confronted with two inescapable problems. The first of
these was how it was to replenish the vast stock of material
productive forces destroyed or exhausted during the revolution and
the civil war. The second was how was it to reconstitute the 'human
labour apparatus' and produce 'a new social equilibrium in
production' which would reforge the links between town and
country and those between workers, managers and technicians.

To overcome the first problem the regime would have to resort to
what Bukharin now chose to call 'socialist primitive accumulation',
which he understood as the systematic appropriation by the state of
all economic surplus above the bare subsistence needs of the people
and its rationally planned allocation to industrial rehabilitation. It
was entirely obvious that such a grandiose project, which assumed
'the mobilisation of the living productive power' of the whole of
society as its 'basic moment',[42] would entail a prodigious growth of

the administrative and coercive agencies of the state. In dealing with the second problem Bukharin now openly acknowledged that many of the organisations and attitudes of mind which were constitutive of the earlier revolutionary period, but which were inimical to centralised planning and direction, would not voluntarily be relinquished; they would have to be purged. As coercion, particularly of the peasantry, would have to be used wholesale, in the process of 'socialist primitive accumulation', so it would have to be employed against the proletariat to oblige it to organise itself in a new way and to accept the new patterns of authority that the new organisational mode embodied. Force, Bukharin argued, had always, in all revolutions, been necessary not merely to put down the opposition of hostile classes but more positively, to 'promote the formation of new production relations'. Indulging his predilection for imposing generalisations Bukharin went a good deal further. He produced the classic formula vindicating the total, untrammelled, economic, political and coercive power of the proletarian state during the transition period. The greater the power it exercised 'the smaller are the "costs" of the transition period . . . the *shorter* is this transition period, the faster appears a social equilibrium on a new base, and the quicker the curve of productive powers begins to rise'.[43] Hostages to fortune with a vengeance!

As we have seen, the socialist revolution was, in Bukharin's view, not primarily concerned with dissolving the legal and political relations of domination which had typified class society but rather with eliminating these same relations from the economic base of society. The patterns of power and authority which connected directors to managers, managers to foremen and the technical intelligentsia, and these to the workers; all the old socio-technical bonds *of a hierarchical nature* had been dissolved by the revolutionary activity of the proletariat. Only the bonds of unity within the working class itself had been preserved and strengthened. What was lacking was 'a new combination of split social groups',[44] for without it industrial disorganisation and technological backwardness would continue to reign. Proletarian class self-confidence, and the camaraderie which the revolutionary process had produced, could not of themselves make good the enormous costs of the revolution. These characteristics had been vital to the first, destructive phase of the revolution, but had become dysfunctional in its second positive phase in that the proletariat had acquired a virulent prejudice against managers, experts, bourgeois specialists and one-man management. Some means would have to be found whereby the spirit of egalitarian solidarity which the revolution had produced in the proletariat could be integrated with the vital expertise of the technical intelligentsia: 'this is the decisive, one could say the basic, question of the structure'.[45]

In the first phase of the revolution, power had been diffused to a myriad self-acting groups. Factory committees of workers had assumed the control and direction of production in particular plants, local soviets operated as virtually autonomous agencies of administration, cooperative societies had taken over distribution on a local scale, detachments of militia had operated as the policing power in the localities, and in the army the power of the officers had been replaced by a system of committees and soviets. This loose structure had the advantage of involving everybody in administration and therefore of carrying the dissolution of the old authority patterns down to the grass roots. It also had its costs. It had resulted everywhere in 'decentralisation and splintering of responsibility'. It had certainly roused the masses and invigorated the lower cells of the nascent apparatus of administration, but it had not articulated a comprehensive plan for further development. 'Decomposition of the old apparatus and rough draft of the new one – that is the model of administration we observe.'[46]

The costs of what we might term the commune model were, according to Bukharin, first exposed in the organisation of the army. The revolutionary decomposition of the old authority patterns of the Tsarist army was necessary in the first stage to break the old coercive structure and begin 'the schooling of and preparation of active organisational powers for the future proletarian army' but, Bukharin went on, 'No one can maintain that the regimental committees make the army able to fight.'[47] When it came to the real crisis point, when the army was obliged to organise itself to fight for the life of the young republic, then, Bukharin argued, almost in modern structuralist terms, the very objectives and situation of the army dictated its organisational structure:

Therefore, as a result of the conditions for existence of this organisation itself, a specific model of this organisation is required here: the greatest exactitude, unconditional and undisputed discipline, speed in decision-making, unity of will, and therefore minimal consultation and discussion, a minimal number of councils, maximal authority.[48]

In precisely the same way he argued that factory committees and workers' councils could and did dissolve the old capitalist relations of production, but this was 'bought at the price of constant errors in administration itself' and encouraged localised as against social production. The objective of the first phase was the revolutionary decomposition of the old and the beginning of the schooling of the mass in administration. The objective of the second phase was radically different: it was to make good the costs of the first period and prepare the ground for the technological revolution. This entailed amassing resources through primitive socialist accumulation, which in turn demanded the planned mobilisation of the available labour power and its most efficient deployment: 'The principle of far-reaching *eligibility* from below upward . . . is replaced by the principle of the painstaking *selection* in dependence on technological and administrative personnel, on the competence and reliability of the candidates.'[49] The task in hand was, therefore, 'the discovery of such a form of administration which guarantees maximal efficiency'.[50]

With the transition to the positive task of maximising productive efficiency, it followed, in Bukharin's view, that the diffuse collegial authority patterns created in the first phase would have to be transformed. Arguing from a similar sort of structuralist analysis to that employed in considering the army, he held that the very exigencies of the modern productive process demanded that engineers and technical experts be given considerable authority within the work process. The technical intelligentsia could not, therefore, be made subordinate to the workers *qua* workers. 'Must not an engineer or technologist issue commands to the workers and consequently stand *above* them? Just as an officer in the Red Army must stand above the common soldier.'[51] The formal dominance of the technical intelligentsia would, therefore, have to be re-established but it would be subordinate 'in the last resort to the collective will of the working class, which will find its expression in the state-economic organisation of the proletariat'.[52] The power of the proletariat, hitherto dissipated in a profusion of more or less autonomous structures, would have to be centralised and concentrated in the state in order to produce equilibrium in the new system, make good the costs of the critical epoch and prepare for the next stage of the ascent to communism. Only the state could undertake the gigantic tasks of mobilising and restructuring the entire labour force of society, tasks which, as we have seen, Bukharin considered to be necessary entailments of primitive socialist accumulation. 'For this reason, *revolutionary* state power is the mightiest lever of economic transformation.'[53] Bukharin had already, in 1921, articulated the major theoretical revisions which Stalinism was to appropriate as its own. In particular he had provided a quite sophisticated justification for the state power of the proletariat during the transition period, being not merely independent of the economic and social base but dominating and moulding it.

Bukharin had at last resolved his 'basic question of the structure'. The split social groups were to be reintegrated through the mediation of the proletarian state. As in the model of finance capitalism, it fell to the state to create and guarantee equilibrium within the social and productive systems.

The paradox was that the state power, which was, *ipso facto*, the organised coercive arm of the dominant class, would, under the dictatorship of the proletariat, have to be extensively employed against the proletariat itself. Just as the imperialist state had been utilised to enforce 'new production relations' in order to guarantee the cycle of capitalist reproduction during critical epochs, so the proletarian state was similarly obliged to act.

> State capitalism saved the *capitalist* state by an active and conscious intervention in production relations. Socialist methods will be a continuation of this active process of organisation, but solely for the salvation and unfolding of the *free* society.[54]

In the first phase of the revolutionary process the revolutionary decomposition of the hierarchical patterns of authority deriving from the power of capital had created a critical situation in which the conditions for the completion and repeatability of the cycle of social production had entirely vanished. And yet, for broad strata of the proletariat, these very same conditions – the absence of central direction and autonomy of individual plants, the collegial form of management and contempt for one-man management and the authority of the 'specialists' – were to be jealously guarded as the real and lasting gains of the revolution. Compulsion, Bukharin concluded, would therefore have to be applied 'even to the ruling class'.[55]

The proletariat, Bukharin argued, was not all of a piece. 'The proletariat arrives at its domination as a class. But this in no way signifies a unified character of this class in which every member represents an ideal cross-section.'[56] It consisted of different strata with differing levels of consciousness. It was, he maintained, illusory to believe that the entire proletariat had a proper conception of the essential interests and goals of the class. Within it there were 'groups which have been completely corrupted by capitalism, with maximal narrow egotistical motives. But even relatively broad circles of the working class bear the stamp of the capitalist commodity world.'[57] As always it was the proletarian vanguard, the more advanced members of the class, which led the other strata. 'It is a purposeful, organising force operating deliberately', enjoying the active support and sympathy of the 'middle stratum', but obliged to force the backward stratum of workers into organisational forms which expressed their real or essential interests.[58] It followed, according to Bukharin's logic, that, insofar as substantial numbers of workers resisted the measures necessary to the transition period, they did so against the essential long-term proletarian interest. To force them to comply with these measures was, therefore, to force them to realise their own true interests. Bukharin ends up, as he was bound to, so long as the distinction between real and felt interest was central to his thought, forcing men to be free. The application of force, in this account, did not impede man's freedom, it simply obliged him to follow his real will. Though this might have the appearance of an external power working on him it was essentially his own self-realisation. We have to invoke this paradox of freedom in order to make Bukharin's pronouncements intelligible:

> This 'concentrated force' turns *inward*, by constituting a factor of the self-organisation and the compulsory self-discipline of the working people.[59]

> It is obvious that this element of compulsion, which is here the self-compulsion of the working class, grows from the crystallised centre towards the significantly more amorphous and dispersed periphery. This is the conscious power of cohesion of the little parts of the working class, which power represents for some categories, subjectively, an external pressure, which constitutes for the entire working class, objectively, its accelerated *self-organisation*.[60]

In the *transition period* the self-activity of the working class is present along with the force which the working class, as a class for itself, introduces for all its parts. The contradiction between force and self-activity expresses the self-contradictory character of the transition period itself. . . .[61]

The proletariat then, in Bukharin's account, could exist as a class for itself – that is, as a class aware of its historical objectives and organised to fulfil them – only by assuming its most purposive all-embracing form as a proletarian state dictatorship. Only in this way could the parochialism and craft particularism of its elements be overcome. Only through the state could its limited forces be organised and efficiently directed. The state form appropriate to the transition period would therefore be not the transcendence of the imperialist state as the initial project he had canvassed, but the creation of its mirror image:

> Now we must investigate the general principles of the building of communism. It is completely clear that the next epoch must be the epoch of the *dictatorship of the proletariat*, which will *formally* have *similarity* with the epoch of the dictatorship of the bourgeoisie, i.e. will be *state capitalism* turned upside-down, its *dialectical reversal of poles into its* own opposite.[62]

As the bourgeois state had emerged in the imperialist epoch as the organiser of labour and director of production, all-embracing and total in its pretensions, so too the proletarian state would, even more emphatically, have to assume the same roles and pursue an even more thorough-going organisation and centralisation of all available human and material resources in order to make good the costs of the revolution and prepare for socialism. The proletarian state could be nothing other than the 'concentrated application of force'[63] and consummate centralised organisation. In this project it followed that all the autonomous, self-acting organisations of the working class appeared now as so many obstacles to centralised direction mobilisation and planning. As in the model of the imperialist state, and for similar reasons (i.e. to produce stability and equilibrium in the productive process), they became the fodder to nourish the insatiable appetite of the growing state power which was the only organisation capable of articulating and realising the essential interests of the class.

It is absolutely clear that the same method is formally necessary for the working class as for the bourgeoisie in the epoch of state capitalism. This organisational method consists in the coordination of all proletarian organisations with one all-encompassing organisation, i.e. with the state organisation of the working class, with the *Soviet state of the proletariat*. The étatisation [*ogosudarstvlenie*] of the trade unions and the effective étatisation of all mass organisations of the proletariat arises from the internal logic of the process of transformation itself. The minutest cells of the labour apparatus must transform themselves into agents of the general process of organisation, which is systematically planned and led by the collective reason of the working class, which finds its material expression in the highest and most all-encompassing organisation, in its state apparatus. Thus the system of state capitalism dialectically transforms itself into its own antithesis, into the state form for workers' socialism.[64]

The model of legitimate authority proposed by Lenin and Bukharin, before, during and immediately after the revolution, was that of radical direct democracy. Universal participation in all the processes of arriving at decisions and implementing them was the end of alienation and of separate bodies of armed men, bureaucrats and managers. This model necessarily entailed the broadest diffusion of authority and power to a multiplicity of self-acting organisations of the popular mass, its animating principles being camaraderie and spontaneous self-organisation.

The model which Bukharin arrived at in 1920 and which Stalin's practices were to confirm throughout the thirties and forties, was a model of necessary power rather than one of legitimate authority. Its legitimising principle was based on the distinction between the real or essential interests of the proletariat and their currently recognised interests. In Marx's account the reconciliation of real and felt interest was immanent within the historical process – as the class matured it would come to full consciousness and recognise its essential objectives.[65] Bukharin's argument in 1920 was that, if the proletariat, at a critical juncture, failed to recognise its essential interest, then its vanguard, concentrated in the state and expressing its 'collective reason', would have to intervene with force. The legitimacy of the superordinate power of the proletarian state power derived, therefore, from a view of a necessary historical process from which the essential goals of the class could be adduced.

Bukharin's new synthesis, which identified the class for itself with the state, which would tolerate no independent organisations standing between the state and its atomised citizens, and which narrowed the concept of socialism to a Saint-Simonian efficiency in which self-management, camaraderie and spontaneity were replaced by one-man management, efficiency and centralised planning, was no more than a forthright and coldly logical statement of what the Bolsheviks already, in 1920, had done or were aspiring to do. He did no more than provide the theoretical gloss (which Lenin, in all essentials, heartily endorsed) to prevailing Bolshevik practice. Theory once more cohered with practice but in the process the initial project of Lenin and Bukharin, to transform all the old relationships of domination and subservience among men, had all but withered away.

NOTES

1. N. I. Bukharin, 'K teorii imperialisticheskogo gosudarstva', in *Revoliutsia prava, Sbornik pervyi*, no. 25 (Moscow, 1925; referred to hereafter as 'K teorii'). This article was written in 1916, and various parts and abstracts of it were published in that year – for details see S. Heitman, *Nikolai I. Bukharin: A Bibliography* (Stanford, Calif., 1969) pp. 29–30 – but it was not published in full until 1925. Not available in translation.

2. N. Bukharin, *Ekonomika perekhodnogo perioda, chast' 1. obschchaya teoriya transformatsionnogo protsessa* (Moscow, 1920). An anonymous English translation, with Lenin's critical remarks, has been published under the somewhat misleading title *Economics of the Transformation Period* (New York, 1971). For the convenience of those who do not read Russian, I will cross-reference on the following model: *Ekonomika*, p. 7 (*Economics*, p. 11). The translation of this text by Oliver Field, with Introduction by K. J. Tarbuck (London, 1979), came to my notice only after completion of these notes.

3. 'K teorii', p. 8. See F. Engels, *The Origin of the Family, Private Property and the State*, (Chicago, 1902) p. 206.

4. Karl Marx and Frederick Engels, *The Manifesto of the Communist Party*; in *Collected Works*, 50 vols (London, 1975–) vol. VI, p. 499: 'Capital is, therefore, not a personal, it is a social power.'

5. 'K teorii'; p. 11.

6. N. Bukharin, *Mirovoe khozyaistvo i imperializm*, with an Introduction by Lenin (Moscow, 1917). References in the text are to the English translation, *Imperialism and World Economy* (London, n.d. [1929 or 1930]).

7. R. Hilferding, *Das Finanzkapital*, in M. Adler (ed.), *Marx-Studien, Dritter Band* (Vienna, 1910). References in the text are to the Russian edition, *Finansovyi kapital* (Moscow, 1914).

8. Ibid., p. 430.

9. Ibid., p. 476.

10. 'K teorii', p. 29.
11. Ibid., pp. 26–7.
12. Ibid., p. 30.
13. Bukharin, *Imperialism*, p. 167.
14. V. I. Lenin, *Collected Works*, 45 vols (Moscow, 1960–70) vol. xxxv, p. 231.
15. Ibid., vol. xxii, pp. 185–304.
16. Karl Marx and Frederick Engels, *Selected Works*, 2 vols (London, 1942) vol. ii, pp. 315–426. I have resorted to the *Selected Works* for those texts not yet covered by the *Collected Works* (see note 4).
17. Marx–Engels, *Selected Works*, vol. ii, p. 412.
18. Ibid., p. 413.
19. Lenin, *Collected Works*, vol. xxvi, p. 411.
20. Ibid., vol. xxv, p. 415.
21. Marx–Engels, *Selected Works*, vol. i, pp. 502–3, quoted in Lenin, *Collected Works*, vol. xxiv, p. 69.
22. Ibid., pp. 169–70.
23. Without big banks socialism would be impossible. 'The big banks are the "state apparatus" which we need to bring about socialism, and which we take ready-made from capitalism. . . . A single State Bank . . . will constitute as much as nine-tenths of the socialist apparatus. This will be wide book-keeping, country-wide accountancy of the production and distribution of goods, this will be so to speak, something in the nature of the skeleton of socialist society' – Lenin, *Collected Works*, vol. xxvi, p. 106.
24. Ibid., vol. xxii, p. 205.
25. Ibid., vol. xxv, pp. 425–6.
26. Ibid., vol. xxx, pp. 339–40.
27. Ibid., vol. xxix, p. 365.
28. 'What happens is that the Party, shall we say, absorbs the vanguard of the proletariat, and this vanguard exercises the dictatorship of the proletariat' – ibid., vol. xxxii, p. 20.
29. Trotsky's vindication of the forced militarisation of labour and his identification of the military model as the model of socialism was also written in 1920 and published as *Terrorism and Communism, A Reply to Karl Kautsky* (Ann Arbor, Mich., 1961).
30. A useful, if somewhat exhaustive, account of the manner in which these agencies of working-class self-administration were rapidly usurped by the party–state apparatus is given in Charles Bettelheim's *Class 'Struggles in the USSR*, vol. i: *1917–1923* (Hassocks, Sussex, 1977).
31. Bukharin, *Ekonomika*, p. 48 (*Economics*, pp. 56–7). (Hereafter, page numbers in parentheses refer to the English text.)
32. Ibid., pp. 15–16; cf. pp. 91–5 (p. 21; cf. pp. 102–5).
33. Ibid., p. 74 (p. 82).
34. Ibid., p. 36 (p. 42).
35. Ibid., p. 37 (p. 43).
36. Ibid., pp. 95–6 (p. 106).
37. Ibid., pp. 97–8 (pp. 106–7).
38. Ibid., p. 98 (p. 107).
39. Ibid. (p. 108).
40. Ibid. (p. 109).

41. Ibid.
42. Ibid., pp. 101–2 (p. 111).
43. Ibid., p. 139 (pp. 150–1).
44. Ibid., p. 52 (p. 61).
45. Ibid., p. 65 (pp. 72–3).
46. Ibid., p. 117 (p. 126).
47. Ibid.
48. Ibid., p. 118 (p. 128).
49. Ibid., p. 120 (p. 130).
50. Ibid.
51. Ibid., p. 66 (p. 74).
52. Ibid., p. 67 (p. 75).
53. Ibid., p. 139 (p. 151).
54. Ibid., p. 64 (p. 69).
55. Ibid., p. 141 (p. 154).
56. Ibid., p. 142 (p. 155).
57. Ibid., p. 143 (p. 156). Cf. Lenin: 'The workers were never separated by a Great Wall of China from the old society. . . . The workers are building a new society without themselves having become new people or cleansed themselves of the filth of the old world; they are still standing up to their knees in that filth' – *Collected Works*, vol. XXVIII, p. 424.
58. Bukharin, *Ekonomika*, p. 142 (*Economics*, p. 155).
59. Ibid., p. 140 (p. 151).
60. Ibid., p. 144 (p. 157).
61. Ibid.
62. Ibid., pp. 63–4 (p. 71).
63. Ibid., p. 147 (p. 160).
64. Ibid., pp. 71–2 (p. 79).
65. Marx–Engels, *Complete Works*, vol. IV, p. 37.

4 The Spark that became a Flame: the Bolsheviks, Propaganda and the Cinema

Richard Taylor

Long before 1917 the distinction between agitation and propaganda had become a commonplace of Russian socialist theory and practice. Indeed, these concepts had their origins in an earlier generation that preceded the emergence of Russian Marxism, with men such as Herzen, Bakunin, Chernyshevsky and Lavrov, and more particularly with the publication of journals such as Herzen's *Kolokol* (The Bell) or Lavrov's *Vperyod* (Forward). The immense significance of these activities for the revolutionary movement as a whole reflected both its complete exclusion from political power and the absence in Russia of the open political debate through which that power might have been modified or even gradually acquired. Having nowhere else to go, the revolutionaries went underground, and an underground movement, even more than a conventional political party, needs a forum for its theoretical debates and a focal point for its political activities. These were two of the functions performed by the underground press during these years, but the third function, which in the longer term was perhaps to prove the most important, was to attract first the support and later the active participation of ever broader circles of the population.

The failure of the 'Going to the People' movement in the 1870s and the rejection as counterproductive of further acts of terror such as the assassination of Alexander II in 1881 led an increasing number of revolutionary activists to a more acute awareness of the vital role that would be played by agitation, propaganda and organisation in the preparation of the emerging proletariat for its historic task. This awareness was crystallised in Plekhanov's pamphlet, *On the Tasks of the Social Democrats in the Fight against the Famine in Russia*, published in 1892. It was here that Plekhanov first made the distinction that was to become so important for later activists: 'A propagandist presents *many* ideas to one or a few persons; an agitator presents *only one or a few* ideas, but he presents them to a *whole* mass of people.' The two activities were of course closely related and intertwined:

> In general it is not easy to draw the line between agitation and what is usually called propaganda. Agitation is also propaganda but propaganda taking place in particular circumstances, that is, in circumstances that compel even those people who would not normally have paid any attention to them to listen to the words of the propagandist. Propaganda is agitation conducted in the normal everyday course of the life of a particular country. Agitation is propaganda, occasioned by events that are not entirely ordinary and evoking a certain upsurge in the general mood. . . . Propaganda, in the proper sense of the word, would lose all historical meaning if it were not accompanied by agitation.[1]

There is an implication in Plekhanov's work that agitation and propaganda were each appropriate to particular stages in the revolutionary struggle, and this point was developed four years later by Kremer and Martov in *On Agitation*.[2] They argued that the revolutionary movement had been engaged in premature propaganda at a time when agitation would have been more appropriate and thus also more effective. The proletariat, in their view, was not yet ready for the heady abstractions of Marxist theory – the propaganda – that had been prevalent in the discussion circles, and this propaganda had actually fragmented and weakened it. The abstractions of Marxist thought would only mean something to the workers if concretely fixed in their own immediate experience. It was thus essential above all else to make the workers aware that their individual grievances over hours of work and rates of pay, and the strikes, lock-outs, fines, dismissals, etc. that ensued, were part of a wider pattern of class conflict between them as the oppressed proletariat and the representatives of the bourgeoisie, the owning class and the autocracy. Lenin shared this interpretation, and in the course of the 1890s he busied himself writing numerous pamphlets designed to provoke in the mass of the workers an awareness of their interests as a class through the extrapolation of localised, often relatively petty, demands.[3] Once agitation had created the basic conditions for such awareness, it would fall to the propagandist to develop that awareness into a coherent class consciousness. It was against this background that the newspaper, *Rabochee Delo*, was prepared in 1895 and *Iskra* (The Spark) and the journal, *Zarya* (The Dawn), were founded in 1900–1. Writing in May 1901, Lenin defined the role of the party press in the now periodised development of the movement: agitation would lead to propaganda, and propaganda would then lead on to the next stage – organisation:

A newspaper is what we most of all need; without it we cannot conduct that systematic, all-round propaganda and agitation, consistent in principle, which is the chief and permanent task of social democracy in general and, in particular, the pressing task of the moment, when interest in politics and in questions of socialism has been aroused among the broadest strata of the population . . .

The role of a newspaper, however, is not limited solely to the dissemination of ideas, to political education, and to the enlistment of political allies. A newspaper is not only a collective propagandist and a collective agitator, it is also a collective organiser. In this last respect it may be likened to the scaffolding round a building under construction, which marks the contours of a structure and facilitates communication between the builders, enabling them to distribute the work and to view the common results achieved by their organised labour. With the aid of the newspaper, and through it, a permanent organisation will naturally take shape that will engage, not only in local activities, but in regular general work, and will train its members to follow political events carefully, appraise their significance and their effect on the various strata of the population, and develop effective means for the revolutionary party to influence those events.[4]

It is small wonder then that the masthead of *Iskra* proclaimed that 'From this spark there shall arise a flame', which had been the Decembrists' reply to Pushkin.

Lenin developed his views in *What is to be Done?*, which he penned in the following months. At this time, 1901–2, when the party's activities were still confined to the secret and the underground, 'the propagandist operates chiefly by means of the *printed* word; the agitator by means of the *spoken* word.'[5] In these circumstances there was scarcely any alternative. But in 1905, following the widespread disturbances of that year, the situation eased somewhat, and it is in this context that we must see one of the most contentious of Lenin's works, *Party Organisation and Party Literature*, published legally in November in *Novaya Zhizn'* (New Life), a newspaper edited by Gorky's wife, Maria Andreeva. But, before examining this seminal article in greater detail, it would be wise to look more closely at the history of the revolutionaries' view of art and its role in society.

There is of course a long history of political and social commitment in Russian literature especially, dating back to Belinsky and beyond, but a spontaneous and voluntary commitment on the part of the artist is by no means the same as a commitment demanded of the artist by, or in the name of, society. In Russia, however, this distinction is one that would appear to have been lost at an early stage. We know from Krupskaya's memoirs that Lenin was a great admirer and avid reader of Chernyshevsky,[6] and we have Lunacharsky's view that 'Vladimir Ilyich considered that art must be "popular", that it must elevate the masses, teach them and strengthen them. In this respect Vladimir Ilyich was a direct descendant of Chernyshevsky.'[7]

Chernyshevsky's view, shared by others, that 'the content of art is the social aspect of life'[8] meant that the intelligentsia, and especially the writer, had a particular duty towards the people, and that duty lay in the area of propaganda. But to the Marxist any work of art must reflect the attributes of its time, and in particular the social and political context in which it is written. Plekhanov and Lenin expounded and developed this view in the early years of this century. For them a belief in 'art for art's sake' (that is, art without any social or political commitment) was explicable only in terms of a rejection of what the painter Repin called 'our vile reality',[9] or, as Plekhanov expressed it, 'The belief in art for art's sake arises wherever the artist is at odds with his social environment.'[10] The idea of separation between the artist and his social milieu is, according to this argument, a sign of decadence: 'The ideology of a ruling class loses its inherent value as that class ripens for doom. The art engendered by its emotional experience falls into decay.' It is a decadence to which bourgeois society had succumbed:

The extreme individualism of the era of bourgeois decay cuts off artists from all sources of true inspiration. It makes them completely blind to what is going on in social life, and condemns them to sterile preoccupation with personal emotional experiences that are entirely without significance and with the fantasies of morbid imagination.

In Plekhanov's words, 'we find that art for art's sake has turned into art for money's sake'.

Although his article was written in 1912, seven years after Lenin's *Party Organisation and Party Literature*, it is appropriate to discuss it first since it summarises decades of Russian, and later of Russian Marxist, thinking on the role of art and of the artist in the historical development of society. In this interpretation a work of art reflected the particular historical epoch in which it was created. The absence of any obvious social import in a work of art – the tendency towards art for art's sake – was merely confirmation of the sickness of that epoch, a sign of the reaction that was to be expected when an epoch was drawing to its close, so that 'believers in the theory of art for art's sake become conscious defenders of a social order based on the exploitation of one class by another'. Plekhanov's conclusions were, of course, based on an analysis of hitherto existing societies, but it nonetheless followed that under socialism the division between art and society would, because of the abolition of class-based relationships, be rendered impossible:

In a socialist society the pursuit of art for art's sake will be a sheer logical impossibility to the extent that there will no longer be that vulgarisation of social morals that is now an inevitable consequence of the determination of the ruling class to retain its privileges.

Further, art could by implication expect to be utilised in the struggle for the creation of that new society, for 'political authority always prefers the instrumental view of art, to the extent, of course, that it pays any attention to art at all. And this is understandable: it is to its interest to harness all ideologies to the service of the cause which it serves itself.'[11] It is clear from *Art and Social Life* that Plekhanov himself also preferred this instrumental view of art: but it is equally clear from *Party Organisation and Party Literature* that Lenin held this view as well.[12]

Those who wish to defend Lenin against this accusation usually refer to the passage in that article where he tries to calm the fears of 'some intellectual, an ardent champion of liberty':

> Calm yourselves, gentlemen: First of all, we are discussing party literature and its subordination to party control. Everyone is free to write and say whatever he likes, without any restrictions. But every voluntary association (including the party) is also free to expel members who use the name of the party to advocate anti-party views. Freedom of speech and the press must be complete. But then freedom of association must be complete too.

This was, however, an assessment of the situation at a time when 'The revolution is not yet completed. While tsarism is *no longer* strong enough to defeat the revolution, the revolution is *not yet* strong enough to defeat tsarism.' But, Lenin maintained, 'One cannot live in a society and be free from society. The freedom of the bourgeois writer, artist or actress is simply masked (or hypocritically masked) dependence on the money-bag, on corruption, on prostitution.' In the pre-revolutionary period, while the revolutionary forces gathered their strength, it was the responsibility of social-democratic literature 'to contrast this hypocritically free literature, which is in reality linked to the bourgeoisie, with a really free one that will be *openly* linked to the proletariat'. Lenin himself answered the obvious question: what would this 'really free literature' be like?:

> It will be a free literature, because the idea of socialism and sympathy with the working people, and not greed or careerism, will bring ever newer forces to its ranks. It will be a free literature, because it will serve, not some satiated heroine, not the bored 'upper ten thousand' suffering from fatty degeneration, but the millions and tens of millions of working people – the flower of the country, its strengths and its future. It will be a free literature, enriching the last word in the revolutionary thought of mankind with the experience and living work of the socialist proletariat, bringing about permanent interaction between the experience of the past (scientific socialism, the completion of the development of socialism from its primitive, utopian forms) and the experience of the present (the present struggle of the worker comrades).

Would there be room for 'bourgeois–intellectual individualism'?

The answer to this question is not made explicit, but it is surely implicit in the whole history of the debate, in the idea that 'One cannot live in a society and be free from society', and in this statement:

> for the socialist proletariat, literature cannot be a means of enriching individuals or groups; it cannot, in fact, be an individual undertaking independent of the common cause of the proletariat. Down with non-partisan writers! Down with literary supermen! Literature must become *part* of the common cause of the proletariat, 'a cog and screw' of one single great Social Democratic mechanism set in motion by the entire politically conscious vanguard of the entire working class.

Clearly the instrumental view of art no longer distinguishes between agitation and propaganda work on the one hand, and artistic creativity on the other.[13] It merely confirms Dobrolyubov's view that 'The measure of the worth of the writer or a work of art [is] the extent to which they serve as expressions of the natural aspirations of the given epoch or people.'[14] Art has a social responsibility and a social function, nothing more and nothing less.

This interpretation is supported by the conversation that Lenin had with Klara Zetkin after the October Revolution had given the Bolsheviks not merely the tasks of agitation and propaganda, but also that of organisation. Art no longer merely reflected society; it had to shape society as well, and to shape it in the revolutionary mould:

> In a society based on private property the artist produces goods for the market; he needs buyers. Our revolution has freed artists from the yoke of these highly prosaic conditions. It has transformed the Soviet state into their protector and their customer. Every artist, anyone who considers himself as such, has the right to create freely, according to his ideal, independent of anything else.
>
> But you must understand that we are communists. We should not stand by with our arms folded and let chaos develop in all directions. We should guide this process and mould its results fully and systematically.

Lenin went on to admit that he found some of the manifestations of modernism in art distasteful: 'I, however, have the audacity to declare myself to be a "barbarian". I cannot bring myself to regard the works of Expressionism, Futurism, Cubism and the other "isms" as the highest manifestation of artistic genius. I do not understand them. I do not derive any pleasure from them.' But, he continued,

It is not our view of art that is important. Nor does it matter what art gives to several hundred, even several thousand, out of a total population numbering millions. Art belongs to the people. It should reach with its deepest roots into the very thick of the broad working masses. It should be understood by these masses and loved by them. It should unite the feeling, thought and will of these masses, and elevate them. It should awaken the artists among them and help them to develop. Should we treat a small minority to sweet refined biscuits while the masses of workers and peasants go short of black bread?

The principal danger to the party's artistic policies after the Revolution came, not from the 'bourgeois-intellectual individualists', but from those, such as the Futurists, who wished to create from scratch a new proletarian culture, destroying all remnants of the old. As will already be clear, Lenin would have no truck with this:

We are far too 'iconoclastic'. We must preserve the beautiful, take it as a model, proceed from it, even if it is 'old'. Why should we turn away from the truly beautiful, rejecting it as the starting point for further development merely because it is 'old'? Why should we bow down before the new, as if before a god to which we have to submit merely because 'it is new'? Nonsense, utter nonsense![15]

In the draft resolution for the Proletkult Congress that Lenin drew up in October 1920 he reiterated this view:

Marxism has won its historic significance as the ideology of the revolutionary proletariat because, far from rejecting the most valuable achievements of the bourgeois epoch, it has, on the contrary, assimilated and refashioned everything of value in the more than two thousand years of the development of human thought and culture.

Nevertheless, Lenin's assessment of the proper role of art in Soviet Russia is made quite explicit in this resolution: art is seen as part of the process of education which, in this context, means political education, or indoctrination: 'All educational work in the Soviet Republic of workers and peasants, in the field of political education in general and in the field of art in particular, should be imbued with the spirit of the class struggle.'[16] The 'small minority' clamouring for 'sweet refined biscuits' clearly has no place in the new order: the Central Committee letter that followed this resolution stated quite simply that 'The Central Committee will achieve the removal of these bourgeois currents.'[17]

The principal task of literature and the other arts after the Revolution was 'always to bear the workers and peasants in mind. For their sakes we should learn to keep house and do our sums. This applies to the fields of art and culture as well. So that art can be closer to the people, and the people closer to art, we should first of all raise the general educational and cultural level.'[18] This meant above all else that illiteracy should be eradicated as soon as possible. In Lenin's words, 'An illiterate person stands outside politics: he has first to be taught the alphabet. Without this there is only rumour, scandal, gossip and prejudice – but no politics.'[19]

He had made much the same point the day after the Revolution when addressing the Second All-Russian Congress of Soviets: 'In our view the state draws its strength from the consciousness of the masses. It is strong when the masses know everything, can make judgements on everything and approach everything consciously.'[20] Four years later he explained to Annenkov that 'the purpose of "liquidate illiteracy" is only that every peasant and every worker should be able to read by himself, without help, our decrees, orders and proclamations. The aim is completely practical. Nothing more.'[21]

The distinction that Plekhanov and Lenin had drawn between agitation and propaganda carried within it the assumption that the party would play a leading, and dominant, role in the proletariat's struggle to achieve socialism: it was an assumption, therefore, of political élitism. If the distinction between party and people were to break down, so too would that between agitation and propaganda, and one might have expected this to happen after the October Revolution. Instead, a significant shift occurred. Whereas before the Revolution agitation had been aimed almost entirely at the urban proletariat, now it had to be aimed at the entire population, urban and rural, bourgeois and proletarian alike. Similarly, the basis for propaganda was also widened: instead of preaching to the converted, propaganda was now directed at the broader mass of those who found themselves, for one reason or another, in the front line of the revolutionary struggle and who, although in a sense therefore still committed, were not committed in the same way, or to the same degree, that their predecessors in the pre-revolutionary underground had been committed. And beyond this broader-based agitation and propaganda the Bolsheviks had also to *organise* the construction of a new political, social and economic order.

In October 1917, however, the Bolsheviks had seized control only of the 'commanding heights' of what remained of the administrative machinery of the Russian state, a machinery that had become rusted, worn and outdated and was certainly no match for the awe-inspiring tasks that the revolutionaries had set themselves. Nor was the Revolution necessarily welcomed by the people who staffed this machinery,[22] or indeed by large sections of the population as a whole. The Bolsheviks, therefore, could not rely on the existing, or remaining, conventional administrative structure of the state to sustain them in power: to utilise it to transform society was quite out of the question. Their position was further weakened by the turmoil that characterised their first three years in power: famine, disease and armed insurrection in the provinces prevented them from establishing, let alone maintaining, lasting contact with the masses in whose name they claimed to act.

To perform their tasks the new rulers obviously required all the means of agitation and propaganda that they could lay their hands on. The conventional realities of political authority were to be obscured by the persuasive mists of revolutionary romanticism. The storming of the Winter Palace was re-enacted, albeit in somewhat enhanced form, for the benefits of the citizens of Petrograd, many of whom participated in the spectacle (many more, in fact, than had participated in the original act), while Mayakovsky urged his fellow poets, 'On to the streets, Futurists, drummers and poets!'[23]

But mass dramatic spectacles were limited both in their appeal and in their effectiveness: they required a tremendous effort of organisation and, however large their 'cast', they could by their nature involve only a relatively small proportion of the population. As Lenin said,

What can this do for the many millions of the population who are untouched by the most elementary knowledge, the most primitive culture? We must admit that, at the same time as ten thousand people here in Moscow, and tomorrow another ten thousand people, will go into raptures over a glittering spectacle in the theatre, millions of people will be striving to learn to count and copy their name, trying to make contact with the culture that would teach them that the earth is round and not flat, and that the world is governed by the laws of nature and not by witches, wizards and the 'Heavenly Father'.[24]

That is some small measure of their enormous task.

Another medium that was available to the Bolsheviks was, of course, the press, and it was a medium that they had utilised to great effect in the days of underground struggle. But, with more than two-thirds of the population unable to read, the scope for successful agitation and propaganda work through newspapers, leaflets and other printed matter was severely limited. It was further restricted by the acute shortage of newsprint. The press would have to continue to fulfil its pre-revolutionary function as a life-line to the committed who, by the very fact of their literacy alone, would act as 'opinion leaders'. It was at best an indirect role, necessary but by no means sufficient. Similarly, the poster was of limited use. It had the advantage that its appeal was primarily, if not entirely, visual and therefore also direct, memorable and universal. But the poster's effectiveness was reduced by difficulties of production, distribution and display, and by the tendency on the part of poster artists to indulge in flights of stylistic innovation.[25] What the Bolsheviks needed was a medium that exerted an essentially visual impact, one that was simple, direct and universal in its appeal. What the Bolsheviks needed was a *mass medium*, and the one that appeared to them to be the most valuable was the cinema.

Why did the Bolsheviks value the cinema so highly? First and foremost, the cinema, which was at that time still silent, was a purely *visual* medium of communication: because of this it was also a simple straightforward medium. What might later become a hindrance to the transmission of a complex message, was a godsend to the revolutionary authorities: the visual nature of the medium combined with its simplicity to make it a particularly effective weapon when the population was predominantly illiterate, spoke numerous different languages and came from a variety of cultural and social backgrounds. The cinema, in this sense, was the great leveller. It was also, as Lunacharsky pointed out, a portable medium: the agit-trains were witness to this.[26] Because of its mechanical basis, the cinema was regarded by many of its proponents as *the* revolutionary art form: 'The cinema is a new outlook on life. The cinema is the triumph of the machine, electricity and industry.'[27] This association enabled the authorities to project an image of modernity and progress which was particularly effective in the remoter areas, at least until machinery became associated with collectivisation.[28] Whereas the poster, also a visual medium, was static, the cinema was dynamic: 'The soul of the cinema is in the movement of life'[29] – and this underlined its novelty. Finally, the cinema was universal in its appeal: apart from its accessibility to audiences of varying linguistic, national or social backgrounds, it appealed to them as individuals in a crowd, and in a crowd individuals are emotionally particularly vulnerable. Because of what came to be known as its 'mechanical reproducibility' the cinema could exert its appeal simultaneously over a wide geographical area, while those in the capital who had controlled the production of a particular film would know precisely what was being shown in the provinces: the cinema was a *direct* medium of agitation and propaganda and a *direct* method of organising the masses. Lunacharsky claimed that 'the power of the cinema is unbounded,'[30] but to what extent was that power actually harnessed?

When the Bolsheviks seized power their principal initial task was quite simply to retain power: they had little or no time to think of the longer term.[31] During the civil war in Russia the use of the cinema for political purposes was largely restricted to the production of short and simple *agitki* that could be shown by the agit-trains as they toured the country.[32] But in November 1920, as the civil war drew to a close, Lenin was able to return to the problems of the longer historical perspective: once the military battle had been won, the Bolsheviks could concentrate on the awesome task of the 're-education of the masses'. He argued that: 'Propaganda of the old type describes and illustrates what communism is. This kind of propaganda is now useless, for we have to show in practice how socialism is to be built. All our propaganda must be based on the political experience of economic development. That is our principal task.'[33] In the same month Lenin advocated 'the more extensive and systematic use of films for production propaganda'.[34] In what has become the most famous and best-documented example of Lenin's interest in the use of the cinema to improve productivity (a technique that he had observed in the capitalist world), he urged the delegates to the Ninth Congress to 'see the film on peat extraction which has been shown in Moscow and which can be demonstrated for the Congress delegates'.[35] However, it was one thing to produce a short *agitka*, quite another to organise a film industry.

There has been some dispute over the kind of films that Lenin wanted the Soviet cinema to produce in the longer term, as it moved from agitation to propaganda and eventually perhaps even to organisation. Again we have to rely on hearsay evidence for Lenin's views. In his directive of 17 January 1922 Lenin urged:

> For all cinema programmes a definite proportion should be determined:
>
> (a) Entertainment films, especially for publicity purposes and for their receipts (without, of course, any obscene or counter-revolutionary content); and
> (b) under the heading 'From the Life of the Peoples of the World', films of a particularly propagandist content, such as the colonial policy of the British in India, the work of the League of Nations, the starving in Berlin, etc., etc.[36]

Lenin's reference to 'a definite proportion' has been seized upon, by Soviet documentary film makers in particular, to support their assertion that the ratio of 'played' (*igrovoi*) films to documentaries was to be set at 75:25 per cent. This has become known as the 'Leninist proportion', but I can find no evidence that Lenin was personally responsible for it. On the contrary, Lunacharsky's recollections of 1928, *Kino na zapade i u nas* (The Cinema Here and in the West), characterise Lenin's views as follows:

> We should pursue three goals overall. The first – a broadly informative newsreel that would be appropriately selected, i.e. it would be visual publicity in the spirit of the line that, let us say, our best Soviet newspapers take. Apart from this, the cinema should, in Vladimir Ilyich's view, assume in addition the character of visual public lectures on various questions of science and technology. Finally, Vladimir Ilyich considered it no less, but on the contrary even more, important that there should be artistic propagation of our ideas in the form of entertainment films, showing fragments of life and imbued with our ideas –

both bringing to the country's attention that which is good, unfolding and uplifting, and hitting out [at that which is not] here and in the life of other classes and other countries.[37]

Behind the tortuous phraseology it is clear that Lenin did not concede supremacy to the documentary: in the cinema, as in the other arts, he rejected, in the words of his draft resolution 'On Proletarian Culture', 'as theoretically unsound and practically harmful, all attempts to invent one's own particular brand of culture'.[38] Far from endorsing the primacy of the documentary, Lenin did precisely the reverse, describing the fictional feature film as 'no less, but on the contrary even more, important', and this genre of film was to stand in the same relationship to the newsreel and documentary as the novel or poem stood to the newspaper article.

The transition from civil war to a period of reconstruction was reflected in a change in the emphasis of agitation and propaganda. Lenin had noted the need for this in November 1920; in the cinema it was marked by a move from the production of short *agitki* to that of feature-length entertainment films, albeit 'imbued with communist ideas'. The move was, of course, facilitated by the importation of new equipment and new supplies of film stock. The overwhelming majority of these films were artistically conservative, based on the conventions established by Hollywood and by pre-revolutionary Russian directors, even if the message was a revolutionary one: Yakov Protazanov's *Aelita*, with its fantasies of a revolution on Mars, is a good example. The Soviet cinema needed to make this kind of film, even if, from Lenin's point of view, such films were 'useless', simply because throughout the 1920s the Soviet cinema had to compete for its own Soviet audience with the films that were still being imported from the capitalist world, and in particular from Germany and the United States.[39] This state of affairs continued until 1928: it had to be tolerated because there was no realistic alternative if the Soviet cinema were to be kept going. It was Lunacharsky who remarked that 'The cinema is an industry and, what is more, a profitable industry.'[40] The reconstruction of the cinema was to be largely self-financed and the imported films were to be used to attract audiences for Bolshevik propaganda. Again, this was no easy task and the party encountered innumerable obstacles, exhorting film makers to make the right kind of films and reorganising the industry in an attempt to ensure that they did.[41]

But the films that are nowadays associated with the 'golden era' of the Soviet silent cinema, the innovatory masterpieces of Kuleshov, Eisenstein and Vertov, were not popular with Soviet audiences who, as long as they had the choice, preferred Chaplin, Keaton, Fairbanks and Pickford, or the kind of 'psychological salon dramas' with which Lunacharsky himself was associated and which later came under fierce attack. But the films of the Soviet *avant-garde* could not be faulted on ideological grounds: they were certainly 'imbued with communist ideas' and in certain ways they also 'reflected Soviet reality'. It was, therefore, in the logic of Lenin's 1905 prescriptions for socialist art that these films should 'serve, not some satiated heroine, not the bored "upper ten thousand" suffering from fatty degeneration, but the millions and tens of millions of working people – the flower of the country, its strength and its future'.[42] This they had patently failed to do. There could be only one possible explanation for this rift between the artist and his audience in a socialist society: the artist had failed to communicate, his art was 'not easily accessible'[43] and not 'comprehensible to the millions'.[44] By the time that these and similar attacks were being made towards the end of the 1920s, the Soviet authorities were in a position to take control of the cinema, and the other arts, in what they proclaimed to be the 'cultural revolution', and what they saw as a necessary adjunct to the economic, social and political revolution of the Five-Year Plan. A Central Committee resolution 'On the Party's Policy in the Field of Literature' of 1925 announced that 'In a class society there is not and cannot be neutral art, though the class nature of art in general and literature in particular is expressed in forms that are infinitely more varied than, for instance, in politics.' It went on to urge that

> The Party must underline the necessity for the creation of a literature aimed at a genuinely mass readership of workers and peasants. We must break more boldly and decisively with the traditions of literature for the gentry and make use of all the technical achievements of the old masters to work out an appropriate form, intelligible *to the millions*.[45]

In March 1928 the party held a conference to solve 'this great problem' in the cinema.[46]

The conference was told that the industry was suffering from the 'hitherto inadequate attention paid to the problems of the cinema by the party and the broad Soviet public'. *October* was criticised as being 'a rather difficult film for the workers and peasants'. But the real problem was encapsulated in a comment on Yutkevich's film *Lace*:

> I have watched this film and I confirm that it is good and ideologically firm. There are extraordinarily interesting formal achievements in it. It seems to me that the designer, the director and the cameraman – all of them – are definitely talented people who can do a great deal. But at the same time the verdict of a workers' meeting that saw this film is fully justified: 'Not interesting. Not gripping'.

Art that was separated from the masses of a revolutionary society was failing in its historic task: even worse, it was dangerously reminiscent of art for art's sake and of what Plekhanov had called 'the extreme individualism of the era of bourgeois decay'. The Soviet cinema was felt to be treating a small minority to its sweet refined biscuits while the masses of workers and peasants went short of their black bread. One speaker told the conference, 'It is time to translate the cultural revolution from the skies of general judgements to the soil of systematic practical work.' In the spirit of the party's 1925 statement on literature one of the conference resolutions confirmed:

> The cinema, 'the most important of all the arts', can and must play a large role in the cultural revolution as a medium for broad educational work and communist propaganda, for the organisation and education of the masses around the slogans and tasks of the Party, their artistic education, and their wholesome relaxation and entertainment.
> The cinema, like every art, cannot be apolitical. The cinema must be a weapon of the proletariat in its struggle for hegemony, leadership and influence in relation to other classes, it 'should be, in the hands of the Party, the most powerful medium of communist enlightenment and agitation'.

The measures taken after the conference, and in particular the decree of 11 January 1929, 'On the Strengthening of the Cadres in the Cinema',[47] were designed to ensure that this time the party's words were translated 'to the soil of systematic practical work'.

Writing in March 1929, Eisenstein, who, despite the criticisms that had been levelled at him, was still considered to be the leading Soviet film director, commented, 'The role of the preacher . . . has merged with the role of the artist. The *propagandist* has appeared.'[48]

To be a good propagandist in the Soviet cinema in 1929 it was no longer enough to make good propaganda films: it was necessary to have impeccable credentials too. The Central Committee Commission set up by the January 1929 decree revealed that 81 per cent of the cinema's creative work force came from a white-collar or intelligentsia background, while only 10 per cent came from worker and peasant families. Similarly, only 8 per cent of the students at the three Cinema Technical Colleges (Odessa, Moscow, Leningrad) were party members. The report concluded that 'the young are not sufficiently firm from an ideological point of view, and to a significant degree they are falling under the influence of pre-revolutionary directors. 97·3 per cent of the directors are of non-proletarian origin.' Recently published evidence demonstrates that these problems persisted in the Soviet cinema well into the 1930s. A Standing Action Committee under the party's Orgburo was established in the spring of 1933, and one of its tasks was to determine the kind of films that should be made. Production plans were submitted by the studios to local party organs for their approval, and completed films were shown to audiences of workers to ensure that the cinema's output was 'comprehensible to the millions'.[49] It seemed that Mayakovsky's dream was being realised:

> I want
> > the pen to be equated
> > > > with the bayonet.
> I want
> > the Politburo reports
> on the efficacy of poetry
> > > > to be read
> alongside those on iron and steel production
> > > > > > by Stalin.[50]

The films of the 1930s were to reflect the official ideology in a way that those of the 1920s had never done: *Chapayev* is a good example.[51]

In 1841 Belinsky had defined art as 'the *immediate* contemplation of truth' but had at the same time insisted that 'spontaneity is not an essential attribute of art – on the contrary it is hostile to it and degrading'.[52] It was in this tradition that Lenin had written, 'One cannot live in a society and be free from society',[53] and Trotsky had maintained that 'you have to sing the song of history as it is'.[54] Experience after the October Revolution had demonstrated, above all, that the commitment to society that the Bolsheviks expected of the artist did not necessarily develop of its own accord. An enormous apparatus had to be established in order to ensure that the Soviet cinema became what Lenin had called '*part* of the common cause of the proletariat, "a cog and screw" of one great Social Democratic mechanism set in motion by the entire politically conscious vanguard of the entire working class'. In 1934, incensed by demands of Goebbels that the Nazi cinema should produce a 'German *Battleship Potemkin*', Eisenstein warned him,

Stick to the instrument you're used to – the axe.
And don't waste time.
You don't have long to wield the executioner's axe.
Make the most of it!
Burn your books.
Burn your Reichstags.
But don't imagine that a bureaucratic art fed on all this filth will be able 'to set the hearts of men on fire with its voice'.[55]

It was a warning that might well have been addressed to his fellow-countrymen, but by 1934 it was a warning that had come too late.

NOTES

1. G. V. Plekhanov, *O zadachakh sotsialistov v bor'be s golodom v Rossii (Pis'ma k molodym tovarishcham)* (Geneva, 1892) pp. 57–8. A translation of part of this work appears in N. Harding and R. Taylor (eds), *Marxism in Russia: Key Documents* (London, 1980). I am profoundly indebted to Neil Harding for his assistance and advice in the preparation of this chapter. Except where otherwise stated, translations are my own, but I give a source for published translations where known to me.
2. A. Kremer and Yu. Martov, *Ob agitatsii* (Geneva, 1896). See the accounts of the reception and significance of this brochure in A. K. Wildman, *The Making of a Workers' Revolution* (Chicago, 1967) pp. 45–57, and N. Harding, *Lenin's Political Thought*, vol. 1 (London, 1977) pp. 110–23.
3. Harding, *Lenin's Political Thought*, pp. 76–7.
4. V. I. Lenin, *Collected Works*, 45 vols (Moscow, 1960–70) vol. v, pp. 22–3.
5. Ibid., p. 410.
6. N. K. Krupskaya, *O Lenine. Sbornik statei i vystuplenii* (Moscow, 1971) p. 75.
7. A. V. Lunacharsky, *Stat'i o literature* (Moscow, 1957) p. 118.

8. Quoted in C. V. James, *Soviet Socialist Realism: Origins and Theory* (London, 1973) p. 22.

9. Quoted ibid., p. 28.

10. *Izbrannye filosofskie proizvedeniya*, 5 vols (Moscow, 1956–8) vol. v, pp. 686–748. English translation, *Art and Social Life* (London, n.d.) p. 11

11. Translations based on *Art and Social Life*, pp. 37, 61–2, 66, 36, 64, 18.

12. Quotations from Lenin, *Collected Works*, vol. x, pp. 45–9.

13. I take the arguments of Boris Thomson, encapsulated in his sentence, 'Art is nothing if it is not human; this is both its strength and its weakness', in his *Lot's Wife and the Venus of Milo: Conflicting Attitudes to the Cultural Heritage in Modern Russia* (Cambridge, 1978) pp. 139–54. See also the points made by Ben Brewster in 'The Soviet State, the Communist Party and the Arts, 1917–1936', *Red Letters*, no. 3 (Autumn 1976) 3–9.

14. Quoted in James, *Soviet Socialist Realism*, p. 24.

15. It is unfortunate that Lenin's most important pronouncements on the arts come to us through hearsay. N. I. Krutikova (ed.), *Lenin o kul'ture i iskusstve* (Moscow, 1956) pp. 519–20.

16. Lenin, *Collected Works*, vol. xxxi, pp. 316–17.

17. *Pravda*, 1 Dec 1920.

18. Krutikova, *Lenin o kul'ture*, p. 520.

19. Lenin, *Collected Works*, vol. xxxiii, p. 78.

20. Ibid., vol. xxxi, p. 256. For some reason the English translators of this volume have inserted the word 'political' in front of 'consciousness', although this does not appear in the original Russian in vol. xxxv of the 5th edn of *Polnoe sobranie sochinenii* (Moscow, 1962), p. 21.

21. Yu. Annenkov, *Dnevnik moikh vstrech. Tsikl tragedii*, 2 vols (New York, 1966) vol. ii, p. 270.

22. S. Fitzpatrick, *The Commissariat of Enlightenment* (Cambridge, 1970) pp. 11–12.

23. V. V. Mayakovsky, *Izbrannye proizvedeniya*, 2 vols (Leningrad, 1963) vol. i, p. 250.

24. Krutikova, *Lenin o kul'ture*, p. 521.

25. A similar tendency limited the effectiveness of the agitational paintings on the sides of the agit-trains. See Dziga Vertov's 'Kinoglaz', first published in 1926 and reprinted in S. Drobashenko (ed.), *Dziga Vertov. Stat'i, dnevniki, zamysli* (Moscow, 1966) pp. 90–1. There were similar difficulties with attempts to replace old statues and create a revolutionary style of 'monumental propaganda' (Krutikova, *Lenin o kul'ture*, pp. 525–6).

26. Cf. R. Taylor, 'A Medium for the Masses: Agitation in the Soviet Civil War', *Soviet Studies*, xxii, no. 4 (1971) 562–74.

27. I. Sokolov, 'Skrizhal' veka', *Kino-Fot*, 25–31 Aug 1922, p. 3.

28. Hence Lenin's emphasis on the need to pay special attention to the use of the cinema in these areas: see his directive of 17 Jan 1922, in A. M. Gak (ed.), *Samoe vazhnoe iz vsekh iskusstv. Lenin o kino*, 2nd edn (Moscow, 1973) p. 42.

29. F. Shipulinsky, 'Dusha kino', in *Kinematograf. Sbornik statei* (Moscow, 1919) p. 20.

30. A. M. Gak and N. A. Glagoleva (eds), *Lunacharskii o kino* (Moscow, 1965) p. 46.

31. Cf. Lenin's reaction to the Hungarian revolutionaries' immediate nationalisation of theatres and cabarets. A. Yufit (ed.), *Lenin. Revolyutsiya. Teatr. Dokumenty i vospominaniya* (Leningrad, 1970) p. 199.

32. Taylor, in *Soviet Studies*, XXII, p. 569.
33. Lenin, *Collected Works*, vol. XXXI, pp. 370–1.
34. Ibid., p. 406.
35. Ibid., p. 510. See also E. Drabkina, 'Arkhivazhneishee delo', *Iskusstvo kino*, Jan 1965, pp. 25–7.
36. Gak, *Samoe vazhnoe* . . ., p. 42.
37. A. V. Lunacharsky, *Kino na zapade i u nas* (Moscow, 1928) p. 64.
38. Lenin, *Collected Works*, vol. XXXI, p. 317.
39. R. Taylor, 'From October to *October*: The Soviet Political System in the 1920s and Its Films', in M. J. Clark (ed.), *Politics and the Media* (Oxford, 1979) p. 34.
40. 'O kino' (1925), in Gak and Glagoleva, *Lunacharskii o kino*, p. 46.
41. R. Taylor, *The Politics of the Soviet Cinema, 1917–1929* (Cambridge, 1979), pp. 64–101.
42. Lenin, *Collected Works*, vol. X, pp. 48–9.
43. Cf. T. Rokotov, 'Pochemu malodostupen *Oktyabr'?*', *Zhizn' iskusstva*, 10 Apr 1928, p. 17.
44. Hence the claim by Eisenstein and Aleksandrov that their next film, *The General Line*, was 'an experiment comprehensible to the millions': 'Eksperiment, ponyatnyi millionam', *Sovetskii ekran*, 5 Feb 1929, pp. 6–7.
45. *Izvestiya Ts K RKP(b)*, 1925, no. 25–6.
46. The report of the conference was published as B.S. Ol'khovyi (ed.), *Puti kino. Pervoe Vsesoyuznoe partiinoe soveshchanie po kinematografii* (Moscow, 1929). The following extracts are from pp. 34, 222, 214 and 430–1 respectively. See also Taylor, *The Politics of the Soviet Cinema*, pp. 102–23.
47. N. A. Lebedev (ed.), *Partiya o kino* (Moscow, 1939) pp. 82–5.
48. 'Perspektivy' (1929), reprinted in S. M. Eizenstein, *Izbrannye proizvedeniya*, 6 vols (Moscow, 1964–71) vol. II, p. 36.
49. This information comes from A. Rubailo, 'Obzor moskovskikh i leningradskikh arkhivnykh fondov o deyatel'nosti Kommunisticheskoi partii v oblasti kino (1928–1936)', *Iz istorii kino*, no. 10 (1977) 8–26.
50. 'Domoi!' (1925), repr. in Mayakovsky, *Izbrannye proizvedeniya*, vol. 2, p. 91.
51. Cf. M. Ferro, 'The Fiction Film and Historical Analysis', in P. Smith (ed.), *The Historian and Film* (Cambridge, 1976) pp. 80–94, and S. Crofts, 'Ideology and Form: Soviet Socialist Realism and *Chapayev*', *Essays in Poetics*, vol. II (1977) pp. 43–59.
52. 'The Idea of Art', in V. Belinsky, *Selected Philosophical Works* (Moscow, 1948) pp. 168, 180.
53. Lenin, *Collected Works*, vol. X, p. 48.
54. L. D. Trotsky, *Literature and Revolution* (New York, 1957) p. 46.
55. 'O fashizme, germanskoi kinoiskusstve i podlinnoi zhizni', *Literaturnaya gazeta*, 22 Mar 1934; repr. in Eizenstein, *Izbrannye proizvedeniya*, vol. V, p. 228. An English translation appeared in *Film Art*, no. 5 (Winter 1934) 7–11.

5 Socialism, Centralised Planning and the One-Party State

Alec Nove

It is essential to make clear what I am *not* discussing in the present paper. It will *not* be concerned with what Marx called 'communism' in its higher form. For most of the readers of this paper, the utopian elements of the Marxian tradition may seem merely nonsensical. Yet sizeable groups of far-left intellectuals, in Germany, Italy, Japan, India, and even nearer home, take it seriously and call it socialism. For them socialism is a society in which the state had withered away, there is abundance and equality, there is therefore no conflict over the distribution of goods and services, there is a high general level of education, the division of labour would be transcended, there would be no commanders and no commanded, and no national boundaries, as this harmonious society would cover the entire world. There would, of course, be no commodity production, money, markets, wages, no specialisation or professionalism. While not everyone would be a Raphael, everyone would be able to paint very well.[1] Is it only because of my own inability to draw that I regard this picture as a cloud-cuckoo-land? Anyhow, this paper is concerned with the political implications of centralised planning within a 'socialism' defined more realistically as state or social ownership of the bulk of the means of production. A revolution has overthrown the capitalist order. However, there is scarcity within national boundaries. Indeed, as Bukharin pointed out, the revolution itself tends to reduce and disorganise production. Human beings differ widely in education and in skills. There is evident need for material incentives, and therefore there is inequality of incomes. There is also conflict of interest, between strata, localities, individuals, which it is the task of the state to resolve. Such categories as economy, efficiency, opportunity-cost, money, are necessarily present, whether or not this is explicitly recognised. Planning must operate in *this* kind of environment and so must political institutions.

Trotsky wrote the following, after citing both Marx and Lenin in his support: 'in so far as the state which aims at a socialist transformation must by coercion defend inequality, i.e. the material advantages of a minority, to this extent it still remains a bourgeois state, though without a bourgeoisie. In these words there is neither praise nor blame; they simply call things by their proper names.'[2] Frequently for the more utopian Marxist a socialist *state* is a contradiction in terms, like 'fried ice', as Plekhanov wrote in another context; so Trotsky may be engaged here in ideologically motivated evasion, but at least he contemplated realistically the necessity of inequality and coercion. He also, as we shall see, stressed the necessity in such a society of monetary calculations of effectiveness, and stressed the *high* probability of one state having to build socialism in isolation, citing Vollmar with approval (Vollmar wrote in the 1880s).[3]

Mention of Trotsky reminds one of the need to distinguish the special circumstances of Russia from the *zakonomernosti* of socialist transformations in general. It is sometimes not too clear, even in the writings of such as Trotsky, whether what is being asserted is specific to the circumstances of a backward country emerging from a ruinous civil war, under conditions of external threat and isolation, or whether the generalisations made purport to apply to any country 'building socialism', in a period of transition. Matters are not helped by the fact that human beings are apt to make a virtue of necessity. Take, for instance, Trotsky's own views about labour direction, in 1920, cited from the recent book by L. Szamuely:[4]

As a general rule man tries to avoid work. We can say that man is a rather lazy animal. . . . The task of social organisation is to insert laziness into a definite framework, to discipline and stimulate it with the help of the social organisation of work. . . . In the military field there exists a proper machinery for compelling soldiers to perform their duty. In one form or another this must also happen with regard to labour. No doubt if we speak seriously about a planned economy, encompassed by a uniform central conception, when labour is located according to the economic plan at a given stage of development, the mass of workers must not be wandering about Russia. They must be directed, nominated, commanded in the same manner as soldiers. This is the basis of the militarisation of labour and without it, under the conditions of devastation and hunger, we cannot speak seriously of any industry standing on new foundations.

After arguing on this basis for the militarisation of trade unions, Trotsky went on to deny that the use of conscript labour would lead to low productivity:

> The arguments raised against the organisation of the labour army are directed entirely against socialist organisation of the economy in our transitional period. . . . Of course . . . we could outline the perspectives for a socialist economy. There coercion would gradually disappear and fade away, and in a well-organised socialist economy the elements of coercion would no longer be felt as such, since work . . . will become a need for every member of society. [However] in the period of transition coercion plays an immense role in the organisation of work, and if forced labour is unproductive this condemns our economy.

The above is taken from Trotsky's speech to the Ninth Congress of the party.[5] Bukharin at the same period had a similar attitude. Thus he spoke of force as a factor of 'the self-organisation and coercive self-developing of the workers'. He went on:

> One of the main coercive forms of a new type in the sphere of the working class is the liquidation of the so-called freedom of labour. . . . The remnants of disorganisation, of individualism, of guild-like seclusion, lack of solidarity, the vices of a capitalist society find expression in the lack of understanding of general proletarian tasks, condensed in the tasks and requirements of the Soviet dictatorship of the workers' state. Since, therefore, these tasks must be fulfilled at any price, it is understandable that the so-called freedom of labour should be liquidated precisely in the interests of the proletariat, in the name of the real and not fictitious freedom of the working class. Indeed freedom of labour is irreconcilable with the correctly organised planned economy.

(This is taken from Bukharin's well-known 'Economics of the Transition Period'.[6])

Neither Trotsky nor Bukharin stated explicitly that the measures they advocated were a response to desperate emergency. Szamuely draws the conclusion that they follow logically from the denial of material incentives. If men and women cannot be *induced* to go where they are needed, and if they have not reached the level of consciousness which would cause them to go of their own volition, they must be *ordered*.

At once this raises the question of *who* is to do the ordering, and the political-social implications of this. It is perhaps not surprising that both Trotsky and Bukharin abandoned these conceptions shortly afterwards. We shall have more to say later on the evolution of Trotsky's ideas, because, on the evidence, they soon ran counter to the views of many who today consider themselves to be his followers.

But let us return to the main theme. Most would probably agree with the following propositions: that central planning plus state ownership of the means of production are necessary conditions for the Stalinist type of totalitarianism. In no other way could the state-and-party machine so completely subordinate to itself the mass of the workers, peasants and intellectuals, because state power is then extended directly to allocation of resources, and to determining incomes, employment, publication, etc. There is no alternative to state employment, and even the state's own managers are dependent on their superiors not only for their position but also for supplies of materials: they can hardly do anything legally without a permit. The state is the only publisher, the only investor, and so on. Thus the negation of democratic and individual rights is *facilitated* by such an economic system. The converse is not thereby proved, and may, indeed, not hold. That is to say, one might have state ownership and centralised planning unaccompanied by Stalin-type totalitarianism. Some vicious despotisms, from Ivan the Terrible to Amin, have not involved total nationalisation (though Ivan did claim that he owned the property and indeed the lives of his subjects). Since there were pathological and non-functional elements in Stalinism as it actually developed, the question to be discussed could be defined somewhat differently: does centralised planning require, or produce a strong tendency towards, authoritarian one-party and/or bureaucratic rule, while weakening democracy? If so, why?

One must surely look at the *functions* of the central planning mechanism, in the knowledge that, with the nationalisation of the means of production and the substitution of central planning for the 'hidden hand', there is a major and necessary function for a complex bureaucracy. This has been little stressed by Trotsky. He tended instead to emphasise *distribution*, which is odd, given that a Marxist training should incline people to look at relations of *production*. The logic of his position would be to deprive the so-called bureaucracy of a *productive* function, i.e. to see them as fundamentally parasitic. Not that the Trotsky view is wholly wrong. It is only incomplete. Poverty and backwardness are involved, he argued, but above all inequality and privilege in the acquisition of goods and services: 'if the state does not wither away, and becomes ever more despotic, if workers' plenipotentiaries turn into bureaucrats and the bureaucracy raises itself above the new society, this is due not to some secondary causes, such as psychological remnants of the past, but through iron necessity . . . to maintain a privileged minority'. And again: 'while a "state of the armed workers" can defend social ownership against bourgeois counter-revolution, it is quite otherwise with the control over inequality in the sphere of consumption'.[7] And still again when he says that the policeman needed to regulate the queue is the foundation of the power of the bureaucracy ('whoever distributes goods never yet forgets himself').[8]

This is certainly a significant point. Whoever allocates, distributes, acquires by this fact a certain amount of authority. He could also deprive, or bargain, or share with other 'allocators' certain advantages. The level of poverty is, however, not so important. In 1920 or 1933, years of hunger, the citizen could be brought to heel by denying him simple necessities, but in more recent years the same result could be obtained by denying or providing access to an apartment, a car, a residence permit, opportunity to travel abroad, or promotion (mass terror, it seems, is not essential, though it helps). There is a further implication, which I have drawn elsewhere:[9] that if goods are rationed, or are sold at prices at which demand exceeds supply, the authorities have means both of control *and* of diversion of scarce resources to their own use, means which are absent if anyone can go to a shop and buy whatever he and she can afford. Though of course 'rationing by the purse' must mean, under conditions of inequality, that some will afford more than others.

But we must return to a functional analysis of the necessary consequences of centralised planning, consequences which are *not* dependent significantly on the level of development, literacy, education or even ideology of the country concerned. It can be argued that a country at a lower level of development, while handicapped by lack of culture of its people, has a simpler job of planning: fewer interconnections, smaller range of products, less specialisation.

What are the 'basics' of centralised planning of the Soviet type? It rests on the principle that the supreme political authorities, acting on behalf of society, ensure that the goods and services required by society are provided when and where they are needed, in the most efficient manner. Private enterprise, with minor exceptions, is barred. The market no longer determines either what is produced or how it is produced. The state mobilises resources (in the Soviet model mainly through profits and turnover taxes arising from the sale of the products of state enterprise), and uses them for a variety of purposes: investment, defence, health, education, etc. The bulk of the labour force is employed by state organs, at rates of pay laid down by state organs. They are paid a money wage, which they are free to spend on the goods and services made available to them at prices which, with few exceptions, are also determined by state organs. It is the task of the central planning organs to identify needs, to aggregate them, to ensure balance between production and supply, and finally to issue *instructions* to the many thousands of managers, so that what is required is, in fact, done. In the absence of a market mechanism, the planners' instructions form the sole criterion for the actions of management and the basis for evaluating their performance. To discuss the inefficiencies to which such a system gives rise is beyond the scope of the present paper. The essential points to appreciate are: the *centralising logic* of a marketless economy, the *immense complexity* of the task of the planners, the *sheer number* of the interrelated instructions which must be issued, and the overwhelming *power* over material resources and human beings which this system concentrates in the supreme political and economic authority – for the Politburo in this sense must be seen as the board of directors of the great firm, USSR Ltd. The political and the economic merge, become indistinguishable.

Let us build up such a plan from first principles. The plan, to be made operational, must be disaggregated until each production unit is slotted in. Plans in their 'micro' aspect must aim to utilise efficiently the productive capacities available and choose between alternative proposals to create new ones. The plan must answer in detail the question 'what?', and then also the question 'how?'. The planning organs must, of course, seek information about wants, but must do so in the knowledge that these will exceed the means available to satisfy them all, and that therefore some will be disappointed. Each productive unit is dependent on a multitude of others. Therefore, in Lenin's words, 'enterprises will be unable to function correctly if there is not a united will, connecting all the groups of toilers into a single economic organ, working with the precision of a clockwork mechanism'.[10] Otherwise, to cite this time Trotsky, the separate units will not know what to do, they will be like 'a telephone whose wires have been cut'.[11] These 'wires', this 'clockwork mechanism', are far more complex than most non-economists seem able to appreciate. In a Western economy, some of this mechanism is administered (through state corporations, large private firms, etc.), but the larger part functions through and by the market: firms and managers decide to produce, to buy, to sell, to invest, by reference to expected profits and through negotiation with customers and suppliers and banks, without receiving plan-instructions. Centralisation involves vast number of interlocking decisions. It would not be inappropriate to cite the former world chess champion, Botvinnik. Writing in *Pravda* (24 Nov 1977), he discussed computerised chess, seen as an aspect of control or management theory, as well as in its own right. Despite the existence of formal rules and the strictly limited number of 64 squares, the number of possible locations on the board for all the pieces is (he wrote) *many* times greater than the number of words uttered by all mankind since the dawn of history. Even after ingeniously eliminating obviously irrational moves, the best chess-playing computer has to consider 400,000 possibilities before deciding on a move in the middle of a game, and this only on the limiting assumption of 'thinking' no more than three moves ahead. This helps to explain why a computerised central plan, disaggregated to the operationally necessary detail, is not a practicable solution – though computers can, of course, help the planners.

To make the task manageable, chess-playing computers (or computerised *or human* decision-makers) have to limit the 'tree of variants' (i.e. to eliminate from consideration a vast number of matters which, for the given purpose, can be treated as irrelevant) *and* to limit the time-horizon, since the longer the period being considered, the greater are the number of variables. For example, moving from chess to economic reality, what in the short run is a fixed quantity or relationship can be changed by longer-term action on the part of the planners themselves. And far from there being 64 squares (8 × 8, on the chess board), there are at present *12 million* different products in the USSR, aggregated for planning purposes into 48,000 'positions',[12] that is to say, obligatory output targets are laid down at some level of the planning hierarchy for 48,000 items, most of which consist of numerous sub-items (different types, sizes, qualities, etc., etc.).

The New Left, such as Charles Bettelheim or Paul Sweezy, wish to eliminate 'commodity production', i.e. production for sale or exchange, and wish to substitute for it the deliberate choice of society, the all-embracing plan. Production shall be controlled by 'the direct producers'. This is indeed what the Bolsheviks tried to do in 1918–20. 'How did we start?' (said Trotsky in 1922). 'There was a market – we liquidated it. Competition? We abolish it. Commercial calculation? Out with it! The Supreme Council for the National Economy allocates everything . . . from a single centre. This failed.' And not just because of Russian backwardness. 'If in Germany the workers were to seize power now, we would not advise them to amalgamate everything and to subordinate it to a [state] economic council.'[13] We shall see that this lesson Trotsky never forgot.

The centralising logic of a marketless economy should be so obvious that it need not detain us for long. Let me approach the question as follows. How, in the name of common sense, can the 'direct producers' decide what is needed by society, if by 'direct producers' are meant actual groups of workers at production units? How can they tell what is the more urgent need to satisfy? How can they encompass all the consequences of their acts or omissions, except if their telephone had wires, connecting them either to a market or to the central planners? To the objection that output should conform to the wishes of the customers and not of the producers, Bettelheim's only possible answer is that the producers are also consumers. So they are, but only in their totality. At the top of the pyramid, at the centre of the economic system, the producer and the consumer are two sides of the same medal. Only at the centre can the various needs of society be considered and reconciled, in the light of information about production possibilities. Links between producers and customers *below* the centre can only take the form of contractual or business deals, exchanges, production for sale and not for use, i.e. commodity production. *Only* a central plan can *substitute* for a market mechanism, in a modern, complex industrial economy.

Now consider the implications. In the first place, those who operate the system face an overwhelmingly difficult task. In order to make it manageable they *must* sub-divide it, creating departments, divisions and other 'instances', they must take decisions in an aggregated form, eliminating from consideration many relevant matters which *cannot* be incorporated into the planning process without creating an impossible informational and decision-making log-jam. The task requires specialists, it requires hierarchy, it generates bureaucratic methods because no other ones are available. All this is independent of the skills, goodwill or social origins of the individuals concerned with the process. Why hierarchy? Because the tasks, the system, are of their nature hierarchical! If ten factories produce ball-bearings, eighty factories use ball-bearings, and a hundred units utilise vehicles and machines into which ball-bearings are incorporated, then some office (with a responsible chief) will plan ball-bearings production, issuing instructions to the factories, and receiving instructions from whomsoever is responsible for ensuring the smooth production of ball-bearing-using factories, which in turn must be producing those things which are needed by other parts of the economy. And within each factory it is simply out of the question for those who are in a particular workshop to decide to alter their product. How could they know the consequences? The reason for their ignorance is *not* stupidity or lack of education, but their place in the production process.

To make the point clearer, let us refer again to the chess-playing computer. *No one*, at any level, can consider everything ('*nel 'zya obyat' neobyatnoye*' – 'One cannot encompass the unencompassable' – to cite the mythical poet Kozma Prutkov.) At *any* level, the human brain, like a computer, can be aware of only a limited number of things. The information and interests of the individual in any factory, office, university, are bounded. Ability to make decisions at *any* level is conditioned by the need to eliminate what at that level appear to be irrelevancies.

Of course, many decisions can be delegated. Thus a minor university administrator can allocate rooms for lectures, because his or her decisions will usually not affect anyone except the university itself. It is already impossible for the stationmaster (or all the staff, including drivers) at a railway station to send off trains at a time which they decide, because this will have effects elsewhere in the system which are beyond their horizon and responsibility, whereas someone else in the railway hierarchy has the duty to know them. Industries depend on deliveries from a multitude of suppliers, any of whom can disorganise the process of production unless a coordinating mechanism prevents this.

Is such a central coordinating mechanism consistent with political democracy? Or could democracy be a solution to the problem of the impossibility of efficient all-embracing central planning? What is its relevance? Is a *one-party* state logically implied?

It is important here, as elsewhere, to be aware of the distinction between the logic of centralised planning *as such*, and the economic problems involved in using the political dominance of the party to 'build socialism' in a post-revolutionary society. It appears to me that these conceptually distinct factors, in fact, coalesce and reinforce each other. In any country in a post-revolutionary situation, the ruling party is faced with the task of changing the structure of the economy and of society. The task of central planning, if it is assumed that market forces are to be reduced or extinguished, will involve a specialised apparatus, which will be pursuing a long-term economic strategy, within which it will have to try to accommodate consumer requirements, technical progress, modernisation, investments, demands by various groups of workers, perhaps the needs of the armed forces too. There will usually be a period of sacrifice, of disappointment of exaggerated hopes of short-term benefits, which can cause unpopularity, of which any legal opposition party (or faction of *the* party) is bound to take advantage. All this would present serious problems anywhere, but was rendered particularly complicated in the USSR because of its peasant majority.

But suppose that the workers were a majority? How could they exercise their 'dictatorship', democratically controlling the economy? The early Bolsheviks expected, in Trotsky's words, 'the *nachal 'nik* [manager or boss] to turn into a simple technical agent' under workers' control.[14] Oddly enough, he added that this did not take place because a revolution had not also broken out in advanced countries, a total *non sequitur*. More to the point is a remark by the Yugoslav Marxist dissident, Mihajlo Markovic:

But Marx did not solve the problem: how will the whole proletariat form its common will and take the step from a 'class in itself' towards a 'class for itself'? How will this alienated and degraded class . . . build up a consciousness about essentially new possibilities, a consciousness that requires enormous general culture and far surpasses official academic scholarship? And if the vanguard of this class does the job, how to avoid the alienation of that vanguard, manipulation of the class by it?[15]

But even he does not explain how the masses, even if not 'degraded', even if they acquire general culture, can actually carry out the tasks for which the self-appointed vanguard takes responsibility. A small group can run its own affairs together. Millions of people in an industrial society are quite a different matter.

A democratically elected assembly *can*, of course, do certain very important things. It can vote on general policy, the 'macro' directions the economy is taking. It can vote on priorities. It can publicise and legislate against blatant abuses. The appalling neglect of housing, for instance, could have been the subject of effective challenge. Individual ministers and officials could be dismissed and others elected in their place. But plainly Mihajlo Mihailov is mistaken in writing that 'the liquidation of the monopoly of the party would at once sharply improve the economic situation, because then the party in power, to avoid losing the election, will do everything possible to activate the national economy. . . . So that feedback [of demand to the producers] can be assured without a market in a politically pluralist society.'[16] The mistake consists in supposing that the reasons why the problems of *micro-economics*, of current management and coordination, are not correctly solved lie in the lack of determination on the part of the leadership to solve them, or that voting and free expression of opinion is a means of replacing market forces. I had a lively correspondence on this topic with Arun Bose,[17] who argued, why not 'registration of clamour' as a substitute for the market? This again shows total misunderstanding. 'Registration of clamour', in the first place, can relate only to consumer goods, and does not help at all in allocating ball-bearings, caustic soda or oil. (Surely no one envisages managers shouting for raw materials?). Secondly, it will only tell us who shouts loudly, and hardly anything about real need. With an acceptable distribution of income, 'voting with the rouble' is a far better guide to need than a measure in decibels can be.

Trotsky understood this long ago:

> In the course of the transitional epoch each enterprise and each
> set of enterprises must, to a greater or lesser degree, orient itself
> independently in the market and test itself through the
> market. . . . It is necessary for each state-owned factory, with its
> technical director, to be subject not only to control from the top –
> by state organs – but also from below, by the market, which will
> remain the regulator of the state economy for a long time to
> come.[18]

It may be thought that this was another instance of making a
virtue of necessity, as this was said in 1922, when the New Economic
Policy (NEP) had just begun. But Trotsky expressed the same ideas
in 1933 and repeated them in 1936. Let me document the
propositions and comment upon them.

Thus here he is in *Byulleten' oppozitsii* (in November 1932):

> If there existed a universal brain . . ., registering simultaneously
> all the processes of nature and society, measuring their dynamics,
> forecasting the results of their interactions, then such a brain
> would no doubt concoct a faultless and complete state
> plan . . . True, the bureaucracy sometimes considers that it has
> just such a brain. This is why it so easily frees itself from the
> supervision [*kontrol*] of the market and of Soviet democracy. . . .
> The innumerable live participants in the economy, state, collect-
> ive, private, must make known their needs and their relative
> intensity not only through statistical compilations of planning
> commissions, but directly through pressure of demand and
> supply. The plan is checked and to a considerable extent realised
> through the market. The regulation of the market itself must base
> itself on the tendencies showing themselves in it. The drafts made
> in offices must prove their economic rationality [*tselesoobraznost*]
> through commercial calculation. The economy of the transition
> period is unthinkable without the 'control' by the rouble.[19]

After noting the necessity and inevitability of conflict between
various strata and objectives he continues, 'only through the
interaction of three elements: state planning, the market and Soviet
democracy, can the economy be correctly controlled in the transition epoch', which will lessen the inevitable contradiction and

disproportions until wider revolutions provide new opportunities. His practical conclusions include anti-inflationary measures and a rouble based on the gold standard.

Later he again speaks of the bureaucracy having freed itself *both* from the control of the masses *and* from 'the automatic control of the chervonets'.[20] Even more strongly the same arguments are put forward in May 1933. Trotsky never fails to stress that he believes in the *ultimate* triumph of communism, and therefore in the disappearance of money in conditions of universal abundance. However, this stage is still very far away:

> The function of money in the Soviet economy can in a certain sense only now expand fully. The transition period taken as a whole means not the reduction of commodity turnover but, on the contrary, its great expansion. All sectors are growing fast and must quantitatively and qualitatively determine their mutual interrelations. . . .

The ending of self-contained peasant household economies causes increased monetisation:

> Keeping stock of all the productive forces of society, the socialist state has the task of giving them their most productive distribution and use for society. The methods of economic monetary calculation developed under capitalism are not rejected, but are socialised. The construction of socialism is unthinkable without building into the planning system the personal interest of producer and consumer. And this interest can manifest itself only if in its service there is a tried and flexible tool: a stable currency. In particular, a rise in labour productivity and improvements in quality of output are impossible to attain without an accurate measuring rod, freely penetrating to all the nooks and crannies of the economy, i.e. with a stable monetary unit.

And again, on the next page: 'economic planning frees itself from financial [or market, *tsennostnyi*] control, just as bureaucratic arbitrariness frees itself of political control'.[21] The same points are made again, often using the same words, in 1936. He also again referred to the advantages of a gold standard.[22]

A parallel could be drawn between the ideas just expressed and the 'overcoming of the division of labour'. Maybe in a future world it will be overcome. Meanwhile, industrialisation and technical progress inevitably increase and deepen division of labour; so also with monetisation and the role of market relations in a semi-developed country. It appears to me that the emphasis was different in Preobrazhensky's work; he saw plan and market ('the law of value') as *opposed forces*.[23]

At no point did Trotsky say that the function of money and market should be all-powerful, but neither did he ever suggest that their function could be meaningfully replaced by some undefined mass action or by democratically elected soviets. His own experience must have shown him the limitations, in practice, of such phraseology as 'control by the direct producers'. Note that decisions by *local* organs within a centralised system cannot be implemented unless the centre allocates the resources required, a process which becomes remote and bureaucratic by the very nature of the function.

It seems axiomatically clear that centralised planning places very large powers in the hands of whoever is in control at the centre. It is also evident that operational control is a highly complex and specialised task, which can only take the form of a bureaucratic mechanism. One eliminates bureaucracy not by incantations, not by denunciation, but by eliminating the *functions* which bureaucracy performs. Thus the Moscow OVIR (visa and registration office) can doubtless be improved and its rules altered, but residence permits cannot be issued by 'the people'. The reason why we in Scotland are free of *this* kind of bureaucrat is that we do not have a residence permit system!

It is a paradox, perhaps, that the more one plans under *political* control the operations of the economy, the *less* possible it is for ordinary citizens to influence affairs. This is because the political organs become locked into their economic-management tasks, which are so interrelated and interconnected that *political* action by 'unofficial' citizens becomes ineffective. Citizens desiring woollen coats or refrigerators can 'reveal their preferences' through the market-and-monetary mechanism. They cannot form a woollen-coat or refrigerator political party. A group of citizen-members of a retail cooperative or catering establishment can vote to acquire coats, refrigerators, cooking-stoves or cabbages, but are only free to act upon their decision if these items are *purchasable*. One can perhaps imagine that under full communism they will be there in abundance in open storehouses which will need no locks. But we are not discussing such a society.

Many Marxists, including Rubin as well as Bettelheim, have correctly pointed out that 'commodity production' (market relations) arise out of the separation between producing units, from their autonomy, and not fundamentally from private ownership. This has given rise to some concern, on the part of such Marxists as Brus and Selucky, about a contradiction between workers' participation and control at the level of the productive unit and the subordination of these units to a central, market-replacing plan. They and others derive from the experience of the USSR a warning concerning the hypertrophy of the state and its bureaucratisation, which they properly link to the economic functions and powers of the central state apparatus. But, it may be asked, why a *one-party* state? After all, even if there is indeed a large body of officials administering micro-economic planning, one could still have competing political tendencies presenting themselves at elections for the central assembly. They would be unable to exercise detailed operational control effectively, but then what central assembly, howsoever elected, ever has? What it can do, so it might be argued, is what elected parliaments can do, only in a more genuinely representative way, reflecting the citizens' consciousness and interests. It could adopt general guidelines, order the dismissal of officials who refuse to carry out their wishes or abuse their position for personal gain, determine priorities.

This seems plausible, but there are objections to such a view, from several angles or at several levels. Perhaps the least convincing is the argument that the powerful economic bureaucracy would find changes in their political masters inconvenient and disruptive. No doubt they would, but the convenience of bureaucrats cannot of itself be decisive. A little stronger is the already-cited proposition that they find it to their advantage to appropriate a disproportionate share of the national product, a procedure which would be impeded by a democratic challenge. But this again only identifies an interest group, without explaining why it should be successful. It is surely unsatisfactory to describe them, as Trotsky does, as a *parasitical* stratum.[24] This completely avoids the necessary definition of the nature of their power, which derives from their (in the circumstances) *necessary function*, one that placed them in positions of power. It may be asked: did the function derive from power, or power from function? Perhaps the only answer is 'both', this being an authentic example of dialectical interaction.

In the USSR, true enough, there were circumstances which strengthened this stratum: a peasant majority, which inhibited mass democratic procedures (since it was felt to be essential to hold on to power, and not to lose it to a peasant-orientated party); low cultural levels; a weak working class without traditions of independent organisation, scattered by civil war and diluted by incomers from the village; the upper strata of the party and of governmental officialdom becoming increasingly merged. All this was important, but surely the key is the *combined* logic of a transformation of society from above (by the party, claiming to be possessors of the sure compass of Marxism–Leninism) *and* the logical necessities of centralised planning. The French semi-anarchist Claude Lefort was surely right when he contrasted the capitalist market economy, in which the various owners of the means of production are interlinked and rendered interdependent through market-based specialisation, competition, division of labour, with the Soviet-type system. One can assert that the 'capitalist' conflicts are functional for the system; markets are a scene of clashes, with victors and vanquished. It has been justly argued that the growth of large so-called monopolist corporations has not diminished the competitive struggle, and in this sense the term 'monopoly-capitalism' is a misnomer. True, the modern state has to intervene to keep the system functioning, but it is not the task of the state in the West to ensure the coordination of thousands of economic units and hundreds of thousands of transactions. This *is* the task of the state in a Soviet-type economy. This in turn leads, for two main reasons, to a one-party state. The first is that the powerful position of the upper strata (party officials, senior managers, 'bureaucrats') depends decisively on their control over state organs, for which their functions prepare and strengthen them. The second is that the essential coordination and coherence of the plan *requires* hierarchical subordination, the reconciliation of various conflicting interests at the summit of the hierarchy. Lefort sees the dominant group or class as being shaped by, and shaping, its relationship to the state as owner of the means of production. 'The state has become civil society, capital has chased out the capitalists, the integration of all spheres of activity is accomplished . . . .'[25] But apart from the consciousness, interest and power of this dominant group, the functional need to integrate and coordinate is itself inconsistent with political competition, with a multi-party state.

Appeals and counter-appeals to the masses, with the right to organise protests and demands, and to utilise politically the contradictions and stresses of the post-revolutionary period, would disrupt an economy so organised, would literally disintegrate it. One might even assert that, in any society that we know, party-political competition is dependent upon the bulk of economic management *not* being subject to political process and domination by political organs. Trotsky seems to have been partly aware of this, when he repeatedly counterposed economic calculation and ar-bitrariness, arguing for 'a rouble independent of the political leadership' ('*nezavisimogo ot vozhdei rublya*').[26]

In fact, the more one reads the real Trotsky, at least the post-1922 Trotsky, the more one has to agree with the statement of Stephen Cohen that Trotsky was really a *Nepist*, not so different in *this* respect from Bukharin.[27] That is to say, he understood the economic 'market' logic of the NEP and saw the politically despotic implications of the alternative. No doubt he saw it the more clearly because the potential despot was a bitter enemy. Yet his ideas on this subject are still insufficiently appreciated, hence the space devoted to them in this paper. Indeed, the East European reformers of the Hungarian type could, without too much distortion, claim to have Trotsky among their forebears, if it were politically possible for such a claim to be made. For was he not plainly advocating the full use of the market mechanism during the transition period, *both* for efficiency *and* as part of the struggle against bureaucratic arbitrari-ness (*proizvol*)?

To avoid misunderstanding, let me make clear that I am *not* asserting that either Trotsky or Bukharin, or any of their supporters, favoured a multi-party state. They were firmly for the Bolshevik monopoly of power, for the suppression of other parties. They realised only too well that, in the Russia of the 1920s, a free election would mean loss of power. Trotsky, it is true, did assert (after his exile), that a one-party state was originally understood as being 'temporary',[28] and he also argued in favour of interest groupings within society being allowed (indeed encouraged) to express their views about economic policies: thus he envisaged 'tractorists', 'oilmen', 'electrifiers' arguing for more resources to be devoted to purposes they favoured.[29] For reasons already explained, this would probably confuse the process of central planning, but then he stressed that even more confusion was actually caused by the suppression of such people and their opinions, and the substitution of bureaucratic arbitrariness. In any event, as has been shown, he was critical of over-centralisation and the precipitate elimination of market forces and of the NEP.

There is another approach to this problem, suggested by a phrase in Mihajlo Markovic's fascinating paper on Stalinism and Marxism, from which we have already quoted. He notes that, in the Soviet Union, 'small production continued to generate bourgeois relations, which was the most important excuse for the political bureaucracy to perpetuate its rule under the disguise of the dictatorship of the proletariat'.[30] This means that, under objective social and economic conditions in which commodity and market relations had a large part to play, their elimination required the continuous use of the state's coercive power. Traders, 'speculators', private workshops, and so on, would continuously arise unless the police stepped in to prevent it. Marx originally envisaged that the petty producers would gradually be squeezed out by the great capitalist corporations before a socialist revolution. He nowhere suggested that this is a task for the police. It is interesting that even at the height of War Communism Bukharin and Preobrazhensky asserted that the petty producers should be neither nationalised nor coerced (see their *ABC of Communism*). The existence of petty producers logically requires a market-type economy in which there is a large segment of unplanned, commercially orientated economic activity. Since small-scale private activities in industry, agriculture and distribution exist even in the most highly developed countries, their elimination would have police-state implications even there, let alone in the less-developed world or in the Russia of the 1920s, where the bulk of the population was *not* engaged in large-scale industry, was in fact 'petty-bourgeois' in status.

It is well worth while to shift attention to China, the China of the Cultural Revolution. For surely what was being attempted there was a deliberate challenge to the whole of the argument of the present paper. They claimed to be eliminating hierarchy, limiting severely the role of material incentives, the market and bureaucracy. Inevitably, direction of labour became widespread. Attacks were launched on the 'capitalist-roaders', Liu-ists, who would travel the road traversed by the USSR towards revisionism. A fascinating article by Ambrose Yeo-chi King[31] traces the consequences: economic confusion, inconsistent both with elementary efficiency and with the logic of one-party rule, or indeed with elementary political order. The actions taken by Hua and his comrades after

Mao's death are wholly understandable. Eventually, the objective organisational structural necessities must assert themselves as against revolutionary voluntarism.

Finally, what conclusion can one come to? Certainly it must be clear that the discussion has touched on only one of the causes and purposes of the one-party state of the Lenin or Stalin type. Since Leninism, in one of its most important aspects, is an adaptation of Marxism to a backward country, and since Trotsky's 'permanent revolution' concept is also explicitly related to backwardness, as has been clearly shown in Knei-Paz's admirable study,[32] the Soviet version of the one-party state could be said to be inherent in the notion of seizing power in order to *create*, from above, the preconditions for socialism in a country with a peasant majority. It is also noteworthy that the one-party state was firmly established *before* the centralisation of planning occurred, and therefore the latter could not cause the former. In such a context, the effect of centralisation and the elimination of the market would then be not to *cause* a one-party state to arise, but rather greatly to increase the size and all-pervasive power of the dictatorship, while reducing or eliminating the rights and possibility of ordinary people (workers too) to set limits to the power of the party-state machine.

But to end on such a note would be incorrect, as it leaves the implication that the analysis relates to Russia or to backward countries only, or that the outbreak of a revolution in an advanced country could have altered the equation. This, however, is not really so.

Let us follow Trotsky's thoughts about a German revolution, cited on p. 84 above, to their logical conclusion. Imagine Liebknecht and Luxemburg organising a *German* nationalised economy in the 1920s. The much higher level of development, compared with the Russia of the period, would make far more complicated the task of central planning. There would be more wires and more telephones, a greater number therefore of potential crossed wires. One must agree with Trotsky's view that commercial calculation, a stable currency, market relations, are irreplaceable on practical grounds during what he liked to call the transition period, i.e. until the material and social preconditions for communism came into existence, presumably on a world-wide scale, and therefore several generations hence (if at all). Some contemporary pseudo-Trotskyist 'ultras' in West Germany put up posters demanding 'the elimination of commodity production and the wages system', apparently as a programme for action. I doubt if Trotsky would have agreed with such slogans. Can we not say that also in Western Europe today, the political pluralism now apparently advocated by Eurocommunists, the necessities of efficient economic management and planning *and* the effective participation of the workers in decision-making at their place of work, all point to the need to limit the functions and powers of centralised planners, and to leave a function for market forces? True, Yugoslav experience shows that *their* species of self-management, with minimal powers for the centre, carries with it dangers and distortions of which we must take cognisance. But to deal with these would require another paper.

NOTES

1. Marx's remarks on communism were collected, collated and commented on by Bentell Ollman in his useful article 'Marx's Vision of Communism: A Reconstruction', *Critique*, no. 8 (Summer 1977) 4–42.
2. Lev Trotsky, *Chto takoe SSSR i kuda on idyot* (Paris, 1974). This is a facsimile reproduction of the original manuscript of Trotsky's *The Revolution Betrayed*.
3. Ibid., p. 241.
4. Laszlo Szamuely, *First Models of the Socialist Economic Systems: Principles and Theories* (Budapest, 1974) pp. 41, 43.
5. For the original, see *Devyatyi syezd RKP (b). Protokoly* (Moscow, 1960) pp. 91, 93, 97–8.
6. See Nicolai I. Bukharin, '*Economics of the Transition Period*', *with Lenin's Critical Remarks* (New York, 1971) pp. 157–8. This translation renders the phrase *svoboda truda* as 'freedom to work'; 'freedom of labour', employed by Szamuely's translation, is a more correct rendering of the original.
7. Trotsky, *Chto takoe SSSR i kuda on idyot*, pp. 49, 78.
8. Ibid., pp. 91, 92.
9. See Alec Nove, 'Market Socialism and Its Critics', *Soviet Studies*, II (1972) 120–38.
10. V. I. Lenin, *Polnoe sobranie sochinenii*, 5th edn, vol. XXXVI, p. 157.
11. Trotsky's speech to the 4th Congress of the Comintern, cited from Szamuely, *First Models*, p. 95.
12. N. Drogichinsky, in *Voprosy ekonomiki*, 1977, no. 12, p. 5.
13. *Odinnadtsatyi syezd RKP (b). Stenograficheskii otchyot* (Moscow, 1961) p. 12.
14. Trotsky, *Chto takoe SSSR i kuda on idyot*, p. 57.
15. Robert C. Tucker (ed.), *Stalinism: Essays in Historical Interpretation* (New York, 1977) p. 312.
16. *SSSR: demokraiicheskiye alternativy* (Achberg, 1976) p. 46.
17. Bose is the author of *Marxian and Post-Marxian Political Economy* (Harmondsworth, 1975).
18. Speech to 4th Congress of the Comintern.

19. *Byulleten' oppozitsii*, ii, no. 31 (Nov 1932) 8.
20. Ibid., no. 33 (Mar 1933) 2.
21. See ibid., no. 34 (May 1933) 5–6.
22. See Trotsky, *Chto takoe SSSR i kuda on idyot*, e.g. pp. 58, 66.
23. See E. A. Preobrazhensky, *The New Economics*, trs. Brian Pearce (Oxford, 1965).
24. Trotsky, *Chto takoe SSSR i kuda on idyot*, p. 190.
25. C. Lefort, *Eléments d'une critique de la bureaucratie* (Geneva, 1971) p. 153.
26. Trotsky, *Chto takoe SSSR i kuda on idyot*, p. 226.
27. See Stephen F. Cohen, 'Bolshevism and Stalinism', in Tucker, *Stalinism*, p. 22.
28. For instance, Trotsky, *Chto takoe SSSR i kuda on idyot*, p. 202.
29. *Byulleten' oppozitsii*, i, no. 10 (Apr 1930) 17.
30. Mihailo Marković, 'Stalinism and Marxism', in Tucker, *Stalinism*, p. 311.
31. Ambrose Yeo-chi King, 'A Voluntarist Model of Organisation', *British Journal of Sociology*, xxviii, no. 3 (Sep 1977) 363–74.
32. Baruch Knei-Paz, *The Political Thought of Leon Trotsky* (Oxford, 1978).

6 Political Myth and Stalin's Quest for Authority in the Party

Graeme Gill

Lenin's death in January 1924 produced a vacuum at the apex of the Bolshevik political structure. It not only deprived the new state and the party of its chief driving force, but it also highlighted the unique position Lenin had occupied in the Bolshevik movement and the special problems that this created for his successors. Lenin's dominance over the movement which he led for almost a quarter of a century had not rested on his incumbency of any particular office in the party, but upon the force of his personality and his role in the growth of Bolshevism. This personalised basis of his leadership[1] meant that in purely institutional terms his death created no problem; power and authority within the party lay with the formal party organs, the Politburo, the Central Committee and the party congress, just as they had during his lifetime. However, the personalised nature of Lenin's authority created a significant practical problem for those with aspirations to personal dominance in the post-Lenin period. It meant that his would-be successors could not gain similar authority through the occupation of a specific leadership position within the party. Consequently, the Lenin succession struggle did not focus on capturing control of any such position. Instead, it involved two main aspects. The first was the struggle for power within the political hierarchy, a struggle which, with hindsight, we can see was weighted in Stalin's favour by his strategic location in the party structure. The course of this conflict was greatly influenced by a second aspect of the succession struggle, the search for authority within the party. In the absence of authority formalised through succession to office, authority had to be sought by association with the mythology, the symbols and the achievements of the regime, with those forms through which the regime sought to establish the legitimacy of its monopoly of power. Much of the history of the 1920s and early 1930s concerns Stalin's attempt to bring about a coincidence between his organisational power and the mantle of authority within the party. It is upon the latter aspect, the quest for authority, that this paper will concentrate.

In the period after the Bolshevik seizure of power in October 1917 Soviet public life was characterised by the emergence of a complex fabric of political mythology. In essence, this consisted of a romanticised account of the party's rise to power. The central strands of the developing myth were Lenin, the party and the proletariat, all woven inextricably together as the force which brought about the explosion into the new era, the Great October Socialist Revolution.[2] As this heroic myth of October continued to unfold during the 1920s, increasingly it came to be dominated by the figure of Lenin, particularly following his incapacity and eventual death in 1924, and the subsequent denigration of the only figure whose role in 1917 rivalled that of Lenin, Leon Trotsky. Despite his disapproval of personal adulation,[3] the result was a burgeoning cult of Lenin. This meant that when the protagonists in the 1920s sought authority through association with the symbols of the regime, it was primarily to the figure of Lenin which they turned.[4] One of the factors in Stalin's eventual success was his ability to evoke an image of his relationship with Lenin that was more appealing to the rank-and-file party members than were those of his opponents.

The importance of establishing an image of close association with Lenin in the eyes of the party membership was clear to the potential contenders for power even before Lenin had died. This is evident from the speeches at the Twelfth Party Congress in April 1923, the first since 1917 not attended by Lenin. Although all leaders paid exaggerated obeisance to the sick leader, it was Zinoviev who set the tone for the image of Lenin which was developing in the myth of October:

When we travelled to these congresses, our aim first of all was to hear this speech, since we knew in advance that in it we should find not only the considered experience of the time through which we had lived, but firm directions for the future. You remember with what thirst we always listened to this speech – a thirst like the thirst of a man who, on a sultry summer day, falls upon a deep clear spring to drink his fill.[5]

According to Kamenev, 'His teaching has been our touchstone every time this or that problem, this or that difficult question, has confronted us. Mentally each of us asked himself: And how would Vladimir Il'ich have answered this?'[6] It followed from this position, enthusiastically endorsed by the congress, that Lenin's guidance should not cease with his death; the infant Soviet state should continue to seek its direction and purpose from Lenin's writings. The logic of this view demanded that after Lenin's death an interpreter of his words, someone who could distil the wisdom and apply it to the contemporary situation, was required. For this task familiarity with Lenin, bred by long, close association combined with fidelity to his thought, was needed. Feeling secure in his past close association with Lenin during some of the party's more difficult periods, Zinoviev was able to espouse this principle in 1923, confident that it would be to his own benefit.[7] In this he was mistaken.

While Lenin remained alive Stalin was restrained in his re-ferences to the ailing leader. However, with Lenin's death in January 1924, Stalin played a major part in stimulating the Lenin cult. Upon Lenin's death the press was dominated by eulogistic articles about the former leader. On 26 January the Bolshevik leaders, with the exception of Trotsky, who was still in the south of the country, paid verbal tribute to Lenin at the Second All-Union Congress of Soviets. With the exception of Stalin, all the orators expressed their praise of Lenin in the orthodox terminology of Marxism, and therefore in the same form in which other departed comrades had been treated. Stalin's speech was totally different in form, appearing as a devotional appeal in which each successive behest of Lenin was to be answered by a uniform response from the worshippers. His speech was regularly interlaced with incantations in the following style:

Departing from us, comrade Lenin enjoined us to hold high and keep pure the great title of member of the party. We vow to thee, comrade Lenin, that we will with honour fulfil this thy behest. . . . Departing from us, comrade Lenin enjoined us to keep the unity of our party as the apple of our eye. We vow to thee comrade Lenin, that we will with honour fulfil this thy behest . . .[8]

The religious connotations of this speech were reinforced by the trappings of the Lenin cult inaugurated at the same time: 21 January was proclaimed an annual day of national mourning, the decision was made to embalm Lenin's body and place it in a mausoleum beneath the Kremlin wall, monuments to Lenin were established in the main cities of the USSR, Petrograd was renamed Leningrad, and the decision was made to publish a collected edition of all of Lenin's works. Henceforth the terms 'Leninism' and 'Leninist' became ritualised, connoting the very best, and the figure of Lenin was inflated to such an extent that it came to dominate the symbolism of the regime. The heroic myth of October underwent a transformation in which its major point of emphasis was altered radically: it was almost as though the central point of the myth was not that victory had been achieved in October, but that Lenin had been the one who had made it happen.[9] The primary point of legitimacy in the system thereby became Lenin and only secondarily the events of October. Lenin was transformed into a symbol.

Stalin's funeral oration not only gave a significant stimulus to the development of the Lenin cult, but it also directed that cult into channels which suited Stalin more than his rivals. Through his speech Stalin had placed the party in the position of humble disciple of its dead leader, forever obeying him and continuing his cause to the best of its abilities. Furthermore, by appropriating to himself the ability to define what Lenin had said and to promise in the name of the party to carry it out, Stalin was clearly staking his claim to be Lenin's successor, to lead the party in pursuit of the aims which he claimed Lenin had laid down. He was Lenin's orthodox pupil, the one who best knew Lenin's feelings and understood his ideas, whose personal association with Lenin extended back to the time of the emergence of the Bolsheviks.[10] Stalin attempted to reinforce this image of himself through the publication, initially in *Pravda* and later in book form, of *Foundations of Leninism*. Originally delivered as a series of lectures at Sverdlov University in April 1924, this work contained a more systematised version of Leninism as Stalin wished to present it than had been possible earlier. Stalin's presentation of Lenin's ideas was very formalistic and simplified, presented essentially as a series of canons to be put into practice unthinkingly, and clearly portrayed the author in the guise of chief disciple and authoritative interpreter of Lenin's thinking.[11]

However, Stalin was not alone in his attempt to establish his credentials as the leader closest to Lenin. Both Trotsky and Zinoviev made similar efforts, although the type of image which they projected was radically different from that of Stalin the disciple. Trotsky's *On Lenin*, published in June 1924, and *Lessons of October*, which appeared on the eve of the seventh anniversary of the Revolution, were key documents in the image projected by Trotsky. Both portrayed the relationship between Lenin and Trotsky as one of equality. Lenin was shown as relying on Trotsky for advice and support in the difficult days of 1917 when other members of the Bolshevik leadership vacillated and even directly opposed the course favoured by Lenin. When Lenin was mistaken, it was Trotsky who ushered him back on to the right path.[12] On reading these works it is difficult to escape the conclusion that Lenin's success was due in large part to the efforts of Trotsky. In the case of Zinoviev, too, the image being projected was one of equality with Lenin. In his funeral speech Zinoviev used the more orthodox language of Bolshevism, appearing not as a disciple but as a fellow Marxist philosopher paying his last respects to a departed colleague. This impression was reinforced by Zinoviev's attempt to reassert his position as the chief exponent of orthodox Leninism through the publication in October 1925 of *Leninism: An Introduction to the Study of Leninism*. In this book Zinoviev did not simply give an exposition of Lenin's views as Stalin appeared to have done, but instead used Lenin's ideas as support for his own commentaries and criticisms of current policies. Implicitly to many in the party he appeared to be bringing Lenin's ideas into question: if Zinoviev's criticisms of the current situation were unfounded, were the arguments from Lenin which he cited in support of those criticisms also mistaken? While Stalin appeared to be looking to Lenin the master for guidance and inspiration, Zinoviev seemed to be looking to Lenin his former colleague for intellectual support in an argument.

The contrast between the images fostered by Stalin and his rivals was highlighted in the factional disputes of the 1920s, during which both sides of the successive struggles sought to affirm their Leninist nature while attempting to tar their opponents with the anti-Leninist brush. In numerous keynote speeches[13] Stalin presented himself as the simple adherent of the ideas of the great master, one whose sole goal in life was to guide the Soviet Union along the path outlined by Lenin. In this way he was able to caricature the differences between himself and those who had pretensions to correct Lenin; he was the 'faithful disciple',[14] protecting the Leninist heritage from those who would pervert it. Skilfully Stalin attempted to highlight the points of difference between his opponents and Lenin. He pointed to Trotsky's non-Bolshevik background and his bitter criticisms of Lenin early in the century, the vacillation of Zinoviev and Kamenev over whether the time was ripe for revolution in October 1917, and Bukharin's differences with Lenin during the war and at the time of Brest-Litovsk.[15] Selective quotations from Lenin were cited to damn his opponents.[16] Taking their lead from the General Secretary, at each stage of the successive conflicts Stalin's supporters at all levels of the party took up the charges he laid, expanded on them, and indicted his opponents for the most heinous sin of all, anti-Leninism in thought and deed. Although Stalin's opponents tried to attach the same anti-Leninist label to the General Secretary, Stalin's low profile in pre-1924 party history left only limited scope for this. Even when his opponents had a damning indictment of Stalin from Lenin's own pen, their political ineptitude enabled him to turn this back on them.[17] As the 1920s progressed, the image of Stalin as the faithful disciple and defender of Lenin's thought gained strength in the Soviet public arena. The image of Stalin, the Leninist disciple, became a part of the Lenin cult.

This image struck a responsive chord among many party members at all levels. Reliable support among rank-and-file party members was important for Stalin, because he sought to use the authority of party meetings for the condemnation and complete crushing of his opponents. Stalin's control over the power of appointment within the party was an important factor in ensuring a solid core of support at these meetings, but this alone cannot explain the growth of support for Stalin within the party. At the higher echelons his apparent moderation and the policies he espoused gained support among many party functionaries; his policy of 'socialism in one country' was especially attractive to many because of the rejection of revolutionary adventurism which it implied. However, at the lower levels of the party, particularly in the provinces where the literacy level among party members was exceptionally low, the theoretical debates occurring at the apex had little impact.[18] It is here that the images projected by the leading protagonists would have been most important.

The Stalin image evoked a more positive response within the party than those of his rivals because it accorded well with the perceptions of many party members about the party and its role in the developing society and, at a more personal level, about their own part in the construction of socialism. While party members shared a broad uniformity of outlook, various differences in orientation can be discerned. Significant in this regard is the difference between the Old Bolsheviks who had joined the party in the uncertain times prior to the seizure of power, and those recruits who had flowed into the party in the post-1917 period. While these two groups had their own distinctive attitudes toward the developing political system, both were responsive to the image projected by Stalin.

To the Old Bolsheviks the party appeared in symbolic terms as the incarnation of proletarian virtue, the beacon that would lead the workers of the world into the bright future. During the years of adversity when the party was underground struggling for its existence against tsarist oppression or battling to expand its position in the chaos of 1917, when membership could involve real costs, possibly including the loss of one's life, those who joined the party and remained in it were motivated primarily by commitment to the ideals for which the party stood. The purely 'careerist' elements criticised so strongly in later years were unlikely to have joined, with the party's fortunes so uncertain. Those long-time members of the party had devoted much of their lives and energy to the cause which they believed the party embodied. It was the focus around which their lives centred, giving meaning to their existence and direction and purpose to their actions. The party possessed for them a mystique of absolute, unconditional loyalty and devotion; Trotsky's 'My party – right or wrong'[19] accurately summarises this sentiment. For these Old Bolsheviks the symbolic importance of the party was immense.[20]

This attitude to the party was reinforced by the conditions which prevailed during the 1920s. The view of the party as the inexorable wave of the future, initially reinforced by the victory in October, was strengthened by the successful conclusion of the civil war. In both cases a small band of men and women, motivated by high ideals, had struggled against seemingly crushing odds and emerged victorious. The Old Bolsheviks' belief that they were the medium through which history would unfold its future course was reaffirmed in their minds. However, the situation which the party found itself in at the end of the civil war did not correspond with this generalised image of the party as the harbinger of the bright new dawn. Party rule was tenuous and confronted by popular hostility throughout large parts of the country. Peasant disorders had broken out in many areas, urban discontent was rising, and even the sailors of Kronstadt had raised the banner of revolt. The party was like a beleaguered garrison, surrounded by a surly populace whose feelings toward the new regime were all too obvious to party members. The result was an acute sense of isolation, a feeling heightened by the disappearance of any prospect of imminent revolution in the west.

This sense of isolation was exacerbated for many Old Bolsheviks by developments within the party and state machines in the post-revolution period. The demands of governing in a hostile environment led to a dilution of the Bolsheviks' utopian ideals as the party's emphasis on revolutionary transformation shifted to one on order. This shift, signified most clearly by the replacement of War Communism by NEP, meant not only a practical downgrading of those ideals to which the Old Bolsheviks had dedicated their lives, but it also involved a change in the necessary qualifications for power within the political structure. No longer was service to the party in the hard times prior to October a ticket to power and influence. With the emphasis on government and order, an increasingly important place in governing circles was being occupied by those more at home in the realm of organisation and administration than of revolutionary transformation. Many of the long-standing members of the party were not equipped to handle this new situation. In Lenin's words,

> The point is that the responsible communist – even the best, the unquestionably honest and devoted, who endured penal servitude and did not fear death – cannot trade because he is not a smart dealer, he has not learnt this and does not wish to learn it, and does not understand that he must learn from the ABC . . . the responsible communist and the devoted revolutionary not only does not know this, but he does not even know that he does not know.[21]

With the party unable to recruit efficient administrators in the numbers required from among the Old Bolsheviks, it turned to former Tsarist officials who were willing to serve the new masters of

Russia. The bureaucratic machines which emerged after 1917 included a significant proportion of former tsarist functionaries.[22] Many of those with long party careers now found that positions of power and influence were being filled by representatives of the regime which they had struggled for so long to overthrow.[23] Many Old Bolsheviks neither had the skills to adapt successfully to the new administrative emphasis in the party's operations, nor were sufficiently high up the hierarchy of power for it not to matter that they had little talent for administration. They were thus effectively redundant, crushed by their inability to play a meaningful role in the new non-revolutionary party that was emerging.

This decline in the position of the Old Bolsheviks within the party was reinforced by the rapid growth in party membership in the decade and a half following the Revolution. The Old Bolsheviks were drawn from the 390,000 members of the party at March 1918, and particularly the 24,000 who were members at the beginning of 1917.[24] However, with the expansion of party membership to 1,677,910 by January 1930, those veterans who had participated in the party's rise to power had become a minority within its ranks. They had been swamped by new recruits, as yet largely untried and untested by the smoke of battle, and yet it was many of these new arrivals who were moving into leading positions in the political hierarchy.

For the Old Bolsheviks the 1920s was thus a time of dramatic change and, for many, of great disappointment. The revolution had not been the key to the immediate glorious future which many of them had imagined it to be. Beset by frustration and disappointment many Old Bolsheviks were potentially receptive to any appeal phrased in terms which made their lives appear more meaningful. The heroic myth of October fulfilled this function. Instead of the increasingly bureaucratised and routinised present in which they felt superfluous, the myth enabled them to fix their gaze on the glorious, heady, semi-anarchic days of 1917 when everything appeared, in retrospect, clear-cut and simple, and when they were central figures in the struggle for communism. They preferred to see the party not as the bureaucratic machine it was becoming but in the form in which it had existed for most of its life, the small dedicated band devoting their lives to the quest for a better way of life for all. A past in which they felt their lives fulfilled was far more attractive than a present in which they felt irrelevant. The heroic myth of October which flourished naturally in the wake of the

Bolshevik consolidation of power thus struck a very responsive chord among Old Bolsheviks.

This myth also appealed to many of those who joined the party after October 1917, although perhaps without the intensity engendered by personal participation characteristic of the Old Bolsheviks. Many of these newer members, having no personal experience of the party's struggle in 1917, had little accurate knowledge of the course of events in the revolutionary year and were seriously hampered in their quest for such understanding by their low level of literacy.[25] For these people, acceptance of the myth of October provided a ready explanation of the past and a justification of the present. As the principal vehicle for the regime's claims to legitimacy, the myth constituted a rationalisation of the post-1917 political structure and, therefore, their own positions in it. Furthermore, overt acceptance of the myth was essential for these newer members if they were to live down the 'Johnny-come-lately' image which many of the Old Bolsheviks attached to them: they had to appear more firmly Leninist than these veterans if they were to remove doubts about their political loyalty. Even those recruits who had joined the party from purely careerist motives must have been aware of this link between the myth of October and their personal positions in both society at large and the party. This instrumental attraction of the myth would have been reinforced for those who accepted the ideals which the myth embodied by the emotional satisfaction and sense of purpose which such acceptance generated. Many of the post-1917 recruits thus shared with the Old Bolsheviks a potentially receptive attitude to any appeals couched in terms of the myth of October.

The importance of the myth of October for the Lenin succession lies in the increasingly dominating position within it that was occupied by the figure of Lenin. The image of Lenin as the source of success in 1917, and as the infallible guide at all times, determined the reactions of many party members to the images being projected by the leading protagonists in the post-Lenin succession struggle. The image of Stalin as the disciple, follower and defender of Lenin evoked wide support within the party because it did not bring the figure of Lenin into question. Unlike Trotsky, Zinoviev, Kamenev and Bukharin, Stalin appeared neither to question Lenin's infallibility nor to diminish his role in 1917. The image of Stalin effectively constituted a reaffirmation of the essence of the myth of October and, by 'correctly' interpreting and defending Leninist orthodoxy, an expression of confidence in the future. This message was far more attractive to party members than that which flowed from his opponents' apparent questioning of this basis of system legitimacy.

The formal capitulation of the right opposition in November 1929 left Stalin in a dominating position in the party. All of his most prominent opponents and their followers had been discredited, although the party was not yet the pliant instrument in his hands it was to become in the 1930s. It was at this time that the image of Stalin underwent a major metamorphosis, with the emergence of the Stalin cult in its own right. Previously the figure of Stalin had not been particularly prominent in the mass media; references to him appeared no more frequently than to other leaders, and there was no laudation of his person. However, in mid-December 1929, the press was dominated by a flood of eulogistic articles celebrating his fiftieth birthday. The issues of *Pravda* for the week beginning 18 December were filled with laudatory articles about Stalin and hortatory greetings from an adoring populace. Although the glorification of Stalin did not continually run at such high levels,[26] henceforth it remained a significant element in Soviet public life. The figure of Stalin came eventually to dominate all aspects of life in the Soviet Union, and his name was rarely mentioned without being qualified by a hortatory epithet.

The significance of the cult for Stalin's search for personal authority derives less from the degree to which the cult dominated Soviet society than from the image of Stalin which it projected. In line with the criteria for leadership established in the early 1920s,[27] the cult emphasised Stalin's relationship with Lenin. In its first full flowering the cult depicted Stalin as Lenin's 'true best pupil', his 'single most reliable aide', with Lenin at all times and always in agreement with him. Unlike other leaders, Stalin appeared never to deviate from Lenin or his teachings while the leader was alive or after his death. Consequently, Stalin was the only true Leninist among the Bolshevik leaders and therefore the one most fitted to lead the party in Lenin's absence. In projecting this image of Leninist–Stalinist unity the cult initially reaffirmed the picture of Lenin's primacy which had existed during the 1920s. However, as the cult developed in the years after 1929, this picture of Stalin's subordinate status became blurred. Stalin ceased to appear solely in the guise of Lenin's follower and subordinate. During the early

1930s a new theme of the cult pictured Stalin as Lenin's equal. All successes prior to Lenin's incapacity became the result of the Lenin–Stalin duo, while Bolshevik rhetoric was punctured by such epithets as 'the party of Lenin–Stalin', 'the cause of Lenin–Stalin', 'the banner of Lenin–Stalin', and 'the teachings of Lenin–Stalin'.[28] Stalin was the living embodiment of Lenin's ideas, and therefore automatically guiding the country along the Leninist path.[29] This sentiment is admirably summarised by the phrase 'Stalin is the Lenin of today'.[30] The figure of Lenin was transformed into a constituent element of the Stalin cult, and clearly became of secondary importance behind the dominating figure of Stalin. As the 1930s progressed, references to Lenin alone became less frequent in the press, increasingly the party's achievements were attributed to Stalin alone, and from late 1935 the adjective 'Stalinist' began to eclipse the 'Leninist' and 'Lenin–Stalin' epithets which had previously dominated Bolshevik rhetoric: 'Stalinist Central Committee', 'Stalinist government', 'Stalinist epoch', 'Stalinist youth', and, of course, 'Stalin Constitution'[31] are only some examples from this period. The longer the cult continued, the more prominent this theme became, until the figure of Stalin dominated all spheres of Soviet life.[32]

In the process of projecting this image of Stalin, the evolving leader cult effectively recast the heroic myth of October. The dominating figure of Lenin was replaced by the duumvirate of Lenin–Stalin in which Stalin became the more prominent figure. Wholesale historical revision eliminated as important figures everyone except this duo.[33] Even the role of the party was diminished as the events of 1917 were transformed into simply the background against which Stalin's personal qualities and his unity with Lenin could be demonstrated. This revision of the myth, buttressed by a process of historical revision during the 1930s and 1940s, was rendered virtually invulnerable. Following closely upon the disbandment of those organisations in which Old Bolshevism had survived spiritually, the Society of Old Bolsheviks and the Society of Former Political Prisoners in 1935 and the Communist Academy in 1936, came the physical liquidation of many Old Bolsheviks still living. The purges removed from the scene many participants in the events of 1917 who could contradict at first hand the way in which the Stalin cult was remoulding the myth of October. With the elimination of many of the Old Bolsheviks and the cowing of those who remained, the myth being projected by the Stalin cult became impregnable, and the symbolic link between Lenin and Stalin unchallengeable.

As well as recasting the myth of October, the Stalin cult clearly undermined the place of the party in the symbolism of the regime. The downgrading of the party's role in the events of 1917 has already been mentioned. This was complemented by the supplanting of claims for the party as the unique source of success and the embodiment of the proletariat by similar claims for Stalin. Successes in all spheres of life in the Soviet Union were attributed to Stalin personally, to his infallible guidance and consummate wisdom. It was he who was portrayed as omnipotent, omnicompetent and omnipresent, as the sole source of achievement, not the party.[34] He was unerringly leading the march into communism. Furthermore, his intimate knowledge of the people's situation and of their innermost thoughts enabled him always to act in their best interests. He was the diviner of the will of the proletariat and the guardian of its interests, the personification of the chosen class in history.[35] The party disappeared as an independent entity, submerged by the expansion of the figure of Stalin.

As it developed, the cult of Stalin thus transformed three of the basic elements of the heroic myth of October: the events of 1917, the figure of Lenin, and the institution of the party. In this process of transformation these elements were co-opted into the Stalin cult and became subsumed under the dominating figure of Stalin: the events of 1917 became a context for the demonstration of Stalin's unity with Lenin and for the expression of his personal qualities, Lenin was reduced to the minor part of the Lenin–Stalin duo, and the party became an instrument to be wielded by the wise leader. By reshaping the symbolism of the regime in this way, the cult turned the figure of Stalin into the central focus of legitimacy within the political system. In his person was contained all notion of right in the system, from his words all authority flowed; he was the symbol towards which all turned for the justification of the regime's actions and for the direction of future activity. Stalin thus gained personal authority in symbolic terms by arrogating to himself through the leader cult the source of regime legitimacy.

The date of the first full flowering of the Stalin leader cult, December 1929, is significant. With the capitulation of the right opposition in November, Stalin's victory over his Old Bolshevik opponents was symbolically crowned. Although not yet invulnerable, Stalin was securely in the saddle; the leading anti-Stalin Old Bolsheviks had been eliminated as power-brokers in the party. While the Old Bolsheviks had remained influential, Stalin had not attacked the myth in which they were personally significant elements and which had direct personal meaning for them. Instead, he had used the symbol of Lenin to outflank successive opposition groups. The image Stalin presented of himself as Lenin's disciple evoked a positive response from party members at all levels, including Old Bolsheviks, because he seemed to pose no threat to their symbolic universe. However, once Stalin had discredited his leading rivals and restricted their influence in the party ranks, he recast the symbolic basis of the regime by a complete reworking of the political myth at the heart of the legitimacy of the system and of the world view of veteran party members. No longer were prominent oppositionists in a position effectively to contradict the newly emerging mythology, nor were potential questioners of the new orthodoxy at lower levels of the party able to focus upon a figure at the top whose very existence constituted a living contradiction of Stalin's revamped myth of October; few potential oppositionists possessed widely acknowledged revolutionary credentials which could provide the basis for a challenge to the Stalin myth.

The emergence of the Stalin cult reflects Stalin's victory in the intra-élite disputes of the 1920s, disputes which, in symbolic terms, had taken place within the context of the developing Lenin cult. The élite tensions which developed in the 1930s occurred at a time when the Stalin cult was becoming the dominant strand of regime symbolism. This cut the ground from under Stalin's opponents in two ways. Firstly, the saturation of the media and of society in general by the image of Stalin as the perfect leader of genius infallibly guiding the country into the era of communism placed the opposition in an invidious position. If all Stalin's actions could be justified in terms of further advancing the march to communism, any criticism of or opposition to him personally could be interpreted as opposition to communism. Opposition to Stalin based on personal, policy or ideological grounds was thus transformed into treason against the Leninist cause and the fatherland. This was reflected in the widespread use of the charge of treason in the purge trials of the 1930s. Secondly, by projecting an image of Lenin–Stalin unity, the cult ensured that any opposition to Stalin had either to base its attacks on a foundation other than claimed adherence to Leninism, or to dispute Stalin's claim to embody the Leninist heritage. The first alternative was not viable in Soviet conditions. The second alternative involved a direct contradiction of the central message of the cult. However, because the image presented by the cult was closely linked to the myth of October, it was difficult to reject the cult's claim of Lenin–Stalin unity without at the same time rejecting the prevailing form the foundation myth of the Soviet regime was taking, thereby once again leaving oppositionists open to the charge of treason. In this way the cult appropriated to Stalin the only grounds on which political activity could legitimately be pursued. In any case Stalin was hardly troubled by his opponents in the symbolic field because his control over the mass media enabled him to so saturate Soviet society with his message that any opposition which attempted to give effective voice to contrary views was overwhelmed. The cumulative weight of the cult was too great for any opposition to overcome. Thus the transformation of the figure of Stalin into the symbol of regime legitimacy made Stalin unassailable in symbolic terms.

The date of the emergence of the Stalin cult is significant in another respect. It burst on to the Soviet scene at the beginning of the decade in which the country experienced the most significant process of directed socio-economic change in its history. The economic structure was completely revamped by the effort to industrialise and to collectivise agriculture. The major political structures were shaken to their foundations by the purges. This massive upheaval created a favourable environment for the Stalin cult to sink its roots deep into party ranks. For those whose lives were completely disrupted by the changes occurring around them, for those who sought reassurance in the face of the abrupt changes of political line, and for those who were simply bewildered by the new turns of events, the dominating figure of Stalin answered a need. The growing emphasis on Stalin's infallibility, the aura of success that surrounded his name, and the claims for his fatherly concern for the people, conveyed an image of someone in control and directing the vast changes. His image offered certainty in a changing and uncertain world.[36]

The effect within the party that this uncertainty produced was reinforced by other developments at that time. The revolution from above involved the expansion of party control into many areas of life previously unpenetrated, combined with a centralisation of effective decision-making at the apex. The demands that this expansion of responsibility made resulted in a substantial growth in membership.[37] Many of the 2¼ million recruits between 1928 and 1933 had no strong ideological commitment to the party and its ideals. In general, they were characterised by a very low educational level and lacked the formal training that would have equipped them to carry out the tasks with which they were confronted. Many were still stamped with the imprint of the traditional political culture and the image of authority as personalised, autocratic and demanding that this involved.[38] Confronted with unyielding demands from above, conscious of the leader's practice of attributing failures in policy to the incompetence of low-level functionaries,[39] and aware of the swathe being cut through the party by the purges, many of these new party members reacted by offering absolute conformity to the centre; any sign of deviation was certain to bring retribution, while it was hoped that total conformity might be the means of salvation. Such an attitude accorded well with the designs of the leadership. The militarisation of the party reflected in the centralisation of decision-making meant that all levels of the party below the Politburo were unable to make major decisions without reference to Moscow. A 'commandist' mentality resulted, with people both unwilling and unable to make decisions without seeking guidance from above.[40] This created a favourable environment for the Stalin cult. By highlighting the supreme source of authority to be obeyed under all circumstances, the cult provided a source of direction for those at all levels of the party. Stalin was clearly portrayed as the supreme arbiter of all questions that arose and the source of guidance and direction on all matters. The cult thus provided the leadership figure demanded by party members at all levels. Just as the foundation myth of the Soviet regime and the leader cult of Lenin struck a positive chord in the party during the 1920s, so too the cult of Stalin and the image which it projected was particularly suited to the party mood of the 1930s. Rank-and-file acceptance of these images was fundamental to Stalin's ability to clothe himself in the mantle of personal authority with which he sought to complement the political power he had been able to amass by other means.

NOTES

1. This is discussed in terms of charismatic authority in Robert C. Tucker, *Stalin as Revolutionary, 1879–1929* (London, 1974) ch. 2.

2. This myth was projected through the publication of historical and memoir material in book and pamphlet form, through the cinema, and through the press.

3. For example, 'Proyekt postanovleniya politburo TsK RKP (b) o statiyakh A. M. Gor'kogo v zhurnale "Kommunisticheskii Internatsional"', in V. I. Lenin, *Polnoe sobranie sochinenii*, vol. LIV, p. 429.

4. The desire to tap Lenin's personal popularity within the party should not be dismissed in this context.

5. *Dvenadtsatyi syezd Rossiiskoi kommunisticheskoi partii (bol'shevikov) Stenografcheskii otchet* (Moscow, 1968) pp. 8–9. Zinoviev was delivering the speech normally delivered by Lenin.

6. Ibid., p. 523.

7. Many in the party believed this interpreter should be the collective leadership. See Bukharin's remarks in 1925. Stephen F. Cohen, *Bukharin and the Bolshevik Revolution* (London, 1974) p. 224.

8. J. V. Stalin, *Works* (Moscow, 1953) vol. VI, pp. 47–53. For some details of the burgeoning Lenin cult, see E. H. Carr, *Socialism in One Country, 1924–1926* (Harmondsworth, 1970) vol. II, pp. 11–12.

9. A central aspect of this magnification of the figure of Lenin during the 1920s was the destruction of the image of Trotsky as a major actor in the foundation of the Soviet state. This was an essential prerequisite for the image Stalin was later to construct.

10. In a memorial speech at the Kremlin Military School on 28 January Stalin set out to catalogue his early meetings with Lenin. In this speech he claims to have received a 'simple but deeply significant letter' from Lenin in 1903. No evidence of this letter exists, and this claim has the effect of pre-dating Stalin's acquaintance with Lenin by two years. The speech, initially published in *Pravda*, 12 Feb 1924, is reprinted in *Works*, vol. VI, pp. 54–66.

11. In this last respect, see the final section of *Foundations of Leninism*, which discusses the style of leadership necessary in a Leninist party in a way which makes Stalin appear more suitable than his competitors. Ibid., pp. 71–196.

12. Leon Trotsky, *On Lenin: Notes Towards a Biography* (London, 1971) pp. 85–6. For a discussion of the reaction to these books, see Carr, *Socialism in One Country*, pp. 13–14 and 17–40, and Tucker, *Stalin*, pp. 337–54.

13. See, for example, 'The October Revolution and the Tactics of the Russian Communists' (Dec 1924) in *Works*, vol. VI, pp. 374–420; 'The Political Report of the Central Committee, 14th Congress of the CPSU (b)' (Dec 1925) ibid., vol. VII, pp. 267–361; 'Concerning Questions of Leninism' (Jan 1926) ibid., vol. VIII, pp. 13–96; 'The Social Democratic Deviation in Our Party' (Nov 1926) ibid., vol. VIII, pp. 245–310; 'Speech to the Seventh Enlarged Plenum of the ECCI' (Dec 1926) ibid., vol. IX pp. 1–64; 'Speeches to the Joint Plenum of the Central Committee and the Central Control Commission of the CPSU (b)' (Aug 1927) ibid., vol. X, pp. 1–96; 'The Trotskyist Opposition Before and Now' (Oct 1927) ibid., vol. X, pp. 177–211; 'The Political Report of the Central Committee, 15th Congress of the CPSU (b)' (Dec 1927) ibid., vol. X, pp. 275–363; 'The Right Danger in the CPSU (b)' (Oct 1928) ibid., vol. XI, pp. 231–48; 'the Right Deviation in the CPSU (b)' (Apr 1929) ibid., vol. XII, pp. 1–113.

14. This was a term Stalin used to describe himself. Ibid., vol. IX, p. 156.

15. For example, respectively: ibid., vol. VI, pp. 382–4; vol. VIII, p. 226; and vol. XII, pp. 74–80 and 106.

16. For example, see ibid., vol. XI, p. 336. As well as using Lenin's words to attack his enemies, Stalin and his supporters scoured his opponents' writings to find evidence of criticism of Lenin. One of the most damning of all in this regard was a passage from a letter by Trotsky to Chkheidze in 1913: 'The whole edifice of Leninism at the present time is built on lies and falsification and bears within itself the poisonous elements of its own decay' (ibid., vol. VI, p. 365).

17. For details of the role of Lenin's 'Testament' in the factional disputes, see Tucker, *Stalin*, pp. 362–7 and 431–2. At this time Stalin was not widely recognised as a major contender for power in his own right, so there was little incentive to attempt totally to destroy him in a political sense.

18. Merle Fainsod, *Smolensk Under Soviet Rule* (New York, 1958) p. 48. On literacy levels in the party, see Leonard Schapiro, *The Communist Party of the Soviet Union*, 2nd edn (London, 1970) p. 315; and Roger Pethybridge, *The Social Prelude to Stalinism* (London, 1974) p. 156.

19. Speech to the 13th Congress of the party. *Trinadtsatyi syezd Rossiiskoi Kommunisticheskoi Partii (bol'shevikov). Mai 1924 goda: stenograficheskii otchet* (Moscow, 1963) p. 158.

20. One historian speaks of a 'religious, cultist attitude toward such concepts as the Party, the Soviet state, the Revolution, and the proletariat' – Roy Medvedev, *Let History Judge* (New York, 1971) p. 164.

21. 'Politicheskii otchet tsentral' nogo komiteta RKP (b) 27 Marta (1922)', in Lenin, *Polnoe sobranie sochinenii*, vol. XLV, p. 82.

22. Carr cites some interesting figures in regard to the developing state machine: in 1929, 37 per cent of personnel in the Commissariat of Finance, 27 per cent in the Commissariat of Labour, and 26 per cent in the Commissariat of Trade held government positions under the Tsar. In Leningrad, 52 per cent of the personnel of local government offices were former Tsarist officials. Carr, *Socialism in One Country* vol. I, p. 130.

23. Certainly many Old Bolsheviks retained positions of power, especially at higher levels. According to party statistics, in 1927 veteran communists still comprised 85 per cent of senior party secretaries, although at the level of the primary cells over 60 per cent of party members had joined after 1921. Cited in Schapiro, *The CPSU*, p. 315.

24. All membership figures are from T. H. Rigby, *Communist Party Membership in the USSR, 1917–1967* (Princeton, NJ, 1968), p. 52. For a discussion of the problems in establishing the number of members in October 1917, see ibid., pp. 61–3. One recent article cites a figure of 350,000 members in October 1917. 'KPSS v tsifrakh', *Partiinaya zhizn'*, (1977, no. 21, p. 21).

25. In 1927, 91·3 per cent of all party members had received primary-level education or less (Pethybridge, *Social Prelude to Stalinism*, p. 156). It was this low educational level that made Stalin's *Foundations of Leninism* so potent. It provided a simple set of guidelines to what Lenin said, constituting a belief map for the ideologically untutored.

26. The author has analysed fluctuations in the cult of Stalin in his unpublished MA thesis, 'The Cult of Personality and the Search for Legitimacy: The Cases of Mao and Stalin' (Monash University, 1973).

27. These criteria were reaffirmed in theoretical terms in K. Popov, 'Partiya i rol'

vozhdya', *Partiinoe stroitel'stvo*, 1930, no. 1, pp. 5–9.
28. For examples, see *Pravda*, 2 Sep 1933, 4 May 1934, 9 Dec 1935, 25 Sep 1936, 6 Sep 1937, 19 Apr 1940, 23 Feb 1942, 8 Nov 1945, 22 Apr 1946, 5 Sep 1947, 22 July 1949. For a fuller list see Gill, 'The Cult of Personality', pp. 132–5.
29. In 1931, Stalin was referred to as the 'incarnation of the power and genius of the great teacher' (*Pravda*, 10 Nov 1931). In 1946 it was asserted, 'speaking of Lenin, we think of Stalin; speaking of Stalin, we think of Lenin' (ibid., 21 Jan 1946).
30. Ibid., 21 Jan 1938.
31. See, for example, ibid., 22 Oct 1935, 21 Jan 1936, 9 June 1936, 25 June 1936, 10 Aug 1936, 7 Nov 1936, 10 Nov 1936. Even prior to this, references to Stalin which implied his primacy over Lenin began appearing in *Pravda*. For example, 'greatest strategist of the proletarian revolution' (22 Jan 1934), 'greatest man of all times and epochs' (2 Feb 1934).
32. One qualification should be added. Despite the overwhelming of the 'Lenin as leader' image by that of Stalin, the former did not disappear entirely. For example, it was claimed in 1950, 'Comrade Stalin, guided by Lenin, came forward as Lenin's closest disciple, his most faithful follower, as, after Lenin, our Party's greatest theoretician, organizer, and Party builder' – L. Beria, *The Great Inspirer and Organizer of the Victories of Communism*, (Moscow, 1950) p. 5.
33. The baldest statement of this trend occurs in the Biographical Chronicle of vol. III of Stalin's *Works*, p. 451: 'October 24–25, V. I. Lenin and J. V. Stalin direct the October armed uprising.'
34. See Gill, 'The Cult of Personality', pp. 145–67. For example, 'all of our successes . . . are wholly and completely linked to Stalin' (*Pravda*, 20 Dec 1939).
35. The flavour of this theme of the cult is suggested by the following verse: 'He remembers us / at every hour, / Works, builds, / lives for us. / He loves each and every one, / like a kind father, / And in his heart he carries / millions of hearts' – cited in T. H. Rigby, 'Some Aspects of the Stalin Myth', *Melbourne University Magazine*, 1949, p. 84. See also Gill, 'The Cult of Personality', pp. 185–92.
36. See the statement by A. Pis'mennyi, cited in Medvedev, *Let History Judge*, pp. 365–6, for a personal reminiscence regarding the link between uncertainty and belief in Stalin.
37. Party membership increased from 1,535, 362 full and candidate members in 1929 to 2,306,973 in 1939. The number entering the party at this time was greater than these figures suggest because of the large swathe that the purges cut through party membership during this decade (Rigby, *Communist Party Membership*, p. 52). By 1939 only 8·3 per cent of full members had joined the party prior to the end of 1920; 70 per cent had joined after 1929 (Schapiro, *The CPSU*, p. 441).
38. By 1939 80 per cent of party members still lacked any secondary-level education (Pethybridge, *Social Prelude to Stalinism*, p. 175). On traditional political culture and its image of authority, see Medvedev, *Let History Judge*, p. 429; and Stephen White, 'The USSR: Patterns of Autocracy and Industrialism', in Archie Brown and Jack Gray (eds), *Political Culture and Political Change in Communist States* (London, 1977) pp. 25–34.
39. Even before Stalin began to purge the party, the trials of 1928–31 acted as a warning to these people. For Stalin's direction of blame at lower-level

functionaries, see, for example, *Works*, vol. XII, pp. 197–205 ('Dizzy with Success'), and vol. XIII, pp. 220–39.

40. A 'commandist' tendency in the party had been noted as early as 1923. See Leon Trotsky, *The New Course* (New York, 1965) p. 154.

7 Stalinism and Intellectual Order

A. Kemp-Welch

The conventional wisdom that the source of policy in the Stalin era was Stalin, aided at most by nicely calculated combinations of secretarial subordinates, corresponds quite closely to what we know about the later Stalinism, and most precisely to the phase into which its cultural policies were frozen after the war. Then the attack on Aleksandrov (1948) did take the philosophical establishment unawares, and seemed to illustrate the method of both 'cult of personality' and 'totalitarian leadership' in acting without regard for precedent or established orthodoxy, apparently by caprice. In further cases, arbitrariness was combined with ambiguity, intended to cause fear or isolation amongst the intelligentsia. Thus the posthumous attack on Marr (1950) was calculated to bring confusion, provoke faction-fighting and dispute over the 'party line' which extended far beyond the chosen field, linguistics, into all the social sciences, where scholars vied with one another in the 'decoding' of and 'drawing of conclusions' from Stalin's statements. But was this always so? Does the conventional wisdom not stem principally from the memory of these last years, ones of policy stagnation and intellectual decline, which is then projected back in explanation of the pre-war period?

In approaching this question, we take our subject-matter from the makings of the Stalinist intellectual order in the thirties. So little secondary work has been conducted on this decade, beyond the ending of its initial phase (1929–32), which is generally regarded as episodic or transitional, rather than Stalinist itself, that we have a whole area open for analysis. On the basis of the primary materials from journals, the press, unpublished Soviet dissertations, and in archives we try to judge Stalin's role in the founding of 'his' intellectual order. So doing, we consider first the cases in which policy changes can be traced directly to him, and, thereafter, the other forms and sources of policy formation.

To write of order presupposes some disorder that it seeks to remedy, and we find this in the transitionary convulsions of the first five-year plan (1929–32). But it was also present in the ideas of socialism that had been put forward, and argued out, during the previous decade. The twenties were, as Leonard Schapiro has written, 'the golden age of Marxist thought in the USSR',[1] and Soviet scholars were then at the forefront in many areas of intellectual discovery. Through such outstanding talents as Preobrazhensky, Chayanov, Pashukanis and Vygotsky, whole new disciplines appeared – developmental economics, peasant studies, the sociology of law, and new branches of educational psychology[2] – and through such institutions as the Communist Academy, and its innumerable publications, a corpus of thinking was built up, whose implications are not yet exhausted in our day.[3] Without doubt, society under the New Economic Policy (NEP) – acceptance of social and cultural pluralism in conditions of political monopoly – was a powerful enabling factor, but it seems that the nature of Soviet Marxism itself, as then understood, also provided impetus for this explosion of learning. In retrospect, therefore, it was the Stalinist redefinition of doctrine that served to bring this era to an end.

Soviet Marxism, as understood in the twenties, assumed a tension between the ideal and the actual,[4] an outlook that fitted NEP society rather well. Isolated, relatively backward, culturally deprived, ravaged by civil war, internally divided on class lines, the society that the Bolsheviks inherited showed few obvious signs of being able to sustain the ideals which the makers of the Revolution had originally intended. All leaders recognised this, and Lenin did so explicitly in justifying the compromise with society that made NEP possible. Trotsky took the analysis further, and seemed to conclude in his later exile that the same social backwardness which made the Revolution possible had also frustrated its final socialist completion.[5] But it was Stalin alone who made a virtue of necessity, and, rather than let Bolshevism founder on the rock of recalcitrant social reality, came forward, cautiously at first, as its great saviour – as a new Lenin – and revised its purpose in the process.

Socialism, he implied, is what Soviet Russia has: state ownership of trade and industry (later agriculture), no more, no less. In consequence, 'utopian' prospectuses for the future: workers' control, dismantling of bureaucracy, the withering away of the state and law, were not 'socialist' at all, but anarchist, romantic day-dreaming of book-worms and theologians, 'wild talk' without relevance to post-revolutionary reality. Such visions were at best futile, and at worst fatal to the party's programme, which should concentrate exclusively on 'building socialism' – that is, on the economic and social development of the country.[6] The part of intellectuals in the transformation need not be negligible, he added, provided they ceased interminable discussions, gave up their rodent-like activities in archives, and turned their practical skills over to 'socialist construction'.[7] We shall return to Stalin's notion of 'practicality' presently, after taking note of his personal injunctions as to how the re-establishment of intellectual order was to be carried out.

The first set of intellectual interventions by Stalin was aimed at the 'school' of Bukharin, which it intended to displace. At first by innuendo, then by general theory, and finally by naming names (after the displacement had been effected) a 'Right danger' was introduced in politics.[8] Thus Stalin's entrance into the 'Bukharin bailiwick',[9] the Institute of Red Professors, nominally to speak on grain problems before collectivisation, was understood by all politically cognisant to mark the opening shot in a new campaign. Selected members of his audience were secretly enrolled in theory 'brigades' to comb the works of Bukharin for evidence of what would later be declared his 'deviation'.[10] Following this, Stalin began to put major revisions of Bolshevik theory on record, undramatically at first, but with major consequences for policy later on. Thus his idea that 'class struggle intensifies' as socialism approaches,[11] which amounted to the statement that enemies grow stronger the more they are defeated, was the basis later 'for the grossest violations of socialist law and for mass repressions'.[12] In origin, however, it was simply a blow against the notion of peaceful development, which lay at the heart of the NEP, and had been elevated by Bukharin to permanent status in the party's programme.

Needless to say, Bukharin replied in kind, and accused Stalin at the July Plenum of 1928 of wanting to create a police state, as he put it, 'barracks socialism',[13] based, he added later, on 'military-feudal exploitation of the peasantry'.[14] Bursting in on Kamenev unannounced, he declared, with what his interlocutor described as 'understanding born of revelation', that Stalin was a Genghis Khan, who would 'drown the Revolution in a sea of blood'.[15] Stalin, he now noted, was a mediocrity and knew it, which led him to detest all signs of excellence in others.[16] But, mediocrity or not, he trounced Bukharin in the power struggle.

Why Stalin won is amply documented in the Western literature, and may safely be summarised in three main aspects. First, of course, was his manipulation of the party through its apparatus, which enabled him to remove all potential opponents by 'administrative measures'. This the entire Bukharin school discovered during its enforced diaspora of 1928–9.[17] Second, was his appeal to millennial aspirations that the NEP frustrated. Since 1921 the party's policy had been compromise: the 'great break' of 1928–9 promised action at last, the fortress-storming spirit that had made the Revolution was relevant again. More than history was involved here. To young party members and Komsomols, the campaign to collectivise was not just War Communism, this was their civil war – against the peasantry.[18] Lastly, and the immediate consequence of the defeat of Bukharin and his supporters, were the career prospects that Stalinism opened up for those who would create it. Now the 'commanding heights' of the intellectual and publishing world lay open for advancement.[19] It went without saying, that promotion rested on utter loyalty to the twists and turns of the General Secretary.

When, therefore, the 'Right' had been defeated, and Stalin suddenly returned to 'Trotskyism' as the main danger to the party, taking as his example the smuggling of unorthodox interpretations of party history into *Proletarskaya revolyutsiya*,[20] supporters followed suit. Giving up the 'Right danger', his faithful followers now set about the 'Left danger', and sought to capture Trotskyist 'contraband' in historiography and the social sciences.[21] This done, the terminology fell out of favour for a while, as symbolised by the 'Congress of Victors' in 1934.[22] But it reappeared in time for the show trials, when all dangers were amalgamated into a 'united Bukharinite–Trotskyite' opposition.

These labels were meaningless, and served only to foreclose political discourse. But the onset of Stalinism in politics did not mean that the Soviet Union, post-Bukharin, found itself without ideological debate. In fact, the rout of the 'Right' had consequences that the party leadership may not fully have foreseen.[23] Students still had to be taught, and their number expanded vastly during the first five-year plan;[24] newspapers and journals needed editing; and a fast-increasing party membership[25] had to be told not only what the future of socialism would be, but also what party history and ideology were. These practical matters presented Stalinism with the urgent problem of self-definition. This involved a shift of level from the high political to the cultural, a reworking of the NEP framework into a new shape, thus taking Soviet Marxism in some un-anticipated directions.

Not hitherto a noted intellectual in the party, Stalin made his main theoretical début at the Society of Marxist Agronomists, in December 1929.[26] On this occasion he took intellectuals to task for their remoteness from 'practical activities', and called for a thorough re-examination of the intellectual front. The main goal was to make theory 'catch up' with life, in all spheres, starting with agronomy and economics. In answer to questions, some two months later, Stalin elaborated his critique into one of the 'Rubin school' in economics and, more generally, to all proponents of 'mechanism' on the economic front.[27] As he had done in the leadership struggle, Stalin first indicated a broad area of struggle, then, following an interval, associated specific leaders with it, accompanying the latter with sharp administrative measures to purify the particular 'front'. His comments were enlarged on by Molotov, who stressed the 'Menshevik–idealist character' of Rubin's economics,[28] and by the prosecutors in the Menshevik trials of 1930–1, which confirmed that this tendency amounted to a form of counter-revolutionary wrecking.[29] In the meantime, the charge of mechanism was pressed on other fronts.

Of all these debates, that in philosophy was the most important, for it established the ideological context in which the others were conducted. Moreover, such guidelines as were worked out in the first years of the thirties have remained essentially unaltered to this day. This, though, poses problems for the researcher: no Soviet scholar, even during the Khrushchevian thaw, has been able to publish a full account of how the seminal discussion was conducted.

According to the Moscow thesis of B. T. Ermakov, the remarks of Stalin to Marxist agronomists were immediately taken up within the philosophical section of the Institute of Red Professors, where the dominant school of Deborin offered some routine self-criticism. This was not accepted by a clique of younger philosophers, who insisted on a sterner re-examination in line with Stalin's statements.

Following Stalin's more specific denunciation of mechanism, in February 1930, these militant vigilantes tried to bring the case into the open within the party bureau of the Institute, but were thwarted by the philosophical majority. Self-criticism was again blunted. At this point, however, the party press opened its pages to the growing opposition, with the leaders Mitin and Yudin writing a joint denunciation of Deborin in *Pravda*. Their main assertion was that Deborin represented the mechanistic danger on the philosophical front.[30] And when the majority boycotted a speech by Mitin at the philosophical section of the Institute, he ominously remarked that express sanction from above would be sought for an about-turn (*povorot*) on the philosophical front. Shortly afterwards, members of the party bureau did indeed meet Stalin, who broadened his criticism into one of a highly serious character. He emphasised, Ermakov reports, 'not only the anti-scientific nature of the Menshevik idealism', but also its 'anti-party character'.[31] This latter dictum was sufficient to end the Deborinite domination. Resolutions against the majority were rapidly passed by the Institute and by the Communist Academy, and were confirmed by the Central Committee of the Party on 25 January 1931. The party resolution displaced Deborin and put Mitin and Yudin at the head of new leaderships in philosophical institutes and journals. A flood of attacks on 'Menshevising idealism' followed,[32] and, after an interval of silence, Deborin and others were obliged to utter self-criticisms.[33]

The theme was then taken up in the remaining social sciences. In law, the outstanding jurist Pashukanis was obliged to make the first of many damaging recantations, in which, in line with contemporary practice, he steadily withdrew his earlier expectations about the 'withering away' of the state and law under socialism.[34] And while he was arrested, in 1937, as what *Pravda* called 'a symbol of the defeated revolution of the law',[35] his successor Vyshinsky introduced his peculiar version of a 'Soviet legal culture', a major constituent of the Stalin order.[36] In literary theory, as we see later, the statements of Stalin were taken as the basis for discussion of theory and practice. Finally, historiography became the object of further personal attention.

Following the letter to the journal, *Proletarskaya revolyutsiya*, and an intensive investigation of the historical front, Stalin (together with Kirov and Zhdanov) initiated the *Pokrovshchina*. Started secretly in 1934,[37] this posthumous attack on the outstanding

Marxist historian of the Soviet period caused dismay to many of his colleagues and pupils. As A. M. Pankratova pointed out, Pokrovsky had trained an entire generation of historians, and others spoke openly about the confusion his denunciation was causing. Cadres were now asking whether his classic works should still be read or if they were to be withdrawn.[38] Some of the most critical were arrested, and executed in 1937, after denunciation of the Pokrovsky school as a 'nest of Trotskyites and wreckers'.[39] This was the denouement of Stalin's denunciation of 'Trotskyist contrabandists' in 1931.

The outcome of this and many other ideological campaigns was to transform the position of the scientific intelligentsia. From having been, in the twenties, the most forward-looking and critical element in the old intellectual order, they were conscripted into the service of the new. Some flourished, such as Vyshinsky, prosecutor in the show trials, others perished, but a majority of survivors were obliged to take mundane occupations. Social science assumed an apologetic character, and helped to purvey some of the mysterious and quite powerful mythologies which sustained the Stalin order.

Common sense suggested that as the Soviet Union accelerated its industrial development, and undertook social transformations that were, literally, without precedent, its leaders would need all the specialist advice that could be given. Since, moreover, this was being done in 'one country' first, it seemed that such advice would principally be Soviet. Our brief account of the twenties suggested that such expertise was, potentially, available. Economists, for instance, had advanced many valuable insights into planning and provided a rich debate between 'genetic' and 'teleological' development. Social theorists were in a position to analyse the impact of industrialisation, and calculate the skills and retraining that would be necessary. A political sociology of Stalinism, first sketched out by Bukharin, could have been used to analyse the sources of bureaucracy and help to reduce the bewilderment after 1929 of many Bolsheviks, who found that they were building nothing more quickly than a new Leviathan. It was, however, left to a handful of historians to hint, in Aesopian language, that this was happening.[40]

In practice, scholarship was subordinated to the requirements of the Stalin state: exhortation, mystification and order. First, facts were suppressed, whether statistical accounts of the economy or population, or unpleasant truths about collectivisation.[41] Then minor myths made their appearance: of the role of Stalin in the civil war, on 'sabotage' and 'wrecking'. Finally, a new doctrine appeared on the ruins of the old: the state and law had to be strengthened. Far from withering away, they would last indefinitely.[42]

To turn now to other sources of policy formation is to see at once a complex and more differentiated picture. For while it is true that Stalin's guidelines were designed to point officials and intellectuals in the right direction, equally the tasks of 'decoding' and 'drawing the conclusions' left room for interpretation. Though this had degenerated into hair-splitting and Talmudism in Stalin's later years, there was considerable opportunity for influence in the earlier, formative period.

Our first point is that intellectual life was an area in which party officials of lower rank felt bold enough to initiate policy changes on their own, and to push proposals upwards as a conscious act of insubordination to their immediate superiors. The origins of the letter to *Proletarskaya revolyutsiya* may be a case in point. According to Avtorkhanov, then a junior official in the Central Committee, the basic ideas of the letter, including that of 'contrabandists', was proposed to Stalin by a middle-ranking functionary of the Press Department, a certain Ingulov, over the heads of his departmental superiors Kerzhentsev and Stetsky. He comments, somewhat paradoxically, that these were 'the Stalinist ideas, not yet formulated by Stalin himself' of a sharp reversal of policy on the historical front.[43] Although this is unconfirmed by other sources, some indirect evidence may perhaps stem from the career of Ingulov, who shortly afterwards replaced Kerzhentsev, and following this was promoted still further, to head the censorship.[44]

A somewhat different case of local party initiative was the role of the Leningrad apparatus, in 1936, in inspiration of a top-level resolution. The target here was pedology, a branch of pedagogy. It opened with the local party bureau investigating the 'damaging research methods' of this science, as practised at the Leningrad Pedagogical Institute, on 8 April 1936. In May, a local resolution declared the findings to be of 'more than Leningrad importance', and called a plenary session of the party for June, at which the city's pedagogues and pedologues would have to explain themselves. By this time, Zhdanov had become involved in the affair, and explained to the June session that the matter was of 'all-Union importance'.[45] This was the signal for a Central Committee

Resolution of 4 July 1936, which condemned the 'pedological distortions' of the Commissariat of Education (Narkompros).

A press campaign began to 'unmask' and 'probe' the researchers and popularisers of this subject, and the writings of Blonsky, Zalkind, M. Sokolov and Vygotsky were worked over in the newspapers. As usual in such a campaign, the size of the problem and alleged mistakes were exaggerated out of all proportion. According to unpublished files, the numbers of pedologues employed by the Ministry were tiny: 320 in Moscow, 204 in Leningrad and none in the countryside. This is confirmed by reports from local *Obkom* Secretaries, who stated that they could not take the 'necessary measures' since, in their schools, the problem of pedology had never arisen.[46] But this did not halt the campaign, and in 1937 the Ministry itself was extensively purged, following the discovery of a 'counter-revolutionary centre'[47] and the arrest of its Commissar in strange circumstances.[48]

A second point is that policy was also made by communist intellectuals themselves. In another text, it is suggested that the end of NEP was hastened by the quasi-independent activity of communists in the various institutes of higher education (the Institute of Red Professors, the Communist Academy, the RANION institutes), who took over academic life during the five-year plan.[49] The case of linguistics may be instructive here.

Even before receiving any top-level recognition for his theories, Marr had won political ascendancy. His 'Japhetic theory' of languages, according to which all stemmed allegedly from a single root, was discussed in the linguistics section of RANION in February 1928. His main opponent at this session, E. D. Polivanov, demonstrated the shaky empirical foundation of this thesis, even on its chosen basis, the South Caucasian languages, and that the more theoretical elements had been formulated 'long before Marr'. But the head of the Institute, Friche, cut short his exposition with an authoritative declaration that 'the Japhetic theory, in the form it has now, is the only basis for Marxist linguistics'.[50] After this, as Polivanov's Soviet rehabilitators point out, it is obvious that there was nothing to discuss.[51]

The attitude of Friche was characteristic of the new type of party ideologists. No longer deriving arguments from scholarly analysis or logical deduction from stated premises, their methodology was one of dogmatic orthodoxy, culled from superficial reading of the 'classics': Marx, Engels, Lenin and Stalin. Even these texts were used as material for ending argument, rather than for initiation of fruitful discussion. As for the works of others, these were shamelessly pillaged for citations that, torn from context, would serve to 'demonstrate' the wickedness of an opponent's position. Argument itself was reduced to the elementary juxtaposition of opposite extremes, with the abolition of distinctions or intermediate positions.[52] Such characteristics made them at once the originators and the bearers of the Stalinist intellectual order.

The career of Pavel Yudin is a typical example. After his interventions on the philosophical front, which resulted in his becoming head of the Institute of Philosophy of the Communist Academy from which he had graduated eighteen months earlier, Yudin broadened his interests to the cultural field. This led him to literature, where he played a key part in the transition to Stalinism.

The position of writers during the five-year plan was overshadowed by the effort of a proletarian association (RAPP) to gain 'hegemony'.[53] In practical terms this had been achieved by 1931, and its leaders then intended to proceed to a theoretical ascendancy. They put forward, first for theatre, then for literature and the arts, a programme based on dialectical materialism.[54] Before this had been introduced, however, the group was suddenly dissolved by the Central Committee. An accompanying editorial, full of what RAPP responded to as 'false citations'[55] and designed to demonstrate the anti-Leninist content of their teachings, was signed by Yudin.[56] Moreover, it was Yudin who supplied the official alternative to *dia-mat*: socialist realism.

Tradition has it that Stalin formulated this new method, at his meeting with writers in October 1932, but the archival record shows this not to be so. On that occasion, recorded in the Gorky papers, Stalin confined himself to some brief remarks about *dia-mat*: 'I want only to say that if a writer or artist studies dialectical materialism that is well and good, but then he will not have time to be a writer. . . . Seriously, you must not stuff an artist's head with abstract theses.'[57] But he did not go on, as followers have afterwards insisted, to present a defined alternative: his comments were restricted to routine remarks on the need for writers to give a 'truthful presentation of reality'.[58] The task of formulation was delegated to a committee.

To list the membership of this body, which sat for eight months, from the autumn of 1933, is to call the roll of the new communist establishment. Besides Yudin as chairman there were: Mitin and

Usievich (also of the Communist Academy); Lifshits and Shiller (of the Marx-Engels Institute); Rozental of *Pravda*; three literary critics; and three leaders of the former RAPP.[59] No writers were included, nor any other organisers of the Writers' Union. Thus the most decisive aspect of the reorganisation of literature in this period was delegated to a group of intellectuals around Yudin.

A third aspect of policy formation, recently examined by a Western historian, is the role of non-party 'authorities' in the cultural and scientific fields.[60] Not antagonistic to the party, but, nevertheless not of it, these figures were delegated a limited responsibility in their particular spheres. There were two main reasons for this delegation. One arose from the activity of the most militant of communist institutions in the proletarian era. Groups such as RAPP, intransigent in politics and iconoclastic in artistic vision, ill accorded with the more orderly system that had begun to emerge out of the first chaotic stage of collectivisation and the planned economy. This may well have led the party leadership to a more moderate line and to propose a tacit division of function between communist administrators and non-party 'authorities' in the cultural field. A second was simply recognition of the circumstance that, throughout the thirties, a great majority of artists and intellectuals were not communists.[61] The forwarding of 'non-party' figures may thus, at first, have reassured them of the moderate intentions of the party's line.

We must be careful, though, to distinguish between 'dignified' and 'efficient' parts of Stalinist institutions. To co-opt a Gorky, and grant him great glory, is not the same as letting him lay down the party line, and was accompanied by the usual policy of placing party watchdogs alongside 'non-party' authorities. At first Yudin was introduced, perhaps partly to reduce Gorky's power, and 'did great damage' in the latter's view. He accused him, by letter, of fragmenting the groups of party writers, and 'driving non-party writers away' from the incipient Union.[62] Later, after the First Writers' Congress, a different watchdog was appointed, Shcherbakov, who treated Gorky – and all writers – more tactfully. A contemporary saw him as an official of a 'new type': diplomatic and inscrutable, giving nothing away.[63] Such qualities served him well, and from literature, he rose rapidly through the party's upper ranks, to join the Politburo in 1939.

Though not, therefore, exercising administrative control, Gorky nevertheless enjoyed great authority – and privileges – as first

President of the Writers' Union. He was able, where he chose, to dispense patronage, in editorial matters, over obtaining passports, and other favours.[64] Although not managing to deliver, as he had intended, a definitive account of socialist realism, he did see that the doctrine contained the main tendencies found in his own work, arising from the 'critical realism' of the nineteenth century.[65] His international standing was enhanced, particularly through stage-management of the Writers' Congress.

In the last years, in the silence of his dacha, he did ruminate on the political complexion of the country, and from remarks addressed to his secretary, seems to have concluded that he had had the worst of his pact with Stalin. A sense of powerlessness invaded him, as he meditated on despotism in historical perspective.[66] But it would be rash to imagine that – had he lived – any statements would, or even could, have emanated from him in opposition to the show trials.

Similar to that of Gorky, and promoted by him, was the role of Makarenko in pedagogy, our next example of non-party authority. His 'Pedagogical Poem' (1935), and subsequent 'Book for Parents', described work with delinquent children in labour communes of the GPU. With the success of these works, and prominence within the Writers' Union, Makarenko was given wide scope to impose his ideas upon the educational establishment.[67] Being idiosyncratic and anti-intellectual, a man of experience who loved to disdain the theories of 'academics', Makarenko took on what remained of educational orthodoxy after 1937, and reshaped it into his own practical and disciplinarian mould.[68] But it is far from clear that educational practice was much altered by his writings.

Turning to the natural sciences, we see a more effective case of 'non-party' authority, in Lysenko, whom Stalin had helped to recognition. Originating in biology, the repercussions of his outlook were soon felt throughout the 'scientific front'. Moreover, purely magical elements entered in, suggesting, as Joravsky argues, that his broad appeal was not only to the Bolshevik belief in science as such, but also to the wider regard for canny peasant wisdom, which his pithy formulae appeared to present.[69]

We may see this in his special method of 'Yarovisation', for treating wheat germs, which began as an assault on scientific rivals. Not content to denounce those who queried his evidence as 'class enemies', he also proposed his scheme to the party leaders as a rapid panacea for agricultural problems, thus dispensing with intellectual hesitations. This may explain Stalin's reaction, the interpellated comment 'Bravo, comrade Lysenko, bravo',[70] as well as the licence given to him later. Following this high-level sanction, he went on to reduce all discussion of genetics to a matter of 'wrecking', and the whole discipline to a tool of Goebbels.[71] The outcome was a ban on genetics for a generation, and repressive measures in such fields as biology, medicine and agro-chemistry.[72]

This general pattern of the penetration of science by self-made men, fanatics, charlatans and 'double-dealers' may seem, *ab initio*, to rule out discussion of our fourth and final category of policy formation: specialist and professional opinion. Were, indeed, the spread of Lysenkos and Marrs a universal one, such would be the conclusion. Yet this, too, may merit consideration.

So little is known about the professions in the Stalin era that we must approach the subject with extreme caution. Any attempt to aggregate 'specialist' and technical advice and to present it as a major influence on policy formation would be premature. Indeed, a recent investigation of penal legislation found no influence at all exerted by criminologists or criminal law specialists during the pre-war period.[73] This puts in its proper context the pomp and public circumstance that surrounded promulgation of the 'Stalin Constitution' in 1936. From some selected specialists of the technical intelligentsia, however, there may have been a greater contribution.

Here, town planners are an illustration. Obviously well suited to 'socialist construction', these soon found their niche within the colossal urban development of the thirties.[74] The Moscow plan of 1935, with its broad boulevards and vast housing complexes, provided priority employment to such specialists and practical scope for initiation and design by architects who worked with them.[75] The fruits of their cooperation are still much in evidence today.

A more general account of the technical intelligentsia might well reveal their role as important exponents of professional opinion. The first phase (1928–31) had been 'proletarian', intended to recruit a 'new technical intelligentsia' at high speed, on the basis of 'specialist-baiting' and educational discrimination.[76] In 1931, such policies were reversed abruptly, and the old and new enjoined to collaborate on the patriotic work of industrial development.[77] In financial aspects, at least, they were accordingly rewarded.[78] How far they obeyed instructions rather than initiated is hard to judge –

certainly the spectre of repression always hung over them. Nevertheless, as Stalin well knew, this technical intelligentsia was an essential social stratum on which both economic progress and, eventually, political stability rested, and its formation shows Stalin's conscious social engineering.

At the apex of the scientific effort was a transformed Academy. Whereas the social scientific institutions were repeatedly purged, and the Communist Academy, following its initial growth of 1928–31[79] was rapidly reduced in size and status, the Academy of Sciences rose from strength to strength. Prudently admitting political nominations, on threat of dissolution, in 1929,[80] it survived to take over the research sections of the Communist Academy.[81] Scientific work was more fully integrated into the requirements of the national economy, and the Academy gained recognition as the 'supreme scientific institution of the USSR'.[82]

An inner logic operates throughout the thirties, whose sudden shifts and intermittent madness represent the alternation of order and disorder. At the first stage (roughly 1928–31), the social structure was unhinged, and every area of intellectual life was thrown into disorder by subterranean forces 'unleashed', but far from fully regulated, 'from above'. Then, in the neglected era, 1932–6, order returns: social and intellectual life settle down; ideas are established; institutions are consolidated and become regular in their activities. Finally, disorder, signalled by the death of Kirov in December 1934, returned with a vengeance in the period of terror (1936–9).

Stalin's interventions conform to this alternating pattern. Stalin's rule was not that of a dilettante who indulged his vanity in one field or another, though this was prominent in later years. At earlier stages he consciously manipulated the 'social forces', astutely harnessing each new one to himself – first 'proletarians', then former specialists, and ultimately the security apparatus – to secure his rule. It is quite possible that this pattern was continued in the forties, with the broadening of the bases of his power through concessions to society in the 'great patriotic war', and the formation and consecration of the technically trained and financially privileged middle-class intelligentsia in the post-war period. While far from directing everything, Stalin alone had the authority – and skill – to swing the entire Soviet system in a new direction.

This, though, should not disguise the role of other actors. Our account of the neglected phase, roughly 1932–6, discloses the institution of an 'order'. This should not be surprising: Stalinism was not simply terror, but became a huge, elaborated system, whose main pillars – those most visible in the thirties – were the ideas, institutions and individuals who constituted it. We identified: the party organisers in various fields (such as Cult-prop and the Leningrad apparatus); ideologists and troubleshooters (for instance Friche, Yudin and Shcherbakov); non-party authorities in many spheres (notably Gorky, Markarenko and Lysenko); and specialists with professional opinions. There is plenty of evidence that actors in all four of these categories had wills of their own, and they would be miscast if simply seen as puppets manipulated by Stalin behind the scenes.

NOTES

1. L. B. Schapiro, *The Communist Party of the Soviet Union* (London, 1960) p. 343.
2. In English: E. Preobrazhensky, *The New Economics* (Oxford, 1965); *A. V. Chayanov on the Theory of the Peasant Economy* (Homewood, Ill., 1966); E. B. Pashukanis, *Law and Marxism: A General Theory* (London, 1978); and L. G. Vygotsky, *Mind in Society* (Cambridge, Mass., 1978).
3. An intellectual history of this era remains to be written.
4. I am indebted to Neil Harding for assistance with this section.
5. This seems to be the central thesis in Baruch Knei-Paz, *The Social and Political Thought of Leon Trotsky* (Oxford, 1978).
6. This passage summarises ideas to be documented later on.
7. The *locus classicus* is J. V. Stalin, *Sochineniya*, vol. XIII, pp. 141–72.
8. His masterful manipulation of a 'Right danger' is described by R. V. Daniels, *The Conscience of the Revolution* (Cambridge, Mass., 1960).
9. Stephen F. Cohen, *Bukharin and the Bolshevik Revolution* (London, 1974) p. 285.
10. An eye-witness was A. Avtorkhanov, *Stalin and the Soviet Communist Party* (London, 1959).
11. Stalin, *Sochineniya*, vol. XI, pp. 179–80.
12. *Pravda*, 30 July 1956.
13. A partial stenogram is in the Trotsky Archive T1901 (Bukharin's speech).
14. *Shestnadtsataya konferentsiya VKP (b) Stenograficheskii otchyot* (Moscow, 1962) pp. 744, 807.
15. T1897 (Bukharin–Kamenev memorandum).
16. Ibid. The same point was made by Trotsky.
17. Only Stetsky, of some twenty major *shkol'niki*, was retained. He defected to Stalin (Cohen, *Bukharin*, p. 308) and became cult-prop secretary in 1930.
18. Some 50,000 were dispatched to the countryside from 1930 to 1934 (Schapiro, *The CPSU*, p. 455).
19. Bukharinists were dismissed from *Pravda*, *Leningradskaya Pravda*, *Bol'shevik*, *Revolyutsiya i kul'tura*, and other journals. The party schools and higher institutes were similarly purged.

20. Stalin, *Sochineniya*, vol. XIII, pp. 84–102.
21. John Barber, 'Stalin's Letter to the Editors of *Proletarskaya Revolyutsiya*', *Soviet Studies*, XXVIII, no. 1 (1976) 22–5.
22. The lapse may indicate Stalin's political weakness in face of a 'Kirov tendency', but the existence of this has never been proved.
23. It unleashed an army of 'cultural revolutionaries' and militants.
24. The number rose from 160,000 to 511,000 over this period, largely through the expansion of workers' faculties. See M. P. Kim (ed.), *Kul'turnaya revolyutsiya v SSSR, 1917–65 gg*. (Moscow, 1967) pp. 134, 164, 187.
25. From 1.3 million (1928) to 3.5 million (1933). See Schapiro, *The CPSU*, p. 435.
26. Stalin, *Sochineniya*, vol. XIII, pp. 141–72.
27. Ibid., pp. 184–96.
28. *Bol'shevik*, 1930, no. 5, pp. 16–17.
29. These trials are discussed by Roy Medvedev in *Let History Judge* (London, 1972) pp. 110–37, where he rejects their legality.
30. *Pravda*, 7 June 1930.
31. B. T. Ermakov, 'Bor'ba K.P. za perestroiku raboty nauchnykh uchrezhdenii v gody pervoi pyatiletki' (candidate's thesis, Moscow, 1955).
32. The victors published their account, *Za povorot na filosofskom fronte* (Moscow, 1931), under the imprint of the Communist Academy.
33. Deborin recanted last. See *Pod Znamenem Marksisma*, May–June 1933.
34. *Vestnik kommunisticheskoi akademii*, 1931, no. 12, p. 9.
35. *Pravda*, 9 Apr 1937.
36. A. I. Vyshinsky, *K polozheniyu na fronte pravovoi teorii* (Moscow, 1937).
37. *Pravda*, 27 Jan 1936.
38. Discussions within historical institutes are documented from archives by L. M. Zak, 'Stroitel'stvo sotsialisticheskoi kul'tury v SSSR' (doctoral dissertation, Moscow, 1966).
39. *Pravda*, 28 Mar 1937.
40. Ia. V. Starosel'skii, *Problema yakobinskoi diktatury* (Moscow, 1930), for instance, quoted in Schapiro, *The CPSU*, p. 470.
41. In 1934 Yudin dismissed these as 'food shortages'.
42. Vyshinsky, *K polozheniyu . . .*, p. 54.
43. Avtorkhanov, *Stalin and the Soviet Communist Party*, p. 186.
44. *Vsya Moskva*, 1933.
45. Zak, 'Stroitel'stvo sotsialisticheskoi kul'tury . . .'.
46. Ibid.
47. A. Binevich and Z. Serebryansky, *Andrei Bubnov* (Moscow, 1964) pp. 78–9.
48. Ibid.
49. For these and other party actors (writers organised by RAPP and militants of agit-prop), see my article 'NEP in Culture', *Journal of Contemporary History*, 1978, no. 3.
50. E. D. Polivanov, *Stat'i po obshchemu yazykoznaniyu*, comp. A. A. Leont'ev, (Moscow, 1968) pp. 23–4.
51. Ibid.
52. See L. Kolakowski, *Main Currents of Marxism* (Oxford, 1978) vol. III.
53. On RAPP see S. Sheshukov, *Neistovye revniteli: Iz istorii literaturnoi bor'by 20-kh. godov* (Moscow, 1970); and Edward J. Brown, *The Proletarian Episode in Russian Literature, 1928–32* (New York, 1953).

54. A. N. Afinogenov, *Tvorcheskii metod teatra. Dialektika tvorcheskogo protsessa* (Moscow–Leningrad, 1931).
55. *Na literaturnom postu*, 1932, no. 12, p. 8 (15 May 1932).
56. *Pravda*, 23 Apr 1932.
57. 'Vstrecha pisatelei s I. V. Stalinym u A. M. Gor'kogo' (26 Oct 1932), unpublished manuscript in the Gorky Archive, Institute of World Literature (IMLI) Moscow.
58. Ibid.
59. IMLI f. 41, opis 1, ed. khran. 445, Manuscript Division, Institute of World Literature (IMLI) Moscow.
60. Sheila Fitzpatrick, 'Culture and Politics Under Stalin: A Reappraisal', *Slavic Review*, xxxv, no. 2 (1976) 224–30.
61. T. H. Rigby, *Communist Party Membership in the USSR, 1917–1967* (Princeton, NJ, 1968) pp. 441–4.
62. Correspondence with Yudin from the Gorky Archives (14 Apr 1934).
63. N. Mandelstam, *Hope Against Hope* (London, 1971) pp. 140–1.
64. See N. Babel (ed.), *Isaac Babel: The Lonely Years, 1925–1939* (New York, 1964).
65. Trotsky noted this.
66. I. Shkapa, *Sem' let s Gor'kim* (Moscow, 1964) pp. 249–50.
67. See Fitzpatrick, *Slavic Review*, xxxv, 226.
68. Idem.
69. David Joravsky, *The Lysenko Affair* (Cambridge, Mass., 1970) pp. 94–5.
70. Ibid., p. 83.
71. *Pravda*, 12 Apr 1937.
72. Zak, 'Stroitel'stvo sotsialisticheskoi kul'tury . . .', pp. 719–20.
73. P. H. Solomon, *Soviet Criminologists and Criminal Policy Specialists in Policy-Making* (London, 1978) pp. 19–20.
74. Contrast S. Frederick Starr, 'Visionary Town Planning during the Cultural Revolution', in Sheila Fitzpatrick (ed.), *Cultural Revolution in Russia, 1928–1931* (Bloomington, Ind., and London, 1978) pp. 207–40.
75. Anatole Kopp, *Town and Revolution: Soviet Architecture and City Planning, 1917–1935* (New York, 1970).
76. Kendall E. Bailes, *Technology and Society under Lenin and Stalin* (Princeton, NJ, 1978).
77. Stalin, *Sochineniya*, vol. xiii, pp. 69–73.
78, On their privileges, M. Lewin, 'Society and the Stalinist State', *Social History*, ii (1976) 172.
79. *Vestnik kommunisticheskoi akademii*, 1932, no. 1–2, p. 13.
80. Loren R. Graham, *The Soviet Academy of Sciences and the Communist Party, 1927–1932* (Princeton, NJ, 1967) pp. 110–14.
81. *Izvestiya*, 8 Feb 1936. The teaching functions were transferred to the inner party apparatus: *Partiinoye stroitel'stvo*, 1935, no. 21, p. 56; ibid., 1936, no. 14, p. 40.
82. *Ustav Akademii nauk SSR* (Moscow, 1936) pp. 3–4.

8 The Power of the General Secretary of the CPSU

Archie Brown

During the sixty-two years of its existence, the Soviet Union has had only four undisputed leaders. We may reasonably leave out of account Georgiy Malenkov who was senior secretary within the Communist Party of the Soviet Union (CPSU) for little more than a week and Chairman of the Council of Ministers of the USSR for less than two years.[1] Iosif Stalin died on 5 March 1953 and by 14 March Malenkov's supreme power was over. In the two years which followed, there was some ambiguity as to who was the top man in the Soviet Union, but gradually it emerged that the senior party secretary (known for most of Soviet history as the General Secretary, but from September 1953 until April 1966 as the First Secretary) commanded greater political resources than anyone else in the land.

This was not always so, for if the Soviet Union has had four confirmed leaders, the first and greatest of these, Vladimir Il'ich Lenin, was not General Secretary (or even a secretary) of the party. Lenin's dominance of the original five-man Politburo was not by virtue of any party office held but on the basis of his colleagues' recognition of him as their *de facto* leader. The office he chose for himself after the October Revolution was that of Chairman of the Council of People's Commissars (the ancestor of the present Council of Ministers). 'Lenin's "Cabinet"', as T. H. Rigby has observed, 'was not the Politburo, but Sovnarkom – the Council of People's Commissars'.[2] So long as Lenin was alive, there could be no mistaking the successive party secretaries, Sverdlov, Krestinsky and Stalin, for the supreme leader in the country.

The General Secretaries who have also been *de facto* heads of executive within the Soviet Union are reduced to three: Stalin, Nikita Khrushchev and Leonid Brezhnev. This immediately brings to mind the difficulty evoked in Hume's rule: 'What depends upon a few persons is, in a great measure, to be ascribed to chance, or secret and unknown causes: what arises from a great number, may often be accounted for by determinate and known causes.'[3] If, however, the base for generalisation about the powers of the General Secretary of the CPSU is rendered uncomfortably narrow by the number of holders of the office, that does not render useless comparison over time or exclude the emergence of certain tendencies and patterns. (Indeed, their political longevity is itself a pointer to the political resources at the disposal of these office-holders.) We are, after all, dealing not only with three men but with their interaction with a great many people and with the interplay of various institutions. It is important to consider the great differences between one General Secretary and another, while not ruling out all generalisation – especially since some of the powers, and constraints upon the powers, of the General Secretary bear comparison with those of heads of executive elsewhere.

At the risk of a little over-simplification, the following pattern may be noted: each General Secretary has wielded less individual power over policy than his predecessor, but *within* his period of office his power *vis-à-vis* his colleagues has grown. (That general trend does not, of course, mean there have been no ups and downs within each incumbency, nor should it be taken to exclude some slight tailing off in the exercise of power as each leader reached the final stage of his political career.[4]) The mid-twenties, the mid-fifties and the mid-sixties may be characterised as periods of oligarchy; the last twenty years of Stalin's life (with the partial exception of wartime) as an era of tyrannical rule; and the late fifties and early sixties, together with the seventies, as years in which the General Secretary became more than a first among equals, widening the gulf between himself and his colleagues, though retaining – in Brezhnev's case at least – the essentials of collective leadership.

The emergence of this pattern raises questions about continuity and change in the sources of the General Secretary's power and in the constraints placed upon him. Though it will be necessary later to make distinctions between different areas of policy and to consider the relationship between style of government, on the one hand, and power and authority, on the other, the changing relationship between the General Secretaryship and other political institutions is a natural starting-point for our enquiry. A good general guide to the degree to which the General Secretary's rule is a personal one is the frequency or infrequency of meetings of the collective bodies charged with policy-making responsibility. Khrushchev, in his 1956 'secret speech' and in his later memoirs, has provided ample confirmation of the drift into moribundity of party institutions in Stalin's time. As he put it in his speech to the Twentieth Party Congress:

> Whereas, during the first few years after Lenin's death, party congresses and Central Committee plenums took place more or less regularly, later, when Stalin began increasingly to abuse his power, these principles were brutally violated. This was especially evident during the last 15 years of his life. Was it a normal situation when over 13 years elapsed between the 18th and 19th Party Congresses, years during which our party and our country had experienced so many important events?[5] . . . It is true that there was an attempt to call a Central Committee plenum in October 1941, when Central Committee members from the whole country were called to Moscow. They waited two days for the opening of the plenum, but in vain. Stalin did not even want to meet and talk to the Central Committee members.[6]

In his later years, Stalin's meetings even with the Politburo were rarely formal ones. Attendance at meetings depended on being in Stalin's favour. On occasion Voroshilov, Kaganovich, Molotov and Mikoyan were excluded.[7] The times and places of political discussion were often between reels of films in the Kremlin theatre and, more extensively, at what Khrushchev called those 'interminable, agonizing dinners' at Stalin's dacha.[8] According to Khrushchev, 'Neither the Central Committee, nor the Politbureau, nor the Presidium Bureau[9] worked regularly. But Stalin's regular sessions with his inner circle went along like clockwork.'[10]

The story of how Stalin built up his position within the party apparatus, used the power of appointment of personnel and control of execution of policy vested in the secretariat against all other organs of government, and finally subordinated the party apparatus to his personal secretariat and to the security forces has been told on numerous occasions.[11] By the time Khrushchev entered Stalin's inner circle, the latter had long since ceased to rely on his formal position of party leadership. This applies also to the titles he accumulated from 1940.

In that year he assumed the office of Chairman of the Council of People's Commissars (from 1946 Council of Ministers). During the war he became Commissar (later Minister) of Defence, Marshal of the Soviet Union and Generalissimo. This concentration of state, as distinct from party, offices in Stalin's person suggests that his power had come, increasingly, to depend upon the state apparatus rather than the party apparatus. In fact, however, these titles probably had more to do with the further build-up of Stalin's prestige and authority (partly with an eye on the outside world) than with the real basis of his power. Certainly, it was not through the ministerial network that Stalin had built up his position of supreme power, though in his later years he appeared to work through the ministerial machinery to a greater extent than through the party apparatus. In that connection it is worthy of note that in the late forties, in contrast with the late fifties or late seventies, more Politburo members presided over parts of the state political machine than over the party apparatus.

It is still important, however, to go one step back and ask how Stalin came to wield so much power as he had attained by the late 1930s. Initially (from 1917 to 1923) Stalin had a position in *Sovnarkom* as Commissar for Nationalities, but more important was his institutional foothold, after he had joined the secretariat of the Central Committee as General Secretary in April 1922, in the three key party institutions at the time of Lenin's death: the Politburo, the Orgburo and the Secretariat.[12] In one of the latest attempts to explain how Stalin came to possess the power he had within his grasp by the period of 'high Stalinism', Niels Erik Rosenfeldt has, however, put still greater emphasis on the role of Stalin's personal secretariat and the 'special sector' of the Central Committee apparatus.[13] He does not dispute the widely-accepted interpretation of Stalin's rise to power in terms of his control over cadres, his tactical skill, his talent for 'finding political formulae which appealed to wide circles within the Party', his mastery of the party apparatus and control of the state security forces, but notes that the account leaves questions unanswered. In particular, 'the inner logic of the traditional interpretation seems to place an inhuman work-load on *Stalin himself*'.[14]

It is the power of the 'special sector' and of Stalin's personal assistants (*pomoshchniki*), of whom the most prominent was

Poskrebyshev, which is one of the features of Stalin's rule that marks it off from the Khrushchev and Brezhnev periods. The successor organ to the 'special sector' of the Central Committee is, as Leonard Schapiro has shown,[15] the General Department, but though its head has an especially close relationship with the General Secretary, this Central Committee department (in a decisive break with the practice of its predecessor) evidently serves as a secretariat for the Politburo as a whole. The head of the General Department, in terms of the functions he performs and his responsibilities to the Politburo, and also in terms of his daily contacts with the General Secretary, appears to be the functional equivalent of the Secretary of the Cabinet in the British system. In the late 1970s, however, the General Department head since 1965, Konstantin Chernenko – a Brezhnev protégé – has greatly increased his political standing by becoming a Secretary of the Central Committee in October 1977 and a full member of the Politburo in November 1978. Chernenko has thereby come to share in collective responsibility for high policy – which is very different from enjoying the irresponsible power of a Poskrebyshev. Stalin's successors, as Schapiro has noted, dismantled the special department precisely 'in order to limit the power of the Party First Secretary and to facilitate the establishment of collective leadership'.[16]

Though in the later stages of Khrushchev's First Secretaryship there was resentment within the Central Committee and among ministers over the influence wielded by *his* personal advisers (notably, Adzhubei, Shevchenko and Lebedev),[17] there was no question of the establishment of a link between his personal secretariat and the security forces to the danger of other leaders. One aspect of Khrushchev's revitalisation of the party was the subordination of security to party organs and of the KGB leadership to the Politburo collectively. Another was the revival, including a return to regular meetings, of party committees at all levels. The Central Committee has met at least twice a year (as it is supposed to do, according to the party statutes) every year since Stalin's death. More important from the standpoint of collective leadership, the Politburo under Khrushchev became a regular forum for discussion and debate, meeting weekly.[18]

The great power wielded by Khrushchev within the Politburo and Secretariat is not, of course, in question, but it is equally clear that Khrushchev often had reason to feel that his policies were not being fully implemented and that one impediment to them was the bureaucratic inertia represented by the ministerial network. There seems no reason to doubt that Khrushchev felt that adding the Chairmanship of the Council of Ministers to his party First Secretaryship in 1958 would also add measurably to his power. A year earlier his attitude to the ministries had been in effect: if you can't beat them, abolish them![19] Now, it was: if you can't beat them, join them and knock their heads together! (If these actions may be regarded as rounds one and two to Khrushchev, it may be noted that round three went to the disgruntled state bureaucrats, for they were undoubtedly part of the coalition which strove for, and welcomed, the removal of Khrushchev in 1964.[20]) The dominance of party organs over ministries is not in question, but a party *leader's* control over policy is likely to be less comprehensive if he is *not* Chairman of the Council of Ministers as well as General Secretary. It was because other leading politicians in the Soviet Union recognised that the linking of these two offices concentrated a greater power in the General Secretary's possession that the October plenum of the Central Committee in 1964 resolved that they should henceforth be in separate hands.[21]

Brezhnev's style of leadership has been very different from Khrushchev's, but in terms of frequency of meetings of collective policy-making bodies there has been a considerable measure of continuity with the Khrushchev period. The Central Committee has spent on average fewer days per year in plenary session in the Brezhnev era than in Khrushchev's time, but the Politburo has met at least as frequently. Figures given by Brezhnev at the 25th Party Congress on the number of meetings held by the Politburo and the Secretariat of the Central Committee since the 24th Congress indicated that – apart from longish gaps during holiday periods – both bodies had been meeting weekly, the Politburo having had ten more meetings during those five years than the Secretariat.[22] Interestingly, it seems as if in the period since the 25th Party Congress the number of twice-weekly Politburo meetings may have increased. In an interview in August 1979 the Chairman of the Council of Nationalities of the Supreme Soviet of the USSR and member of the Central Committee of the CPSU, V. P. Ruben, stated that the Politburo met on Tuesdays and Thursdays and the Secretariat on Wednesdays.[23] The information that Wednesday is the normal meeting day of the Secretariat is new, but in an interview in 1973 Brezhnev stated that Thursday was the usual day for Politburo meetings and that the sessions lasted from three to six hours.[24] Possibly because the volume of business coming to the Politburo has become greater since then, or perhaps because the rise in the average age of the Politburo membership in the meantime has reduced the stamina of members for marathon meetings, the number of twice-weekly meetings has apparently grown. It would seem that Politburo practice is remarkably similar to that of the British Cabinet. That body, too, normally meets on Thursdays (three hours being a fairly typical length for the meeting), but in weeks in which there is a lot of business, an additional meeting is held on Tuesdays.[25]

Notwithstanding the key role still played by the party's highest collective bodies, Brezhnev's power and influence within the Soviet leadership have grown during his lengthy incumbency of the General Secretaryship. Some of the honours and titles he has accumulated are more relevant to his status and prestige than to his policy-making power. This is surely true, *inter alia*, of his various Hero of the Soviet Union and Order of Lenin awards; of his Lenin Peace Prize of 1973; as well as of his acquisition of the rank of Marshal of the Soviet Union in 1976, and of the award of the highest military honour, the Order of Victory, in 1978. Even the remarkable choice of Brezhnev in 1979 to be the recipient of the Lenin Prize for Literature (by way of acknowledgement of the merits of his memoirs) is not likely to lead to his emergence as an adjudicator on issues of literary policy or matters of artistic taste.[26]

The most important accretion to Brezhnev's party leadership has, of course, been the Chairmanship of the Presidium of the Supreme Soviet which he assumed in June 1977. Two reasons were advanced by the General Secretary in explanation of this move in a speech to the Presidium of the Supreme Soviet on 17 June 1977,[27] and they were echoed in a *Pravda* editorial two days later.[28] First, making the party leader formal head of state was interpreted as a reflection of the development of the party's 'leading and guiding role', emphasising its determination of the political line 'in the solution of all the major problems of state life'.[29] Secondly, the General Secretary, as Brezhnev himself pointed out, had on a number of occasions to represent the Soviet Union 'in international relations, in talks on the cardinal questions of the strengthening of peace and guaranteeing the security of peoples'.[30] That practice (whereby he represented the country), added Brezhnev, was now being given its 'logical legalization'.[31]

While the second of the reasons carries the greater weight, the first should not be completely discounted. In a sense, making the party leader Chairman of the Presidium of the Supreme Soviet merely continued a process whereby prominent party officials have been playing a greater part in the life of the Supreme Soviet in a period in which the role of that body, and especially of its Presidium and permanent commissions, has been given greater emphasis.[32] The raising of the status of the Supreme Soviet has apparently been connected with the party's drive to enhance its control over the ministerial system and Brezhnev's accession to the Chairmanship of the Presidium fits very well into that framework. It adds a constitutional power to that which the party's 'leading and guiding role' (now enshrined in Article 6 of the 1977 Constitution) already gives him *vis-à-vis* the Council of Ministers and its Chairman. For constitutionally (Article 130) the Council of Ministers is responsible to the Supreme Soviet and in between sessions of the latter to the Presidium of the Supreme Soviet.

More generally, Brezhnev's accession to the headship of state set him further apart from his colleagues in the Politburo, but the main reason for the move was almost certainly that strongly hinted at in Brezhnev's own account and in *Pravda*'s – namely, to enhance the General Secretary's status internationally. Its purpose was to put him on the same footing as those heads of executive elsewhere (and, above all, the American President) who are also heads of state. The fact that Brezhnev was signing treaties before he became President had attracted some adverse foreign press comment, and precise application of protocol had sometimes meant that Brezhnev's official reception abroad was deliberately kept on a lower key than would be accorded a head of state.

Willy Brandt has recalled that when, as Chancellor of the Federal Republic of Germany, he first had talks with Brezhnev, many Germans 'could not grasp that, as General Secretary, Brezhnev was senior to the Chairman of the Council of Ministers'. Brandt was asked 'in what capacity we had conferred – for instance, as Chairman of the SPD and leader of the Soviet Communist Party?' Similarly, when Brezhnev visited Bonn in 1973, 'the gentlemen in charge of protocol found the set-up too mystifying to unravel. The General Secretary was obliged to forgo a gun-salute on arrival although he had long ago been greeted in Paris with all the honours befitting a head of state . . . .'[33]

For General Secretaries concerned with their dignity (and there is ample evidence that they have been) the combination of General Secretaryship and Chairmanship of the Presidium of the Supreme Soviet has an advantage over combining the party leadership with the Chairmanship of the Council of Ministers. Even after Khrushchev had taken over the latter post, he could not be sure of receiving the highest category of official receptions on his travels abroad. Mohamed Heikal, who had numerous meetings with Khrushchev and in 1964 accompanied him by boat from Odessa to Alexandria, noted Khrushchev's worries on this score. 'They are applying protocol to me', Khrushchev complained on arrival in Alexandria. 'Nasser is in Cairo and only Marshal Amer will meet me because I am not a Head of State.' When Heikal was able to confirm that President Nasser would be meeting him, 'Khrushchev was delighted. . . . He was always very concerned about these details.'[34]

The combination of General Secretaryship with the headship of state rather than with the headship of government has two other advantages – one for the General Secretary personally, the other for the political system as a whole. Party organs at the All-Union level cannot be criticised in the Soviet Union, but ministries can be and frequently are. A General Secretary who is not also Chairman of the Council of Ministers can more easily stand aloof from this criticism, avoid being tainted by it, and indeed, join in the criticism himself. If he is head of the government as well as party leader, this has the double disadvantage of inhibiting some deserved criticism of the ministries and of implicating him more directly than he is at present with responsibility for things that go wrong. The very fact that Kosygin is still Chairman of the Council of Ministers diminishes Brezhnev's ability to determine policy in certain areas, as compared with Khrushchev, but this sacrifice of some policy-making power – especially in the sphere of economic policy and planning – may well have contributed to Brezhnev's security of tenure.[35]

This leads into the question of the style of rule of successive General Secretaries and of their role in policy-making. Even Stalin, needless to say, did not determine *all* major policy. As Joseph LaPalombara has put it (colourfully, but with only a little exaggeration):

. . . never in history – not even in the heyday of absolute monarchies or the so-called totalitarianisms of Hitler or Stalin –

were public policies made except on the basis of complicated, often Byzantine conflicts among administrative and bureaucratic elites.[36]

We must be careful not to attribute to Stalin superhuman powers. There were only twenty-four hours in the day even of the great *vozhd'* – and in his later years at least a large part of that time was taken up, as noted earlier, by those 'interminable, agonizing dinners'. T. H. Rigby has observed that what distinguished Stalin's dictatorial rule from the 1930s onwards from 'the oligarchical pattern of power before and afterwards' was not 'that Stalin personally decided everything, which would have been physically impossible, but that he personally decided anything he wanted to, unconstrained by the power of any individual, group, institution or law'.[37] While this describes clearly Stalin's position within the leadership, it perhaps unwittingly implies a greater independence from all social groups than even Stalin could possess. In general, however, if Stalin took a personal interest in a particular area of policy, there is no doubt that he had the power to impose a binding decision. In that sense, he was far more powerful than the rest of the Politburo put together. 'Stalin', said Khrushchev, 'did everything himself, bypassing the Central Committee and using the Politbureau as little more than a rubber stamp. Stalin rarely bothered to ask the opinion of Politbureau members about a given measure. He would just make a decision and issue a decree.'[38]

When Stalin spoke, he spoke *ex cathedra*, but he did not always speak. And in the breaks between his pronouncements, which became increasingly lengthy as he grew older, some semblance of real political life went on. Economic policy in the Soviet Union in the post-war part of the Stalin era was decided largely on the basis of argument between ministries, but with a certain amount of debate in which even academic economists were able to join.[39] In the 1930s, when Stalin's vigour was much greater, the fact that other individuals and groups did not succeed in constraining him does not mean that all policy options were open. Even a tyrant's power rests to some degree upon opinion as well as upon coercion[40] and Stalin could not pursue policies which alienated all social strata or which were rendered impossible by the pertaining level of cultural and economic development. It is also clear that in such an area as cultural policy, and in many spheres of intellectual life, the policy which ultimately received Stalin's stamp of approval in the 1930s had often come from middle-ranking functionaries, ambitious to take the place of their present overlords. Not all policy initiative came from above.[41]

From the Second World War onwards, General Secretaries of the CPSU have had to devote a disproportionate amount of their time to foreign policy. Relations with other Communist states have a high priority, but the General Secretary has also become increasingly involved in the conduct of diplomacy with the non-Communist powers. This is part of a secular trend connected with the greatly increased speed of communications whereby heads of executive generally have become key participants in the foreign policy-making process. It holds true of every American President from Franklin D. Roosevelt on, and of every British Prime Minister after Baldwin. That Stalin was no exception to this rule has been made clear by, among others, Djilas[42] and Khrushchev in their memoirs. In Khrushchev's words: '[Stalin] jealously guarded foreign policy in general and our policy toward other socialist countries in particular as his own special province. He had never gone out of his way to take other people's advice into account, and this was especially true after the war.'[43]

So far as Khrushchev's policy-making power as First Secretary is concerned, there is scarcely an area of policy in which he did not have an impact. He was able to do more once he had defeated the 'anti-party group' and had his own majority in the Presidium of the Central Committee, but even then policies he was able to force through (in the sense that they were formally approved by the Central Committee or Council of Ministers) were not always fully implemented. The point is sufficiently demonstrated in studies which have been made of Khrushchev's educational[44] and agricultural[45] reforms. In general, it is easier for a political leader to change a policy when it costs nothing to do so. Khrushchev – and Brezhnev after him – found it particularly difficult to effect a radical redistribution of resources. Apart from the necessity (already noted) for general secretaries to spend a great deal of time on foreign policy, both Khrushchev and Brezhnev (this time in contradistinction to Stalin) devoted much attention to agriculture. But both found it necessary to complain on more than one occasion that even after a specific share of resources had been allocated to agriculture, Gosplan – in alliance with the heavy industry sector – succeeded in diverting some of these resources away from agriculture.[46] The fact that two successive General Secretaries put their weight behind a policy of raising the status of agriculture, improving the working conditions of those employed in it, and increasing investment in agriculture (especially for the production of chemical fertilisers) has, of course, had a big impact. But both Khrushchev and Brezhnev had to struggle to get their higher targets for investment in agriculture adopted and, once adopted, to get them implemented.

In foreign policy, though Khrushchev was critical of Stalin's domination in this sphere, his own style of personal diplomacy left him open to the same charge. Two of the most important decisions of the Khrushchev era – the decision to wreck the Paris summit meeting with Eisenhower, Macmillan and de Gaulle in 1960 and the decision to put missiles in Cuba in 1962 – were, reading between the lines of Khrushchev's own testimony, taken on Khrushchev's personal initiative and without adequate consultation with his Politburo colleagues or expert opinion.[47]

Khrushchev's impulsiveness and his tendency to listen only to advice he wanted to hear has often been criticised in the Brezhnev period (though normally without explicit reference to Khrushchev's name). Brezhnev's close Politburo colleague Konstantin Chernenko has observed that 'the October [1964] plenum of the Central Committee of the CPSU played an outstanding role in the process of restoration and development of Leninist norms of party and state life' and that the enormous service performed by the 23rd and 24th Party Congresses consisted in the creation of the kind of 'moral and political atmosphere in the party and Soviet society in which, as Comrade L. I. Brezhnev says, "people breathe easily, work well and live tranquilly"'.[48]

'Tranquilly' and 'tranquillity' are words which have been much used by leading party spokesmen in the Brezhnev era. They came as music to the ears of party and state officials recuperating from the turmoil of the Khrushchev period, not to mention those whose memories stretch back to the Stalin purges. Though the political contexts are different in many ways, the new emphasis is strikingly reminiscent, in the most verbatim sense, of the attitude of British Conservative politicians at the end of Lloyd George's Prime Ministership. Shortly before the 1922 election which brought him to office, Bonar Law said to Lord Swinton: 'They tell me that we have to have what is called a slogan. What should we have for this election?' Swinton replied: 'Well, I know what the country is feeling, they don't want to be buggered about.' Bonar Law answered: 'The sentiment is sound but we must find a more refined version: let us call it "Tranquillity".'[49]

The feelings of members of many influential groups within Soviet society by 1964 were no doubt very similar to those ascribed by Swinton to 'the country' in the Britain of 1922. Bonar Law fought and won the 1922 British general election on the theme of 'tranquillity', and the same theme and political style have served Leonid Brezhnev well for fifteen years. It is, perhaps, the relative tranquillity of domestic Soviet politics in the Brezhnev era that distinguishes it most clearly from any other period in the history of the USSR.

In the latest volume of his memoirs,[50] Brezhnev himself explicitly contrasts the style of government he favours with that employed by Khrushchev. He describes a meeting in the bureau of the Kustanai *obkom* at which a majority were in favour of building roads rather than railways in the virgin lands of Kazakhstan. Khrushchev (mentioned by name in Brezhnev's account) was present at the meeting and favoured the building of narrow-gauge railways. He refused to listen to any argument against his policy and his conception was later seen to be mistaken.[51] Brezhnev says that his purpose in mentioning this fact is not to show that a party leader or statesman 'must simultaneously be a roadworker, economist, engineer, etc.', but to emphasise the necessity of his not considering himself 'the sole and indisputable authority in all spheres of human activity'. Contemporary economics, politics and social life are so complicated, Brezhnev notes, that they call for 'mighty collective wisdom'. Therefore, 'one must listen to specialists and scholars, and not only of one tendency or one school'.[52]

Though the contrast which is made between Khrushchev and Brezhnev in official Soviet publications does not tell the whole truth (and passes over in silence a number of Khrushchev's merits and achievements), it does tell part of the truth. There is a real contrast to be discerned between Khrushchev's bold and impulsive decision-making and Brezhnev's cautious, consensus-seeking style.[53] Brezhnev has preferred to postpone a decision rather than take a risk, and this style has survived into the middle and late 1970s,[54] when his strength within the Politburo has been greater than in the 1960s.

Important evidence on Brezhnev's position in the late 1960s has come from a particularly well-placed observer, Zdeněk Mlynář, who was a Secretary of the Central Committee of the Communist Party of Czechoslovakia in 1968 and (more briefly) a member of the

Czechoslovak Politburo. He was also one of those who took part in the tense and prolonged talks in the Kremlin in August 1968 following the Soviet military intervention in Czechoslovakia. Mlynář suggests in his memoirs that Brezhnev was among the more reluctant invaders, but that by postponing a decision, as he did throughout the Spring and Summer of 1968, he laid himself open to removal in a coup, in which the more hawkish members of the Soviet leadership would win over some of the waverers, possibly by the offer to one of them of the General Secretaryship. Mlynář believes that Brezhnev and the more moderate group within the Soviet leadership eventually took the initiative (to prevent their removal) by uniting with the 'hawks' in favour of armed intervention.[55]

During the talks in the Kremlin between 22 and 26 August 1968, Mlynář relates, Brezhnev told those members of the Czechoslovak Politburo who had been taken there that when he was preparing a speech, he passed it to all the members of the Politburo, requesting their comments. 'Isn't that true, comrades?' Brezhnev asked the whole Politburo who were sitting in a row alongside him, and they confirmed the truth of his words with a nod of the head and a mumble of assent.[56] More significant evidence of the real limitations on the General Secretary's power – in the late sixties at any rate – is given by Mlynář when he reports a conversation which Brezhnev had with Bohumíl Šimon, who was at that time a member of the Politburo of the Czechoslovak Communist Party and leader of the Czech delegation to the October Revolution celebrations in Moscow in 1968. Brezhnev, he says, told Šimon:

> You thought that if you had power, you could do what you wanted. But that is a fundamental mistake. Not even I can do what I like – perhaps I can manage about a third of what I'd like to do. If I had not raised my hand in the Politburo when I did for military intervention – what would have happened? You certainly wouldn't be sitting here now. And possibly not even I would be sitting here![57]

Brezhnev has, of course, strengthened his position within the Soviet leadership since then. Indeed, 1968 should probably be seen as a turning-point. The very fact that Czechoslovakia assumed the importance it did, the fact that it was an inter-party matter and so Brezhnev rather than Kosygin (who had been engaging in summit talks with Western statesmen up to that time) had to become principal Soviet spokesman, began a process which led to Brezhnev's clear supremacy in the foreign policy sphere. The change was still to be a relatively gradual one. Willy Brandt detected a definite development of Brezhnev's power *vis-à-vis* his colleagues, and in his command of foreign policy, between 1970 and 1971. In August 1970

> [Brezhnev] made rather a wary impression and spent considerable periods of time referring to his written material, whole passages of which he read aloud. But this was clearly the stage at which Brezhnev had resolved – and been empowered – to take personal charge of important aspects of Soviet policy towards the West. At the time, he and Kosygin struck me as the Kremlin's '1A' and '1B'. A year later Brezhnev's definite and undisputed supremacy could not escape the eye or ear. He was also a master of his material.[58]

One of the most important aspects of the power of the General Secretary of the CPSU is his power – and the constraints at different times on that power – of appointment and dismissal. It is such a large question, one on which much has been written but on which much remains to be written, that it can be touched upon but briefly here, and with reference only to the Politburo. According to the party statutes the Politburo is, of course, elected by the Central Committee and in the post-Stalin period that formal position has not always been a *mere* formality. Essentially, though, the process has been one of collective co-option by the existing Politburo within which the voice of the General Secretary can be seen to have counted for more than that of any of his colleagues. Apart from the period of 'high Stalinism', however, the General Secretary's power of appointment to, and dismissal from, the Politburo has never been an absolute one. There have been great variations over time in the General Secretary's ability to intimidate, cajole or persuade his colleagues into making changes.

The more senior Politburo members have their own supporters within the party *apparat* or other *apparaty* and it is to prevent them from attempting to mobilise that support that the final moves against a member so often take place when he is far from Moscow. Marshal Zhukov learned that he had been dismissed as Minister of Defence and from the Politburo on his return to the Soviet Union from Yugoslavia in October 1957. Aleksandr Shelepin was removed immediately after his return from Britain (as head of a Soviet trade union delegation) in April 1975. Nikolai Podgorny was dismissed a little over a month after coming back from an extensive African tour and it is probable that advantage was taken of Podgorny's absence from the Soviet Union in late March and early April 1977 to broach within the Politburo the proposal that Brezhnev be given the presidency. These instances demonstrate not only that absence does not necessarily make the heart grow fonder but that removing a senior man from the Politburo is a delicate business and one to be handled with caution.

The importance of the person concerned being absent from Moscow is all the greater if it is a case of other Politburo members attempting to remove the General Secretary. The 'anti-Party group' moved against Khrushchev while he was in Finland and his defeat in the Politburo[59] (to be followed by his victory in the Central Committee) took place immediately after his return. The later successful organisation of his removal in October 1964 was carried out when Khrushchev was on holiday in the Crimea.

It is noteworthy that the Politburo turnover has been slower under Brezhnev than under either of his predecessors. This probably reflects *both* his more cautious style *and* the desire of his colleagues to maintain some counterweights to him within the Politburo. It is a reasonable inference that Brezhnev would not have retained in the Politburo until well into the 1970s such non-admirers and potential rivals as Shelest, Shelepin and Podgorny if he had felt strong enough earlier to propose their removal without risk to his own position.

Though Stalin's power was by no means absolute in the 1920s, of the seven members and three candidate members elected to the Politburo after the 11th Party Congress in 1922, only two of the ten – Molotov and Kalinin – in addition to Stalin were still there by the time of the 16th Congress in 1930. (Kalinin survived in the Politburo until his death in 1946 and Molotov remained a member until four years after Stalin's demise when he was expelled not only from the Politburo but from the Central Committee as a member of the 'anti-Party group'.) With the sole (and no doubt deserving) exception of Beria, Khrushchev did not shoot sacked Politburo members, and most of those dropped from high party and state posts in his time had relatively soft landings. It is, nevertheless, of interest that by the summer of 1960, apart from Khrushchev himself, there was only one survivor of the ten-man Politburo in office immediately after Stalin's death – namely, Mikoyan – and of the four candidate members in 1953, three had disappeared from the political scene and only the fourth (Shvernik) had been promoted to full Politburo membership.

In contrast, of the ten full members of the Politburo who held office immediately after Khrushchev's removal from office in October 1964, seven were still there at and beyond the 24th Party Congress of 1971 (indeed, their number was not reduced until 1973). Of the six candidate members of the Politburo immediately after Khrushchev's fall, five held either candidate or full membership at and beyond the 24th Congress. In 1979, fifteen years after Brezhnev's accession to the General Secretaryship, there were still three full members of the Politburo, apart from Brezhnev himself, who had been there since Khrushchev's time – Suslov, Kosygin and Kirilenko.

It is true that from 1971, when the size of the Politburo was increased, Brezhnev has been successful in gradually bringing into the leadership a steadily growing number of his known supporters, a process that has continued right up to the end of the seventies. Nevertheless, the presence within the Politburo – and in key positions in the Secretariat in two cases and as Chairman of the Council of Ministers in the other – of men of the party standing and experience of Suslov, Kosygin and Kirilenko,[60] is likely to have acted as a constraint upon Brezhnev's individual power over policy. At the same time, the gradual ageing of the Politburo can be seen in retrospect to have been a remarkably effective way of safeguarding Brezhnev's lengthy tenure of the General Secretaryship. When the only Politburo members with the right career profile to look like plausible successors have had to be ruled out because they are as old as, or older than, the present incumbent, it is not surprising that Brezhnev for so long should have looked indispensable. Given, however, the advanced age and poor health of the General Secretary and the high average age of his colleagues, the leadership has had to remain essentially collective – as a matter of physical, as much as political, necessity.

Perhaps the main general point which emerges from this look at Stalin, Khrushchev and Brezhnev, and some of the powers they wielded, concerns the relationship between style of leadership and power over policy. A head of executive can lead from the front or lead from the middle. Nikita Khrushchev (like British Prime

Ministers Lloyd George and Neville Chamberlain) led from the front – took vital policy decisions and bypassed his colleagues when he deemed it necessary. Leonid Brezhnev (like Baldwin, Attlee and Wilson) leads from the middle. If you follow the first course, you can wield more power while you are in office, but your tenure of office is likely to be shorter, for when things go wrong – as in politics they can be guaranteed to go wrong, sooner or later – it will be too late to seek the security of collective responsibility.

Stalin began as a centrist – and was regarded as such for much of the 1920s – and only later led (in a peculiarly 'Stalinist' way) from the front. But once terror is applied on a mass scale and with the skill of a Stalin, the normal rules of politics cease to apply. The period of 'high Stalinism', however, lasted for some twenty years and the Soviet Union has been in existence for over sixty years. Stalinism, therefore, cannot be identified with the Soviet norm.

Since Khrushchev's abrupt removal, a General Secretary must know that even if he does succeed in appointing many people to responsible positions, if he proceeds to act against their interests, they may still rise against him. Likewise, he will understand (as American Presidents have come to understand) that sharing in the greater power which has accrued to a 'superpower' is far from the same thing as wielding a greater power within the system. The very exigencies of superpower status, which demand that the General Secretary spend a great deal of time on foreign policy, help to diffuse power over domestic policy – and, as Brezhnev's replacement of Khrushchev suggested, present opportunities for self-advancement among those left minding the shop.

NOTES

A version of this chapter was presented as a paper to the 1979 Convention of the American Association for the Advancement of Slavic Studies at New Haven, Connecticut. For their provision of financial support for my participation in that convention, I am most grateful to the Johnson Foundation of Racine, Wisconsin, and to the Inter-Faculty Committee for Slavonic and East European Studies of Oxford University. The theme of the chapter is so large and its time-span of some sixty years so great that I am conscious of neglecting aspects of the problem and of merely touching on certain others. In a comparative study of the powers of heads of executive which I am undertaking, I hope to tackle the issues at much greater length.

   1. Leonard Schapiro, *The Communist Party of the Soviet Union*, 2nd edn (London, 1970) pp. 559 and 561. It could be argued that Malenkov was top man within

the Soviet hierarchy for longer than his occupancy of the party secretaryship and a shorter time than his tenure of the Chairmanship of the Council of Ministers. Until mid-1954, when alphabetical order was adopted, his name consistently appeared first in lists of members of the Presidium of the Central Committee of the party.

2. T. H. Rigby, *Lenin's Government: Sovnarkom 1917–1922* (Cambridge, U.K. 1979) p. x. Rigby notes further that the chairmanships of Sovnarkom and of the Labour and Defence Council (*Sovet Truda i Oborony*) were the only formal positions which Lenin ever held within the Soviet regime. 'It is true', he adds, 'that as the most authoritative member of the Party Central Committee he usually chaired its meetings and those of the Politburo and was its main spokesman at Party congresses. Yet, unlike other Politburo members such as Stalin, Kamenev and Zinoviev, he never came to hold any formal position in the party giving him direct authority over any of its executive machinery' (ibid., p. 108).

3. David Hume, 'Of the Rise and Progress of the Arts and Sciences', in *Essays Moral, Political and Literary* (Oxford, 1963; first published 1741) p. 112.

4. It is at least arguable that Stalin, in his last few years, and Brezhnev, in the most recent period, were both – as a result of failing health – less dominating figures in the policy process than they had been a year or two earlier. A case could be made for regarding the mid-1970s as the zenith of Brezhnev's power. But even if a reduction in his physical strength has led to some subsequent reduction of his political activity, it must also be noted that in the late seventies the number of Brezhnev protégés in leadership positions was continuing to increase. Khrushchev's last years present a still more ambiguous picture. On the one hand, there is ample evidence of Khrushchev pushing policies through against the wishes of his colleagues even when he was within two years of his enforced retirement. On the other hand, these very actions provoked opposition, and the over-confidence which led to the actions provided opportunities for that opposition. The limitations upon Khrushchev's power in the early 1960s have been skilfully depicted (though somewhat *over*-emphasised at the expense of the very considerable powers he still wielded) by Carl Linden in his *Khrushchev and the Soviet Leadership 1957–1964* (Baltimore, Md., 1966) and Michel Tatu, *Power in the Kremlin: From Khrushchev's Decline to Collective Leadership* (London, 1969).

5. The 18th Congress was held in March 1939 and the 19th Congress in October 1952.

6. N. S. Khrushchev, *The 'Secret' Speech*, with an introduction by Zhores A. Medvedev and Roy A. Medvedev (Nottingham, 1976) p. 32. Of course, Stalin had done much worse than not meet the Central Committee. As Khrushchev went on to tell the delegates to the Twentieth Congress: '. . . of the 139 members and candidates of the party's Central Committee who were elected at the 17th Congress [in 1934], 98 persons, i.e. 70 per cent were arrested and shot (mostly in 1937–8)' (ibid., p. 33).

7. *Khrushchev Remembers*, trans. and ed. Strobe Talbott (Boston, Mass., 1970) pp. 275, 278, 280, 281 and 308–10.

8. Ibid., pp. 297–303, esp. 297 and 301.

9. In 1952 Stalin abolished the Politburo and replaced it with a Presidium of twenty-five members and an inner body, the Bureau of the Presidium, which

included nine people. According to Khrushchev (*Khrushchev Remembers*, p. 281) the enlarged Presidium never met, and 'out of the nine members in the Bureau Stalin selected an inner circle of five, according to his will and benevolence'. Apart from Stalin himself, the usual four others were Malenkov, Beria, Bulganin and Khrushchev. Kaganovich and Voroshilov were 'rarely invited' and Molotov and Mikoyan 'absolutely never invited'.

10. *Khrushchev Remembers*, p. 209.
11. One of the best accounts of this process is still Leonard Schapiro's *The Communist Party of the Soviet Union*. The most detailed study of Stalin is Robert C. Tucker's trilogy, of which the first volume, *Stalin as Revolutionary, 1879–1929* (London, 1974) has already appeared. See also Robert C. Tucker (ed.), *Stalinism: Essays in Historical Interpretation* (New York, 1977); Roy A. Medvedev, *Let History Judge: The Origins and Consequences of Stalinism* (London, 1971); and Roy A. Medvedev, *On Stalin and Stalinism* (Oxford, 1979).
12. Cf. Roy A. Medvedev, *On Stalin and Stalinism*, p. 24.
13. Niels Erik Rosenfeldt, *Knowledge and Power: The Role of Stalin's Secret Chancellery in the Soviet System of Government* (Copenhagen, 1978).
14. Ibid., p. 15.
15. Leonard Schapiro, 'The General Department of the CC of the CPSU' in *Survey*, 21, no. 3 (Summer 1975) pp. 53–65.
16. Ibid., p. 65.
17. See, for example, Roy A. Medvedev and Zhores A. Medvedev, *Khrushchev: The Years in Power* (Oxford, 1977) pp. 129–42.
18. There is plenty of evidence of real discussion taking place at Politburo level in the Khrushchev era, though it is also clear that Khrushchev often succeeded in getting his way against the better judgement of his colleagues, since those same colleagues proceeded to criticise and reverse a number of the policies, to which, in principle, they were parties, within a very short time of Khrushchev's removal. These changes have been summarised in my chapter 10 of Archie Brown and Michael Kaser (eds), *The Soviet Union since the Fall of Khrushchev* (London, 1975; 2nd edn, 1978) pp. 218–75, esp. 218–38. For a statement by Khrushchev that the Politburo (or Presidium of the Central Committee as it was known then) met weekly when he was First Secretary, see *Khrushchev Remembers: The Last Testament* (London, 1974) p. 25.
19. In 1957 Khrushchev abolished a majority of the industrial ministries, setting up in their stead regional economic councils (*sovnarkhozy*).
20. Possibly because he realised that it contributed ultimately to his downfall, perhaps because he recognised that becoming Chairman of the Council of Ministers had represented an excessive lust for power on his part, Khrushchev in retirement indulged in some self-criticism of his 1958 move: 'In addition to my duties as First Secretary of the Central Committee, I became Chairman of the Council of Ministers as well. I've often criticized Stalin for allowing a single person to have two posts, one in the government and one in the Party. Therefore my acceptance of the Premiership represented a certain weakness on my part – a bug of some sort which was gnawing away at me and undermining my power of resistance. The final judgment on this question I'll have to leave to the court of history' (*Khrushchev Remembers: The Last Testament*, pp. 17–18).
21. See T. H. Rigby, 'The Soviet Leadership: Towards a Self-Stabilizing

Oligarchy?', *Soviet Studies*, XXII, no. 2 (October 1970) pp. 167–91, esp. pp. 175–6; P. A. Rodionov, *Kollektivnost' – vysshii printsip partiinogo rukovodstva* (Moscow, 1967) p. 219 (cited by Rigby, p. 175).

22. *Pravda*, 25 February 1976, p. 7.
23. During the XIth World Congress of the International Political Science Association, held in Moscow, 12–18 August 1979, a small group of twenty or more political scientists from different countries had a meeting at the Presidium of the Supreme Soviet. I was one of those present at this session in the Kremlin on 16 August which was presided over by V. P. Ruben. In answer to a question from me about the frequency of meetings of various political bodies, Mr Ruben provided information which suggests that a number of the highest party and state bodies are meeting more often than they hitherto were (or than was thought to be the case). Apart from the impression conveyed that it is now normal for the Politburo to meet twice weekly, the IPSA group of scholars were also told that the Presidium of the Council of Ministers meets at least once a week, that the Council of Ministers as a whole meets once a month, and that the Presidium of the Supreme Soviet meets once a month (though, V. P. Ruben added, work was going on all the time, for the Presidium was a '*postoyannyi* organ'). Given that this information is new – certainly different from that previously available from authoritative Soviet sources – it is to be hoped that confirmation, or further elucidation, of the frequency of meetings may be forthcoming. Soviet press reports have no guidance to offer on the frequency of meetings of the Politburo or of the Presidium of the Council of Ministers. They do, however, lend support to the statement that the Presidium of the Supreme Soviet has been meeting monthly of late, though not to the suggestion that the Council of Ministers as a whole has been meeting just as frequently. (To obviate the possibility that the differences might be accounted for by a mishearing on my part, I have checked my notes with those of other scholars present at the meeting, and they have confirmed the accuracy of the reporting.)
24. *New York Times*, 15 June 1973, p. 3; cited in Jerry F. Hough and Merle Fainsod, *How the Soviet Union is Governed* (Cambridge, Mass., 1979) pp. 471 and 650.
25. See, for example, Harold Wilson, *The Governance of Britain* (London, 1976) p. 45.
26. In sharp contrast with his predecessor. See, e.g. Priscilla Johnson, *Khrushchev and the Arts: The Politics of Soviet Culture, 1962–1964* (Cambridge, Mass., 1965); and Zhores Medvedev, *10 Years After Ivan Denisovich* (London, 1973) esp. pp. 119–20.
27. L. I. Brezhnev, *Voprosy razvitiya politicheskoi sistemy sovetskogo obshchestva* (Moscow, 1977) pp. 434–8, esp. 434–5.
28. *Pravda*, 19 June 1977, p. 1.
29. Brezhnev, *Voprosy razvitiya politicheskoi sistemy sovetskogo obshchestva*, p. 434.
30. Ibid., p. 435.
31. Ibid.
32. The general point has been made by Peter Vanneman in *The Supreme Soviet: Politics and the Legislative Process in the Soviet Political System* (Durham, N.C., 1977). Writing prior to Brezhnev's assumption of the presidency, Vanneman pointed to the close links between departments of the Central Committee and

the commissions of the Supreme Soviet, observing (p. 214) that 'the commissions are virtually the legal arm of the Secretariat and practically duplicate it in some respects'. The point that he makes about the commissions could be extended to embrace the role of the Presidium and its Chairman: 'The commissions constitute a second line of supervision for the Party apparatus – legal "kontrol" over the organs of state administration.'

33. Willy Brandt, *People and Politics: The Years 1960–1975* (London, 1978) p. 336.
34. Mohamed Heikal, *Nasser: The Cairo Documents* (London, 1972), pp. 147–8; see also Heikal's *Sphinx and Commissar: The Rise and Fall of Soviet Influence in the Arab World* (London, 1978) p. 135.
35. This is related to the fact that in Kosygin, the General Secretary has had a colleague who has not aspired to his job, has not tried to deflect blame for ministerial shortcomings in his direction, and whose own qualifications for the post of Chairman of the Council of Ministers were unsurpassed – in terms of relevant experience and reputed administrative efficiency – by any of his colleagues.
36. Joseph LaPalombara, 'Monoliths or Plural Systems: Through Conceptual Lenses Darkly', *Studies in Comparative Communism*, VIII, no. 3 (Autumn 1975) p. 317.
37. T. H. Rigby, 'Stalinism and the Mono-Organizational Society' in Robert C. Tucker (ed.), *Stalinism: Essays in Historical Interpretation*, p. 60.
38. *Khrushchev Remembers*, p. 277.
39. See Timothy Dunmore, 'Soviet Economic Policy-Making during the Fourth Five-Year Plan Period 1946–1950', unpublished Ph.D. thesis (University of Essex, 1978).
40. Cf. David Hume, 'Of the First Principles of Government' in *Essays Moral, Political and Literary*, p. 29.
41. See, for example, the chapter by A. Kemp-Welch in the present volume.
42. Milovan Djilas, *Conversations with Stalin* (London, 1962).
43. *Khrushchev Remembers: The Last Testament*, p. 357.
44. See on educational reform Mervyn Matthews, *Class and Society in Soviet Russia* (London, 1972) esp. chs 10 and 11; Nigel Grant, *Soviet Education* (4th edn, Harmondsworth, 1979) esp. pp. 109–17; Joel J. Schwartz and William R. Keech, 'Group Influence and the Policy Process in the Soviet Union' in Frederic J. Fleron, Jr (ed.), *Communist Studies and the Social Sciences* (Chicago, 1969) pp. 298–317; and Philip D. Stewart, 'Soviet Interest Groups and the Policy Process: The Repeal of Production Education', *World Politics*, XXII, no. 1 (October 1969) pp. 29–50.
45. See Sidney Ploss, *Conflict and Decision-Making in Soviet Russia: A Case Study of Agricultural Policy, 1953–1963* (Princeton, N.J., 1965); Werner G. Hahn, *The Politics of Soviet Agriculture, 1960–1970* (Baltimore, Md., and London, 1972); Karl-Eugen Wädekin, *The Private Sector in Soviet Agriculture* (Berkeley, Los Angeles, Calif., and London, 1973); and Martin McCauley, *Khrushchev and the Development of Soviet Agriculture: The Virgin Land Programme 1953–1964* (London, 1976).
46. See, for example, Hahn, *The Politics of Soviet Agriculture*, pp. 113–16, 171 and 194.
47. *Khrushchev Remembers: The Last Testament*, pp. 443–61, esp. pp. 444 and 451; and pp. 509–14; *Khrushchev Remembers*, pp. 489–505, esp. pp. 494–5.
48. K. U. Chernenko, *Nekotorye voprosy tvorcheskogo razvitiya stilya partiynnoi i*

gosudarstvennoi raboty, 2nd edn (Moscow, 1978) p. 6.

49. The Earl of Swinton, *Sixty Years of Power: Some Memories of the Men who Wielded It* (London, 1966) p. 67.

50. The objection is sometimes made to the use of Brezhnev's three volumes of memoirs (*Malaya zemlya*, *Vozrozhdenie* and *Tselina*) that it is highly unlikely that a busy General Secretary could find the time to write such works while still in office. Brezhnev himself has drawn attention to his busy schedule, as, for example, when excusing the brevity of an interview he gave to the editor, Moscow correspondent and three other representatives of *Time* magazine in early 1979, he said: 'I hope you will understand my time budget is extremely tight' (*Time*, 22 January 1979, p. 17). Whether Brezhnev's memoirs were dictated to a recording machine and 'written up' by others or based upon recorded interviews with him is, however, almost immaterial. What is certain is that the final product could not be published without his detailed scrutiny and permission and that it therefore reflects that part of his experience, those views and that image which he wishes to project.

51. Leonid Il'ich Brezhnev, *Tselina* (Moscow, 1978) p. 50.

52. Ibid., pp. 50–1.

53. Cf. Jerry F. Hough, 'The Brezhnev Era: The Man and the System', *Problems of Communism*, xxv, no. 2 (March–April 1976) pp. 1–17.

54. There must, claims a Central Committee spokesman, Valentin Falin, in an interview he gave to the American journalist, Henry Brandon, 'be a consensus [in the Politburo]. If several members have a different view on the same matter, then Brezhnev sums up those differences and suggests a postponement for further study' (*Washington Star*, 15 July 1979).

55. Zdeněk Mlynář, *Mráz přichází z Kremlu* (Cologne, 1978) pp. 217–8. The constraints upon Brezhnev's freedom of political action, and his consciousness of them at that time, are emphasised by a Polish first-hand observer. See Erwin Weit, *Eyewitness: The Autobiography of Gomulka's Interpreter* (London, 1973) p. 177.

56. Mlynář, *Mráz přichází z Kremlu*, p. 304.

57. Ibid., p. 210.

58. Brandt, *People and Politics*, p. 334.

59. The Politburo was at that time known as the Presidium of the Central Committee.

60. It may seem strange to view Kirilenko's presence in the Politburo and Secretariat as a constraint upon Brezhnev's power. It is true that Kirilenko's past relations with Brezhnev have been much closer than those of the General Secretary with Kosygin and Suslov. Kosygin and Suslov made their way to high office in Stalin's time, reaching the top earlier than Brezhnev and independently of Khrushchev. In contrast, both Brezhnev and Kirilenko worked together in the Ukraine for a time and both owed their further promotion to Khrushchev's patronage. This in itself, however, distinguishes Kirilenko from a colleague such as Chernenko who owes *his* position entirely to Brezhnev. Moreover, someone in Kirilenko's post, and with his degree of Politburo experience behind him, acquires great influence in his own right. And as Brezhnev showed when he was the Central Committee Secretary with day-to-day control of the party organisation (the position Kirilenko now holds) in 1964, a General Secretary simply cannot assume that the Secretary to whom such organisational power has devolved will in all circumstances deploy it in support of the party leader.

9 Policy towards Dissent since Khrushchev

Peter Reddaway

The title of this chapter may suggest a subject which is compact and clearly defined. Working on it has shown me however that it needs several books, at least, to do it justice. So the essay which follows is no more than an attempt to map out the main territory and provide pointers for further, more detailed research.

After quoting Brezhnev's interpretation of dissent and his explanation of official policy towards it, the essay discusses how this policy is applied in practice towards an average dissenter 'on the ground' and briefly reviews the dissent-related aspects of foreign policy. We then examine chronologically how these different strands of policy have been applied to major dissenting groups and individuals. Next we attempt to summarise the policy as a whole, and to analyse the limits within which its application has varied over time; also, to assess tentatively the different inputs, domestic and foreign, involved in the policy's formation. Finally, we consider briefly what implications the essay's findings have for the broader study of the Soviet political system, and that system's stability or otherwise in the future.

As will quickly become clear, the essay does not examine in any depth either dissent-related laws, or public declarations of policy, or the policy formation process. Nor does it embark on numerous case-studies which still need to be made, notably some with a strong foreign relations component and/or involving a dissenting group with a difficult native language such as Armenian or Georgian. Nor does it discuss the problem of primary sources, or analyse official ideology. Nor does it explore the element of political culture in the regime – dissenter equation by, for example, making comparisons with the analogous equation in the late Tsarist period. And nor does it consider in any specific way what model of the Soviet system seems to be most clearly endorsed by its conclusions, let alone whether these can offer anything to political theory at a higher level of abstraction regarding, for instance, 'the social bases of obedience and revolt'[1] or 'rewards, punishments and political stability'.[2]

A PUBLIC OFFICIAL STATEMENT ON DISSENT AND DISSENT POLICY

While most official writings about dissent[3] tend to the stridently defensive and vindictive, statements by Politburo members are usually (and probably deceptively) more measured. In a speech of 1977 Brezhnev presented this fairly typical appraisal:

> Our enemies would like to find at least some sort of forces speaking out against socialism inside our countries. But as there are not such forces, there being in socialist society neither oppressed, exploited classes, nor oppressed, exploited nationalities, they invent some sort of Ersatz – through mendacious propaganda they create an appearance of an 'internal opposition' in the socialist countries. Precisely for this reason campaigns are organised about so-called 'dissenters' . . . . In our country it is not reprehensible to 'think differently' from the majority, to evaluate critically these or those aspects of public life. We regard comrades who criticize in justified ways, trying to be constructive, as honest critics and are grateful to them. Those who criticize mistakenly we regard as people who have erred.
>
> It is another matter when a few people who have divorced themselves from our society speak out actively against the socialist system, take the path of anti-Soviet activity, break laws, and, not having a base within the country, appeal for support to abroad, to imperialist subversive centres – both propagandistic and intelligence ones. Our people demand that such – if you permit me – figures should be treated as enemies of socialism, people going against their own Motherland, mercenaries, also as agents of imperialism. (Stormy, prolonged applause.) Naturally we are taking and will take against them the measures prescribed by our laws.[4]

Brezhnev thus implies that dissent is of little or no significance: his regime punishes it mainly in response to popular pressure.

SOVIET POLICY TOWARDS INDIVIDUAL DISSENTERS

To try to keep the appearance of dissenters to a minimum the broad policy applied is one of political socialisation in forms so comprehensive and unified that it can best be called ideological indoctrination. This system, which is intended to have a fool-proof prophylactic effect in relation to dissent, is administered through the familiar channels of the officially-controlled mass media, the Pioneer and Komsomol organisations, the education system, and compulsory lectures at places of work.

Where discontent none the less appears, the first line of defence is the officials most directly involved – those at the workplace or, one level higher, in the local soviet. These are repeatedly enjoined by the regime to deal promptly and fairly with citizens' legitimate grievances. Clearly the leaders of an authoritarian system have an even stronger incentive than those of a pluralistic one to see grievances settled on a bilateral basis between individual and officials. In this way the illegitimate (under authoritarian rule) and potentially dangerous development of aggrieved individuals forming groups can be averted.

If, however, the officials directly involved fail to satisfy the grievance, and if it takes on an even faintly political hue, the KGB, from the office it has in every work-place of any size, steps in. At first its approach is often that of the stern but friendly uncle. But if the protester persists, it escalates by stages, as required, to a mixture of cajoling and threats, then to demotion or dismissal from work, then sometimes to physical attacks, then to formal warnings, then to arrest, then to exerting pressure to obtain a recantation in court, then to imprisonment, exile or psychiatric internment, with, sometimes, vilification in the press, and finally to further pressure to recant during imprisonment.[5] If the dissenter 'fails to take the path of reform' during his sentence, he is subject on release to severe restrictions on his movements and place of residence, or (though this is unusual in the post-Stalin period) he is re-sentenced on some pretext before his term expires.

We should note that the KGB's standing orders clearly include the instruction to avoid making political arrests if at all possible. Numerous samizdat sources show the above pattern of escalation, and some report KGB officials as describing the resort to arrest as evidence of their own failure ('kazhdaya posadka-brak v nashei rabote').[6] There seems no reason to doubt the truth of these statements. Arrests, after all, risk creating both martyrs and undesirable publicity.

DISSENT AND SOVIET FOREIGN POLICY

To look at foreign policy and dissent in even more general terms than those used so far, we may note first that the regime's central aim is to keep foreign support for dissenters to a minimum. To this end it uses its radio stations, publications, diplomats and foreign friends to discredit dissenters and their foreign supporters in a variety of ways. It also puts pressure on governments, national associations and international organisations from UN bodies to the World Council of Churches and the World Psychiatric Association, trying to prevent them from responding to dissenters' appeals for help. And it tries repeatedly to get foreign radio stations broadcasting in languages of the USSR to be less critical of Soviet policy, or to close down altogether.

A CHRONOLOGICAL REVIEW OF DISSENT POLICY APPLICATION

Let us now fill out the generalised picture sketched so far by looking chronologically at some key episodes in dissent policy application.

The Khrushchev leadership, in its dissent policy, had tried to present a sharp contrast to Stalin. Seeking to rule by persuasion, not terror, it had released the vast majority of political prisoners (i.e. nearly ten million people) and claimed that it now held no such prisoners: what few critics remained were mentally ill. And indeed, the rate of political arrests was generally low in the Khrushchev period, rising sharply only in 1956–7 following the Hungarian events, and in 1961–3 to suppress opposition to the official campaigns against religion and 'bourgeois nationalism'.

While Khrushchev's successors retained his broad political strategy, their institutional reforms, their Stalin policy and their political style constituted a systematic reaction against most of the distinctive features of his rule.

The new leadership also became a remarkably stable oligarchy (a type of rule without precedent in Soviet history), largely reflecting, balancing and reconciling the desiderata of the entrenched bureaucracies which make up the Soviet polity. Its order of priorities regarding substantive policy-making was interesting, if perhaps predictable. First came the economy and the 'general political line' (which determines policy on, notably, political control, dissent and ideology): foreign policy and other internal matters were less important and could wait.

Regarding dissent, the new leaders took the interesting step of immediately halting arrests in all categories. From October 1964, with marginal exceptions, no 'mainstream' dissenter was arrested until June 1965, no Ukrainian nationalist until 24 August 1965,[7] no Baptist until February 1966,[8] and no Crimean Tatar until May 1966.[9] More than this, of the nearly 200 Baptists in captivity when Khrushchev fell, over half were, over the next year or so, released early before their sentences were up,[10] and most of the anti-religious press changed gear and published explicit criticism of the official coercion of the preceding years.[11] Also, Crimean Tatar delegations were now received in Moscow with less reluctance and at the highest political levels.[12]

All this amounted, first, to part of the bounty dispensed by the new leaders in their efforts to obtain popular acceptance. It contributed to a lowering of social tensions, and thus distinguished their rule from Khrushchev's. But it also indicated that they had no overwhelming urge to impose a neo-Stalinist discipline on the population, and that their policy on dissent could be worked out with due deliberation.

In mid-1965 the outlines of this policy began their slow emergence. The KGB had already been allowed to adopt a higher profile and re-establish its somewhat diminished prestige.[13] This was presumably to the advantage of its recent head, Shelepin, whose links to his successor were close, and who apparently made a bid for power from his new position in the Presidium in August–September.[14] At all events, in April the KGB had arrested an NTS courier, Gerald Brooke, and got permission – unprecedented in such cases – to give him a show trial. This was conducted, on 22–23 July, so as to demonstrate the security men's vigilance and skill.[15]

In June, as noted above, the KGB were allowed to start arresting dissenters again. Though scarcely known abroad, the people concerned were mostly better known locally than the political arrestees of the Khrushchev years. The process began in Leningrad in June, with seven arrests,[16] and continued in the Ukraine in

August–September with twenty-five more.[17] In September the trend escalated with the confiscation of one of Solzhenitsyn's archives and the arrest of the Moscow writers Sinyavsky and Daniel. Not only were the latter known abroad, if not well; they had, more importantly, relations and friends who broke long-established taboos and set about campaigning both at home and through Western media for their release.[18]

This led to the first Constitution Day demonstration in Moscow on 5 December, another unprecedented event, since regarded as marking the starting-point of the human rights movement.[19]

These unwelcome developments, taken with the related and similarly publicised campaign of early 1966 against the re-habilitation of Stalin, in which leading scientists and writers took part,[20] and with other publicity abroad which was awakening the outside world to the existence of extra-systemic dissent,[21] helped to set limits to the hardening of the general line, and probably undercut Shelepin's position. The cautious new leaders who were feeling their way towards a political style of consensual oligarchy had to take these pressures into account. As a result, they seem to have re-imposed their ban on political arrests, but in a modified form to cover only those which might generate publicity abroad. They thus re-immunised, notably, members of the incipient dissent movement and any dissenters who were likely to have links with it, as the movement's main function was the generation of publicity. The ban, which does not appear to have been clearly noted by observers before, thus operated for these categories, first from October 1964 to June 1965 and then (with only a few very minor exceptions)[22] from September 1965 until January 1967.*

For Shelepin's circles the renewed ban was the complete negation of one of their reported demands of 1965 – the arrest of a thousand

---

* It is important to note that certain categories of Soviet political offenders appear to be penalised automatically and therefore constantly. The major ones are would-be defectors and border-crossers who are caught; and those who succeed in their aim but later return home. Slightly different categories are former anti-Soviet partisans in the Baltic and the Ukraine, and ex-Nazi collaborators, whose actions during and after the war only come to light much later. The prosecution of the first category seems to be much more often automatic than that of the second. Prosecution of Nazi collaborators appears to be mainly contingent on political circumstances, a constant reserve of cases being drawn on whenever, for example, the Politburo hardens the internal political line and therefore wants to shoot some citizens with attendant publicity.

intellectuals in Moscow alone.[23] But the Presidium did, naturally, appease these circles by going at least some of the way to satisfy them – partially rehabilitating Stalin, for example, tightening the censorship to bar serious criticism of him and impose a firmer ideological line, replacing the over-liberal Rumyantsev as editor of *Pravda*, and prescribing heavy sentences for Sinyavsky and Daniel.[24] In the latter case, which had provoked strong protests from abroad,[25] Soviet face could not be lost. The beneficiaries of the protests were thus not the two writers themselves (though Sinyavsky profited later by being released early), but those dissenters who avoided arrest as a result of the Presidium's above-mentioned ban. At the same time the new leaders defused their most awkward single dissent problem of the previous year by allowing the writer Tarsis to make a trip abroad in February 1966 and then quickly depriving him of Soviet citizenship to prevent him returning. His exposé of psychiatric abuse, *Ward 7*, had generated widespread publicity when published abroad in March 1965, something which, at this time, guaranteed him against arrest. He had then exploited his situation to be an active patron of the dissenting young writers' group SMOG and to publicise their samizdat works through, *inter alia*, the unprecedented device of giving press conferences in his own flat.[26]

As the new leadership settled down in 1966, it turned its attention to devising a wider and more flexible range of laws for use against dissent. In particular it was worried by the increasing boldness of the schismatic Baptists and the Crimean Tatars, who had operated organised movements since 1961 and 1956, respectively. These large pressure groups had pioneered precisely those techniques of samizdat, demonstrations and sit-ins, and mass lobbying of local and central authorities which were now spreading to parts of the intelligentsia. And they were pressing the new leaders hard, in the hope that they might prove more responsive than Khrushchev had been.

POLICY TOWARD RELIGION

The regime's response was the well-known legislation of March and September 1966, aimed directly at the above-mentioned techniques. The March laws were so elastic that they could easily be used not only against religious proselytising but also against almost any religious activity which was not purely liturgical or inward. They immediately provoked strong protests from believers, including a Moscow demonstration by 600 Baptists from many parts of the country.[27]

But although the new laws were quickly used against the Baptists (about 170 being arrested in 1966)[28] and other denominations, and have been up to the present, we should note that the overall policy towards religion soon became, and has in essence remained, a rather less militant version of Khrushchev's.[29]

POLICY TOWARD 'MAINSTREAM' DISSENT

On another flank the Politburo found itself faced in autumn 1966 with determined protests by leading intellectuals and Old Bolsheviks against its September legislation (in particular against the new articles 190–1 and 190–3)[30] and by the appearance in Moscow of two substantial samizdat volumes whose young editors and in many cases well-established contributors had been more provoked than deterred by article 190–1.[31]

So in January 1967 it modified its ban on political arrests which might cause publicity. Over the next two months the young editors (Galanskov and Ginzburg) and some 50 other assorted dissenters in Moscow, Leningrad and the Ukraine were arrested.[32] But care was taken to select either young·and unestablished figures, or people unlikely to have links with Moscow dissenters and, through them, the outside world. The hope clearly was that publicity would be minimal and would anyway soon blow over. In 1966 reprisals had been eschewed against the numerous writers and intellectuals who had protested over Sinyavsky and Daniel.[33] And now, as the Fourth Writers' Union Congress of May 1967 approached, the regime held out a tempting vision to them by allowing a liberal writer to publish a call for a drastic and legally enforceable easing of the censorship.[34] It also gave the vision a slight touch of reality by, at this time, starting to allow both the publication in *Molodaya gvardiya* of thinly disguised non-Soviet, Russian nationalist writing, and the polemics which this provoked with *Novy mir* and other journals up to 1970. Its motives in doing this were doubtless mixed. The major purposes were probably to test how effectively a sanitised Russian nationalism could be used against the generally West-oriented liberal intelligentsia, and, more broadly, whether such nationalism could be adequately synthesised with Marxism–Leninism, thus producing a modified official ideology with wider popular appeal.[35]

CENSORSHIP POLICY AND SOLZHENITSYN'S OFFENSIVE

Whatever the case, there is no reason to believe that any substantial change of censorship policy was in fact in the offing. The general trend regarding any topic with political content was for a continued gradual tightening, a tendency which sharpened following the invasion of Czechoslovakia in 1968. This process did not prevent the further refining over the next years of a policy already developed under Khrushchev, namely the quite frequent printing of less orthodox writings in small-circulation or provincial publications, and in duplicated form.[36] Dissenters without too high a profile have often continued to have access to such outlets, the KGB being keen to stave off their unequivocal commitment to samizdat. Their more militant colleagues, by contrast, have found not only that all outlets are barred, but their previously published books and articles are systematically removed from libraries and from sale, by order of the chief censor.[37] An analogous policy has been applied to films and film-directors.[38]

By early 1967 Solzhenitsyn realised that despite the efforts of Tvardovsky and his other supporters the new leaders would almost certainly not – without unacceptable compromise on his part – publish any more of his work. So he decided to cut his losses, come out fully into the open, and put his persecutors on the defensive. In this way he could, he hoped, deter them from jailing him over the manuscripts confiscated in September 1965, and win enough time to complete important research and writing projects, notably the *Gulag Archipelago*.[39] His calculation proved correct. Indeed, because his domestic and foreign support proved greater than expected, he in fact won more time than he apparently at first thought possible.

His first aggressive thrust was his open letter to the Writers' Union Congress of May 1967 denouncing in strongly accusatory terms the literary censorship and the complaisant Union. When a hundred members and Western opinion openly endorsed his stand, he followed it up with further letters pressing (without real hope) for the publication of *Cancer Ward*.

This offensive produced greater pressure on Solzhenitsyn to

denounce his foreign supporters, and no let-up in the calculated campaign of slander against him by official speakers at public and private lectures which had begun in 1965.[40] But it did not bring reprisals against him or his supporters. In December, moreover, it was apparently decided at Politburo level, where the recent appearance of Svetlana Alliluyeva's memoirs had increased the leadership's nervousness about foreign publications, not to exclude the possibility of publishing *Cancer Ward*, and to ease the pressure on its author.[41]

OFFICIAL RESPONSES TO THE EMERGING HUMAN RIGHTS MOVEMENT AND PROTESTS OVER CZECHOSLOVAKIA

Solzhenitsyn's militant stand naturally emboldened the embryonic human rights movement. Its activists had already begun campaigning for a fair and open trial for Galanskov and Ginzburg and their associates, and in spring–summer 1967 they gave considerable support to Bukovsky and others tried for organising a demonstration.[42] The authorities, for their part, hesitated to take reprisals against the campaigners. In May Semichastny had been dismissed, reportedly for – *inter alia* – 'causing small matters to be blown up out of proportion'.[43] This presumably referred to his clumsy handling of cases like those of Tarsis, Solzhenitsyn, and Sinyavsky and Daniel. Not surprisingly then, his successor, Andropov, trod warily at first, reducing political arrests to a very low level and eschewing, until February 1968, any that might cause publicity abroad.[44]

To avoid appearing too weak, however, the authorities handed out a fairly firm sentence to Bukovsky and then, at a trial in January 1968 which mocked justice more than most, to Galanskov and Ginzburg. This provoked the maturing in early 1968 of a loosely organised but determined movement for human rights, with its own journal and growing mutual cooperation, based on an expanding network of, in particular, mathematicians, scientists, writers, literary intellectuals, Crimean Tatars, Jews, Ukrainians and Orthodox laypeople.[45]

This well-documented development produced alarm in the authorities, especially as it gained considerable publicity in the West and also coincided with the 'Prague Spring', which aroused widespread admiration and support among dissenters of different types. The Politburo was thus faced for the first time with open alliance-building among its critics, an activity which even became international as Western and Czechoslovak elements joined in, and as the Soviet dissenters increasingly deployed their most powerful single weapon – the broadcasting of their appeals, protests and other writings to their own country and Eastern Europe by Western radio-stations.

The response was cautious but systematic. The KGB embarked on applying to the nearly 1000 people who had signed various documents, the gradated, individual treatment described earlier. About three-quarters of them yielded to this pressure quite quickly, their dissent usually becoming henceforth either passive or covert. But as the rest could not be so easily intimidated, sanctions were applied: dismissal from the party for virtually all members; finely-graded rebukes and warnings for 35 members of the Writers' Union – after publication of the official intention to conduct expulsions had provoked a threat of mass resignations if this were carried out; widespread dismissals from jobs; administrative commitment of two leading figures to mental hospitals for brief periods; and – to show a touch of greater determination – the arrest of one relatively minor figure in Moscow and two in the Ukraine.[46] All these individual measures were reinforced by a press campaign against the defendants at the January trial – who were portrayed, as at the trial, as morally degenerate pawns of the emigré NTS and thereby of foreign intelligence – and their defenders.[47]

The publication abroad in June of Sakharov's first essay, and its broadcasting to the USSR, seem – because of the author's prestige and his support of the dissenters – to have confirmed for the worried authorities the wisdom of this rather cautious approach.[48] A few weeks later, however, as the decision to invade Czechoslovakia became irreversible, and was promptly perceived by certain dissenters, the Politburo decided with unusual speed that some of these people should be imprisoned at once. So Anatoly Marchenko was arrested on 28 July, within a few days of issuing an incisive warning about the invasion, to be quickly followed into prison by one of the Moscow friends who sprang to his defence and five Leningraders who were apparently drafting a statement to reinforce his warning.[49] Then, when the invasion had duly occurred and a group of leading dissenters demonstrated against it on Red Square the KGB could not avoid making their first arrests of people quite well known abroad since those of Sinyavsky and Daniel three years earlier.

But the volume of condemnation which the invasion provoked abroad and even at home dictated mild sentences for Litvinov and his friends, and very few serious reprisals against other domestic critics.[50] The Politburo decided now, however, to re-impose extensive jamming of broadcasts in Russian by those foreign radio-stations which had been freed of it by Khrushchev, notably the BBC, the Voice of America and Deutsche Welle, but not Radio Liberty. This financially expensive step was a direct, if only partially effective counter to, above all, the dissenters' recently developed method of circumventing censorship.[51] It could, moreover, be implemented without any substantial, clearcut political cost, at least in the short term.

In early 1969 the regime managed to 'normalise' the situation in Czechoslovakia and thus regain self-confidence. It therefore embarked on a much higher level of political arrests at home, to try to contain the dangerous developments of 1968. Among its main targets were the Initiative Group for the Defence of Human Rights in the USSR, the first free association of its type, formed in May, and the most visible linkmen between the human rights movement on the one hand and the Crimean Tatars and Orthodox Christian dissenters on the other.[52] None the less, the 'hard core' of the human rights movement was strong enough to continue expanding its network of informants and correspondents, and thereby also the *Chronicle*.

Another consequence of the regime's regained confidence was the decision to neutralise *Novy mir*, now that less hesitant political tightening-up was clearly required all round and the journal had become so vulnerable: the number of its contributors to have gone beyond the permissible now amounted to many more than just Solzhenitsyn, Sinyavsky and Daniel, and its editorial stance had been too openly sympathetic to the Prague Spring.

So, in a two-pronged action in November 1969–February 1970, Solzhenitsyn was expelled from the Writers' Union, and Tvardovsky and his close colleagues were purged from *Novy mir*.[53] More than this, the authorities showed in a number of ways that they were seriously considering ways of getting rid of Solzhenitsyn abroad.[54] His world repute was apparently now too great for them even to consider putting him on trial. But in 1970 the political cost of his expulsion was raised too high by the award to him of the Nobel Prize for Literature and by his statement that he could not go to Sweden to collect it as he would probably be barred from returning.[55]

CHANGE OF EMIGRATION POLICY FOR JEWS AND OTHERS

The year 1970 saw three further significant developments. First, the KGB created a 'Fifth Main Directorate' to coordinate more efficiently its many and varied efforts to combat dissent and allied phenomena.[56] It thus seemed to acknowledge both the seriousness and the non-temporary nature of the problem. Second, certain curbs were placed on officially published Russian nationalist writings – a subject unfortunately too complex and still too little researched to be discussed in any depth in this essay.[57]

And third, the problem of the Jewish emigration movement exploded. Such (to summarise what I have written elsewhere[58]) were the movement's militancy and skilful organisation, and, from 1970 on, the strength of its foreign lobbies, that the barring of its one aim by the regime soon provoked the formation of underground groups and then a planned attempt to hi-jack an aeroplane. The KGB replied with some three dozen arrests, quickly ferreting out the underground. But the first trial – of the would-be hi-jackers – produced such a storm abroad, when two of them were sentenced to death, that the appeal hearing was held with illegal haste, only six days later, and on 30 December 1970 the death sentences were – clearly at the Politburo's direction – commuted.[59]

With the approach of the 24th Party Congress of March–April 1971, which was to ratify the Politburo's decision to embark on detente with the US, the leaders were thus faced with a problem which was both serious and urgent. They had, in my view, little choice but to yield. The other options must have been unacceptable. To put thousands of Jews in camps was impossible for reasons of foreign and economic policy, given the strength of the American Jewish lobby. (It was anyway no longer, for a fully bureaucratised KGB, an easy task.) But to tolerate the *status quo*, in which the Jews were, with virtual impunity, providing an example of militancy to other oppressed groups in various cities, at the same time that anti-

Soviet publicity was building up abroad and even forcing Western communist parties to become critical of Soviet intransigence, was also impossible. So, on the eve of the congress, the gates were unlocked.[60] By 1979 200,000 Jews had passed through a safety-valve which had been effectively closed for almost fifty years, ever since Lenin and Dzerzhinsky encouraged or forced political opponents into emigration.

This was a radical change of policy, especially as it was soon applied not just to Jews, but also to Germans, Armenians and trouble-makers in various other categories, so that by 1979 the annual emigration rate had risen to about 70,000. The new policy had, as we have seen, been foreshadowed by the treatment of Tarsis and by official intentions regarding Solzhenitsyn. And even though the regime's prestige and self-confidence have since then been undermined by the fact that (a) large numbers of citizens want to leave what its propaganda machine says is the most just and democratic country in the world, and (b) this wish is constantly publicised abroad because the bureaucracy is slow with some applicants and bars others so as to discourage applications from economically valuable people, the policy has been applied with little wavering.

All this reinforces the view that the most important single variable in determining emigration policy towards any group (assuming it has a country willing to accept it) is the level of militancy and resourcefulness of the group's lobbying, demonstrating and samizdat circulation. Next most important is almost certainly the level of its foreign and domestic support, a variable with a direct influence on the first one.

It seems, to sum up, that the Soviet system can neither tolerate a high level of extra-systemic pressure group activity, nor, if the group has strong foreign support, can it suppress it. Emigration, however distasteful, is the only solution.

Not surprisingly, Soviet diplomacy and propaganda try to conceal all this and to make the foreign governments involved believe that emigration policy depends mainly on the pleasure of the Politburo. If, Soviet diplomats reportedly say, the foreign government gives minimum publicity to the emigration issue, and if it manages to get its country's mass media to do the same, and if it grants economic favours to the USSR, then emigration will be allowed. If, however, these conditions cease to be observed, the flow will be sharply cut back. This line appears to have had considerable success *vis-à-vis* the Israeli and West German governments, some-what less with the American.[61]

The above interpretation of emigration policy can, I believe, be documented in detail. But this would require three lengthy case-studies, based in part on careful study of Israeli, West German and American sources. Here, space permits little more than a bald statement of the interpretation.

STRIKES AT MAINSTREAM DISSENTERS AND MINORITY NATIONALISM

During 1971 the substance of the Soviet–American detente package was negotiated. President Nixon's visit to Moscow to sign the agreements was then set for May 1972. The most important of a number of goals on the Soviet side was, in my view, economic advantage. The label 'detente', or (the Soviet term) 'relaxation of tensions', was designed mainly for Western consumption, and was not meant to imply to Soviet citizens the onset of ideological coexistence or milder KGB methods. To thrust home this point and to stress that the relaxation of tensions would, in fact, involve an 'intensification of the ideological struggle', the Politburo acted in late 1971 and early 1972 to tighten political control all round.

Partly because it was reviewing and tightening its nationalities policy in anticipation of the 50th anniversary of the formation of the USSR in December 1972, one of its targets was lax political control, and crime and corruption, in certain union republics. In Georgia the main emphasis was on crime and corruption, which had long ago reached the top of the political apparatus. First party secretary Mzhavanadze was removed and a reported 25,000 arrests carried out.[62] In Lithuania, increased pressure on Catholic dissent pro-voked the opposite of what was sought – the sudden development of a broadly-based movement for national and religious rights.[63] But in the Ukraine the arrest of about a hundred activists successfully snuffed out the *Ukrainian Herald*, a samizdat journal partially modelled on the *Chronicle* and tolerated by party leader Shelest for two years. Shelest and a large part of the party – state apparatus were then purged in 1972–3 for the sins of softness on bourgeois nationalism or involvement in corruption. The drastic treatment of the Ukrainian dissenters, who were mostly given heavy sentences, involved a negligible short-term political cost, as the outside world knew little about them and paid scant attention.[64]

The mainstream dissent movement had in 1970–1 been steadily developing its contacts, and in this way extending its coverage of specially acute human rights issues in the *Chronicle* and related samizdat publications. While from time to time the KGB arrested and tried contributors and editors, new activists regularly replaced them.

This, plus the 'detente' considerations discussed above, formed the background to an important Politburo decision reportedly taken at the end of December 1971: to instruct the KGB to close down the *Chronicle* (and also, as we have seen, the *Ukrainian Herald*). The story of how this was eventually achieved at the end of 1972, if only temporarily, for 18 months, and of how Sakharov and Solzhenitsyn filled the gap in the face of a virulent official onslaught, has been told elsewhere.[65] What need to be stressed here are the following points: (a) the operation against the *Chronicle* would probably not have succeeded if the West had protested less weakly, and if the KGB had not managed to 'break' two key figures, Yakir and Krasin; (b) the level of Western protests in September–October 1973 about the apparent intention to arrest or deport Sakharov and Solzhenitsyn, about political abuse of psychiatry, and about Soviet repression generally, clearly shook the Politburo profoundly;[66] (c) the latter was forced to change its policy on Sakharov for fear of losing the scientific and economic fruits of detente, and to make do henceforth with KGB harassment and threats, sometimes on the life of his family and himself;[67] (d) it delayed executing its intention to deport Solzhenitsyn, already delayed for a second time in March–April 1972, until circumstances became easier in February 1974: deportation was possible in principle because his foreign lobby had less relation than Sakharov's to the fruits of detente;[68] (e) it modified its policy on political psychiatry by – to simplify the conclusions of a detailed case-study[69] – banning its use in any case which was likely to generate significant publicity abroad; and (f) it ended the KGB's drive against mainstream dissent, diverting that organisation's main energies to tightening control in quarters which would attract less attention in the outside world – as discussed below.

The close coordination of the start of the 'detente crack-down' in January 1972 shows clearly in the timing of its key components. *Pravda* heralded it on 13 January with an article about the East–

West ideological conflict which divided dissenters into two categories: ideologically unstable individuals and those who wanted to restore capitalism.[70] Between 11 and 15 January arrests and searches were carried out at 35 homes in Moscow, Leningrad, Kiev, Lvov, Novosibirsk, Vilnius and Uman.[71] And on 14 January new, harsher regulations were issued by the MVD for prisoners in camps (though not published). These were clearly aimed in part at trying to prevent the by now regular smuggling of political prisoners' appeals and other writings out of the camps to the *Chronicle* circles in Moscow; and in part at further undermining the prisoners' health and morale.[72] These aims were advanced still more by additional regulations, also unpublished, issued in December 1977.[73]

LEGISLATIVE AND ADMINISTRATIVE MEASURES AGAINST DISSENT

1972 also saw other legislative and administrative measures directed at dissenters and would-be emigrants. Soon after Nixon departed from Moscow, with the détente agreements safely signed, a decree was passed imposing an education tax on emigrants. A well-educated person had to pay about 20,000 roubles, the equivalent of his total income over (depending on his salary) five to ten years. The tax was presumably a concession to hard-liners, and was probably agreed on in 1971 at the time of the decision to allow emigration, but held back until after Nixon's visit. However, it provoked much bad publicity and contributed heavily to the framing of the Jackson–Vanik amendment. Soon therefore – though it was not repealed for reasons of face-saving – the authorities ceased to apply it.[74]

Another decree provided for the issuing of written warnings to individuals whose civic activities displeased the KGB. This was not published, but quickly began to be applied to dissenters.[75]

And an unpublished order of the Minister of Communications, which leaked into the *Chronicle*, had the clear if not explicit purpose of giving some legal sanction to phone-tapping: 'The use of the telephone communication system . . . for purposes contrary to the interests of the state or to public order is prohibited.'[76]

These measures were only the start of a steady flow of broadly-related legal changes which continued through the 1970s. In 1974, for example, the residence regulations were tightened to make it possible to bar political prisoners sentenced under article 190–1 from settling in or near major cities on release.[77] In 1975 and 1977 the law on 'parasitism' was tightened (in two stages) to make it more easily applicable to dissenters who are dismissed from their jobs and then barred from obtaining others.[78] In 1977 and 1978 the legal controls over printing-presses, duplicators, etc. were tightened in two stages.[79] In 1978 a comprehensive new law on citizenship was promulgated, providing *inter alia* a firmer legal basis for depriving of citizenship people 'who defame the lofty title of citizen of the USSR'.[80] And in 1975 and 1977, respectively, a comprehensive new law on religion and the new Soviet Constitution were adopted.[81]

We should also note here that, if we leave aside a marginal change for the better in the 1971 revision of the 'Directives on the Immediate Hospitalization of Mentally Ill Persons who Represent a Social Danger' – a revision which has had no apparent effect on official practices[82] – there appears to have been no domestic legislation since Khrushchev's fall which substantially and unambiguously improves the situation for dissenters.[83]

However, in autumn 1973, as the regime pursued its efforts to bring about a European security conference, it demonstrated concern for its international image in several ways concerning human rights. It ratified the two UN Covenants on human rights,[84] freed of jamming the radio stations which had been subjected to it since 1968,[85] and, while setting up a monopolistic copyright agency for Soviet and foreign authors, joined the Universal Copyright Convention. The last move, however, was immediately seen as more threatening than helpful to dissenters,[86] and the first as being welcome but of little practical use, as the Soviet authorities could not in practice be made accountable under the Covenants. The only real concession concerned jamming, although, being a purely administrative change, it could, as experience had shown, easily be reversed.

POLICY TOWARDS MAINSTREAM DISSENT FROM 1974

For the mainstream human rights movement the years 1974–6 saw relatively few serious losses and an impressive growth in the *Chronicle*, which extended its coverage to all the known, openly-dissenting groups in the country. The regime was almost continuously on the defensive. Its humiliating retreat of autumn 1973 had been visible to the whole population, as the prolonged media vilification of Sakharov and Solzhenitsyn had made their names, and official intentions towards them, known throughout the country. Further incentive to avoid bad publicity was provided by the Soviet leaders' pursuit of MFN status and, much more important, large quantities of subsidised credits from the Americans. To this end they grudgingly acquiesced in the Jackson–Vanik amendment, using a complex formula whereby the US side announced the fact in October 1974 and then allowed them to appear to deny it. When the Stevenson amendment quickly followed, suddenly cutting by four-fifths the quantity of subsidised credits promised since 1972 by Nixon and Kissinger, they were unpleasantly confronted with the economic price to be paid for Americans' dislike of their regime.[87] But although they had now, in January 1975, to save some face by abrogating the Soviet–American Trade Agreement, they could still not afford to tighten the screws on mainstream dissent, as at last they had secured agreement to one of their main foreign policy aims – a European security conference. Prior to and during this, it was essential to keep their international image on human rights as respectable as possible. This requirement then remained in force *after* the signing of the Helsinki Final Act in August, as persistent Western diplomacy had given the Act a substantial human rights content, and as a follow-up conference was to review compliance with the act in only two years' time.

The pressures increased further when, in October, the award to Sakharov of the Nobel Peace Prize was announced: the regime felt constrained to limit itself to another virulent press campaign against him, lasting two months, and a severe sentence on his friend Kovalyov, imposed during the prize award ceremony in December. As, however, Kovalyov was not known abroad, the authorities had probably planned to punish him quite harshly anyway.[88]

In any case the trial also served to compensate somewhat for the regime's direct, if of course unacknowledged capitulation to an effectively escalated Western campaign to free Leonid Plyushch from a prison mental hospital. The campaign reached its apogee in late October 1975, when the French Communist Party felt compelled to join it, and Plyushch was freed in January.[89] Similar, but much less powerful campaigns were sufficient to extract Valentin Moroz, Pyotr Starchik and Vladimir Borisov from the mental institutions they were put into in, respectively, May,

September and December 1976. Borisov's internment of ten weeks was the longest.[90]

From late 1973 to late 1976 the main action for the KGB had been against individuals not endowed with actual or potential foreign lobbies: first, starting in November 1973, it had arrested members of the Lithuanian and Armenian national movements, then – to name the main groups – Germans, Russian nationalists, Georgians, Crimean Tatars, Baptists, Pentecostals and young Orthodox intellectuals. It had also severely harassed, with a few arrests, a newer category of dissent – 'alternative culture' groups in Moscow and Leningrad, many of whose members were Christians.[91]

December 1976 proved to be a policy turning-point for several quite obvious reasons. First, though, there was a diversion: Bukovsky was suddenly freed from prison and exchanged for the Chilean communist leader Corvalan. This must have seemed to the Politburo a convenient way of showing practical concern for imprisoned communists, and at the same time presenting a more humane face to the West when it had in fact just decided to launch a big new crack-down. It overlooked, however, the effective admission that it did in fact hold political prisoners, and it also established beyond doubt its readiness to barter these prisoners in diplomatic trading.[92]

Belief that this was the case had arisen in 1974 when Silva Zalmanson and Simas Kudirka were released after serving less than half of their sentences, just when Soviet efforts to obtain MFN status and subsidised credits from the USA were at their height.[93] A subsequent case was that of the Jewish doctor Mikhail Shtern. An international tribunal chaired by the chief American prosecutor at Nuremberg, Telford Taylor, was due to review his case in Holland in March 1977. At first the President of the USSR Supreme Court told the Soviet Association of Jurists 'to organize counter-propaganda'. But then Shtern was suddenly released, after serving only a third of his sentence, on the eve of the tribunal.[94]

The practice of using prisoners as diplomatic pawns became still more explicit in 1979 when, at tactical moments in the Soviet campaign to get American agreement to SALT-2, first a group of five imprisoned Jews was released a little early and allowed to emigrate, then the same happened with a more 'choice' and varied group of five, all of whom had powerful lobbies in the USA and elsewhere: Kuznetsov and Dymshits a mainly Jewish one, Vins a

mainly Christian one, and Moroz a mainly Ukrainian one;
Ginzburg had three overlapping lobbies, organised by Christians,
supporters of the Soviet 'Helsinki movement', and the
Solzhenitsyns. While the first four had served half their sentences,
or a little more, Ginzburg had served only a quarter of his. This
showed how far the Politburo's earlier inhibitions about trading its
political prisoners had evaporated. It also held out hope to other
prisoners, while simultaneously causing non-imprisoned dissenters
to feel an additional vulnerability regarding their own possible
arrest and exploitation as hostages.[95]

A new crack-down on mainstream dissent presumably became
inevitable soon after the 'Civic Group to Assist the Implementation
of the Helsinki Agreements in the USSR' was formed in Moscow in
May 1976, and the group, headed by the Yury Orlov, proved to be
vigorous. The KGB reacted at once to the group's formation, issued
a formal warning to Orlov to stop his 'anti-constitutional activity',
and publicised it.[96] However, with the Belgrade review conference
only a year away, the Politburo apparently had second thoughts
about acting severely and decided it would be more prudent merely
to have the group closely watched by the KGB. Soon the latter
presumably reported that the group had compiled and successfully
publicised numerous reports documenting Soviet violations of the
human rights provisions of the Final Act, and then that sister groups
had sprung up in early November in Lithuania and the Ukraine. In
December the Politburo clearly resolved that this expanding
'Helsinki movement' was already harming the Soviet position for
Belgrade and would do so much more in the coming months. So it
ordered the KGB into action.

The new policy was later communicated to a closed conference
for editors of newspapers and journals organised by the Propaganda
Department of the Central Committee. A summary of the speaker's
talk leaked to the *Chronicle*. He said in part:

> The editors of newspapers and journals receive numerous
> demands from Soviet people that, at last, firmness be shown and
> the dissidents silenced. In this connection it has been decided to
> imprison fifty of the most active dissidents and take a tough line
> with their associates. It is time to show strength and not take
> notice of the West.[97]

The KGB struck its first heavy blow, at the Ukrainian group, on

24 December (before the newly-elected President Carter had spoken out about human rights); it followed it up with a second, clearly co-ordinated strike at the Moscow group on 4 January; and opened its offensive against the Lithuanian group on 11 January. The moves were conducted in an aggressive way which usually indicates that arrests will follow within days, and it may be that Carter's speaking out at this time caused the Politburo to hesitate.[98] In any case, arrests did not start until 3 February, and although a press campaign of vilification was now underway and much KGB intimidation of individuals occurred, by the time the Belgrade conference opened in October only eleven members of the by now five Helsinki groups had been arrested (Georgian and Armenian groups were founded in January and April, respectively). As a result, all groups except the Georgian were still active, busily addressing reports, advice and appeals to the conference.[99]

Throughout this period Carter had followed up his first statement by exchanging friendly letters with Sakharov and receiving Bukovsky in the White House. His government had issued protests about some of the arrests and made it clear that it would not compromise on human rights in Belgrade.[100] The congressional Commission on Security and Co-operation in Europe had begun in January a series of public hearings on compliance with the Final Act, which were addressed by experts and recent émigrés like Bukovsky.[101] The American government's lead had also been followed by a number of other Western governments. As a result, in all probability, the Politburo's policy of December 1976 had to be severely modified, and did not therefore achieve its aim: only a quarter of the 50 'most active dissidents' were arrested, the others were not silenced, little Soviet strength was shown, and notice was, after all, taken of the West.

In 1978, after the Belgrade Conference was over, some heavy sentences were imposed on Orlov, Ginzburg, Shcharansky and other members of Helsinki groups.[102] But, as noted earlier, the Politburo began trading them as early as 1979, when it released Ginzburg and showed clear signs of putting others 'on sale'.

DISSENT POLICY – SOME GENERALISATIONS

After this chronological discussion of selected episodes and topics we may now try to generalise about dissent policy. This policy is, I believe, very central to Soviet policy as a whole, if more often implicitly than explicitly: Soviet leaders probably discuss it in any detail or frankness only rarely, accustomed as they are to suppressing their awareness of such unpleasant matters in the back of their minds, and doubtless, most of the time, in their subconscious; but unspoken assumptions about it probably play a considerable role in the policy-formation process regarding many areas of policy. One such assumption is the basic axiom that dissent must unquestionably be suppressed, an axiom based on 'traditional' practices dating from Lenin's time and reinforced by the fear that more liberal policies would make the USSR vulnerable to the sort of political processes which developed in Hungary in 1956 and Czechoslovakia in 1968. However real or unreal this fear may be, the centrality of dissent policy suggests that generalisations about it can best be deployed within a broad framework.

Soviet ideology being strongly teleological, there is an inescapable logic to the process whereby, as time goes on, theory leaves less and less room for the existence of any form of dissent. The nature of the 1977 Constitution and other recent ideological and legal developments makes it clear that Soviet law is having to follow in the wake of ideology, thus gradually reducing the tensions and contradictions between them. These developed as a result of Khrushchev's legal reforms moving the Soviet system, albeit tentatively, towards the rule of law, while his revamped ideology laid out the path to a utopian form of organic communism which has not, in its essentials, been renounced by his successors.

Thus ideology prescribes the natural withering of dissent, while law is used to block each new manoeuvre of dissent while the withering process proceeds. An MVD minister states that 'In the Soviet Union there is an objective absence of a basis for emigration as a social phenomenon',[103] while at the same time his ministry helps to devise and apply laws to impose an education tax, a renunciation-of-citizenship tax and an exit visa tax on would-be emigrants, and other laws to try to prevent those refused emigration (and others) from campaigning for their cause, to control the granting and removal of citizenship, and so on.

Khrushchev used the device of corrupt psychiatry to try to give credibility to his claim that dissent had withered away. His successors have added to it the device of emigration: if dissatisfied citizens who cannot easily be intimidated into passivity can be allowed (even encouraged by official anti-Semitism) quietly to emigrate, then not only is the KGB's immediate job of maintaining political control made easier, but also the regime can more easily sustain, to itself and the population, the illusion that there are no objective causes for social discontent: what the eye does not see. . . . Psychiatry and emigration, in fact, 'explain away' a lot of unpleasant facts. The further facts that many of the emigrants propagate abroad a negative image of the USSR, and few of them return to the USSR, is highly regrettable but secondary: the vital thing is to maintain political control and an appearance of legitimacy at home.

So much for the approach of the ideologically minded to dissent policy. What now of the input from pragmatism? The clear-thinking pragmatists appear to argue like this. The main aim is to maintain maximum political control in a situation where dissent is at least endemic and almost certainly spreading. To contain this situation (a) one must isolate the dissenters through imprisonment, exile abroad and other means, so that their example does not spread and encourage emulation; (b) as samizdat, international publicity and foreign radio render this isolation only partially feasible, one must make dissenters appear as unattractive as possible by smearing them in the mass media; (c) to prevent organised dissent from spreading to the working class, and thus becoming really dangerous, one must carefully avoid excessive oppression of the types which provoked mass riots and demonstrations in Novocherkassk and elsewhere in 1962, in Lithuania in 1972 and 1977, and in Georgia in 1978;[104] more generally, one must try to ensure a steady improvement in living standards; (d) but as economic growth is now dropping close to zero, and as the vast network of bureaucracies which runs the economy is so deeply entrenched in its ways as to be essentially unreformable, it will be necessary for the indefinite future to obtain regularly from abroad large quantities of grain and advanced technology, and cheap credits to pay for them; it will also be necessary to develop and exploit bi- and multilateral exchanges involving science, technology and other fields relevant to living standards; (e) it is therefore important not to offend too much the susceptibilities of the actual and potential sources of these goods, capital and knowhow; (f) one must therefore suppress bad publicity about the Soviet system by all possible means, including the intimidation of dissenters and foreign journalists,[105] the joining and manipulation of international organisations, the Finlandisation of foreign governments and mass media, etc.; (g) proceeding to longer-term policy goals, one must try to subvert, or at least Finlandise, all political systems which express the dissenters' values, and thereby undermine these systems' will to oppose communism (e.g. through their radio broadcasts), disillusion the admiring dissenters, and prove the truth of Soviet ideology;* finally, (h) to help achieve the goals listed under (g), to divert the attention of the Soviet people away from domestic failures and the potential appeals of the various dissenters, and to generate in them a patriotic, even chauvinistic pride which the regime can harness to increase its own legitimacy and discredit the dissenters, one must continue to build up, and progressively exploit, Soviet military might.

As should now be clear, the more ideological and the more pragmatic approaches to policy do not seem at present to be in serious conflict with each other.

THE LIMITS WITHIN WHICH DISSENT POLICY HAS VARIED

The data presented in this essay prompt the conclusion that the specifically dissent-related component in the policy just outlined has remained remarkably stable since 1964 (and indeed, though the Khrushchev period has been little discussed, since the mid-1950s). True, the authorities have felt it necessary to tighten political control every three to five years (if to varying degrees), but these operations have involved only temporary hardenings of policy application, not substantive changes in policy. The periods of tighter control have been late 1956 to 1957, 1961–2, summer 1965 to March 1967, 1968–9, 1972–3 and December 1976 to summer 1978.

If we consider also the number of dissenters sentenced in each year since 1968, as recorded in the far from complete coverage of the *Chronicle of Current Events* (which reported little, for example, about the Protestant sects until recent years), we find that this rough-and-ready method of measuring trends confirms the paucity of change. The highest figure is 102 for 1970 (many of them arrested in 1969), while the lowest is 24 for 1976.[106] But if we add in those people

---

* Increasingly often, it seems, Finlandisation is seen to be preferable, as successful subversion would threaten the vital economic infusions listed under (d); hence the Soviet support for De Gaulle, Pompidou and Giscard d'Estaing at successive French presidential elections.

forced into emigration since 1971 – usually under threat of heavy sentences if they refused to go – the range becomes roughly 40 to 102. The fact that the numbers have not risen, but have even declined somewhat from the peak of 1970 – despite the spread of dissent throughout the period – can be attributed (a) to the success of many dissent groups and movements in gradually mobilising support at home and, especially, abroad, and thus generating increasing publicity and pressure on the authorities; and (b) to the specific achievement of freer emigration.

The Politburo has in fact been forced to tolerate a gradually rising level of unpunished or weakly punished dissent. Since 1969, for example, the number of free associations (like the Helsinki groups) functioning independently of the authorities has steadily increased. Likewise with samizdat periodicals, of which almost 30 were coming out in 1979.[107] And since the early 1970s the practice of giving unofficial press conferences for foreign journalists in private flats has become commonplace: many seminars and a few international conferences have also been conducted in flats.

Official policy still lays down that all this should be either prevented or punished, and sometimes, when the Politburo agrees, it is. But more often, other policy imperatives – especially the need to avoid provoking foreign lobbies and generating bad publicity – take precedence. Perhaps partly to compensate for this frustrating state of affairs, the KGB has apparently been allowed since around 1976 to practise more covert violence than previously, but against unknown or little known dissenters: the number of murders and assaults involving such people and which the police fail to investigate has grown.[108]

Only one very substantial policy switch has occurred since the immediate post-Stalin changes – the decision of early 1971 to allow large-scale emigration. However, this can be seen to flow logically from the broad policy considerations outlined above, and thus simply underlines the consistency of their application. The only other policy changes of great substance have been the decisions in 1963 and 1973 to reduce the number of foreign radio stations subject to jamming, and the intermediate one to increase the number again. These have affected dissenters considerably, though somewhat less than might be thought: the jamming is far from fully effective, and it has never been removed from the one station which gives really extensive coverage to dissent matters, Radio Liberty.

POLICY INPUTS

We have often referred to various policy inputs in general terms, and sometimes more specifically. A systematic analysis of the subject would require, first, a considerably greater number of case studies of different aspects of dissent than we yet have, and second, a close examination of the dauntingly voluminous official Soviet publications relating to dissent in newspapers, journals and books. However, to record my mostly impressionistic conclusions to date, and thus perhaps encourage further research and debate, I have compiled the chart on page 185 (Figure 1). To a reader of this essay the chart largely speaks for itself. But a few further comments may be helpful.

Regarding the intra-societal environment, we should stress first the interaction – intellectual, sometimes 'tactical', often indirect – between some of the openly-dissenting groups and some of the covertly dissenting 'tendencies'. As for the 'more flexible officials' represented among the latter, from the economic sphere they came forward openly during the 'Liberman debate' of the mid-1960s, and it seems likely that they exist in the KGB (as they did in the Tsarist secret police) and in the diplomatic service: these organisations have to deal constantly with the consequences of the present policies, which cannot fail to strike some officials as dangerously negative.

Most of the party–state bureaucracy is probably 'centrist or neutral' on dissent policy simply because they have been trained in a long tradition – only briefly modified by Khrushchev – of uncritical obedience to orders from above. But some middle-level officials probably favour tighter control, perhaps because, unlike their superiors and inferiors, they are not involved in either its foreign policy implications or the problems of administering it on the ground. Ideological bureaucrats also seem to be hard-liners, as their work is greatly complicated by having to explain in lectures and articles the existence of so much unpunished dissent.[109]

As regards operational decisions on policy application, these appear to be taken on a day-to-day basis by the KGB, more important ones being referred to the administrative organs department of the Central Committee or even to the Politburo.

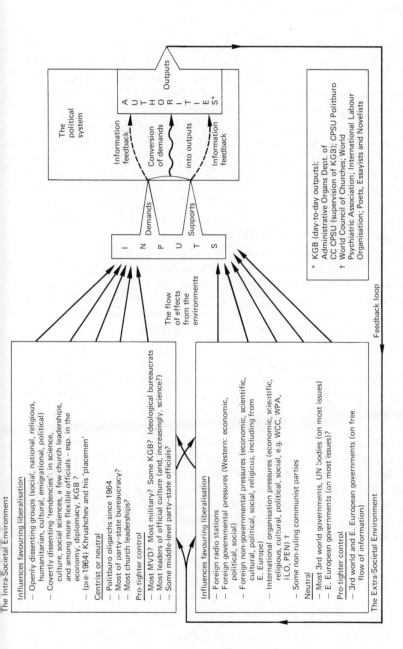

The Intra-Societal Environment

Influences favouring liberalisation
– Openly dissenting groups (social, national, religious, humanitarian, cultural, emigrational, political)
– Covertly dissenting 'tendencies': in science, culture, social sciences, a few church leaderships, and among more flexible officials – esp. in the economy, diplomacy, KGB ?
– (pre-1964) Khrushchev and his 'placemen'

Centrist or neutral
– Politburo oligarchs since 1964
– Most of party-state bureaucracy?
– Most church leaderships?

Pro-tighter control
– Most MVD? Most military? Some KGB? Ideological bureaucrats
– Most leaders of official culture (and, increasingly, science?)
– Some middle-level party-state officials?

Influences favouring liberalisation
– Foreign radio stations
– Foreign governmental pressures (Western: economic, political, social)
– Foreign non-governmental pressures (economic, scientific, cultural, political, social, religious, including from E. Europe)
– International organisation pressures (economic, scientific, religious, cultural, political, social, e.g. WCC, WPA, ILO, PEN) †
– Some non-ruling communist parties

Neutral
– Most 3rd world governments, UN bodies (on most issues)
– E. European governments (on most issues)?

Pro-tighter control
– 3rd world and E. European governments (on free flow of information)

The Extra-Societal Environment

The flow of effects from the environments

The political system

Demands
Supports

INPUTS

Information feedback

Conversion of demands into outputs

Information feedback

Outputs

A U T H O R I T I E S*

Feedback loop

* KGB (day-to-day outputs); Administrative Organs Dept. of CC CPSU (supervision of KGB); CPSU Politburo
† World Council of Churches; World Psychiatric Association; International Labour Organisation; Poets, Essayists and Novelists

FIGURE 1 Dissent in the USSR: the formation of official policy towards it (a tentative application of a chart in David Easton's *A Framework for Political Analysis*)

CONCLUSION

Policy towards dissent, and policy application, have changed remarkably little. The one big safety-valve which can easily be used – emigration – has been partially opened and is likely to stay so, even though it must eventually produce a back-lash accusing the leadership of provoking a deplorable drain of scientific, cultural, academic and moral capital. A much tougher policy seems precluded, under the present type of leadership, by, ultimately, (a) the strategy of placing a lot of economic reliance on the capitalist world in the hope of being able to put off economic and political reform indefinitely, and (b) the limits to the amount of Soviet oppression which the capitalist world finds tolerable. At present both these variables appear fairly stable, though the second shows a slight tendency to move in the direction unfavourable to the Soviets.

A radical change in dissent policy seems likely to occur only if a future leadership emerges which is bold enough either to embark on reform, as the Czechoslovaks did in the mid-1960s, or to set a lower priority on economic progress and pursue a strategy of no reform and little concern about capitalist economic support. In the former case a substantial easing of dissent policy would be probable, in the latter a sharp tightening.

But neither such change looks, on a five-to-ten year perspective at least, very likely. For while this preliminary study supports the view that a number of groups and 'tendencies' have some influence on policy-formation, if mostly at the margins, it also suggests that the macro-features of dissent policy, as of most other policy, are determined by a rather stable equilibrium of forces based on heavily entrenched and highly-conservative bureaucratic interests. In the longer term, however, the stability of this equilibrium seems likely to give way to instability, as the generally rigid and reactionary conservatism of the bureaucratic interests fails to adapt adequately to the inexorable pressures for social and economic change of which dissent in its many forms is a clear symptom.

NOTES

1. See Barrington Moore, Jr, *Injustice: the Social Bases of Obedience and Revolt* (London, 1978).
2. See Uriel Rosenthal, *Political Order: Rewards, Punishments and Political Stability* (Gravenhage, Netherlands, 1978).

3. See, for example, B. Ya. Kantorovich and I. A. Stepanov, *Antikommunizm: Sushchnost' i organizatsiya* [Nauka i tekhnika] (Minsk, 1979); S. T. Tsvigun, *Taynyi front* (Moscow, 1973); KGB General A. Malygin's article in *Molodoi Kommunist* (1969) no. 1; the article by Deputy Procurator-General of the USSR N. Zhogin in *Agitator* (1971) no. 2; the interview by Deputy Minister of Justice of USSR A. Ya. Sukharev in *Novoe vremya* (1976) no. 1; Assotsiatsiya Sovetskikh Yuristov, *Belaya kniga: svidetel'stva, fakty, dokumenty*, Yuridicheskaya literatura, (Moscow, 1979); leading article in *Pravda*, 11 February 1977; Vladimir Lysenkov, 'A Look at some "Dissidents"', *Soviet Weekly*, 30 October 1976; I. Aleksandrov, 'On Real and Imaginary Freedoms', *Pravda*, 20 February 1976; 'Provocation in the Mutualité', *Literaturnaya gazeta*, 27 October 1976; G. Kozlov, 'A Mission not of Good Will', ibid., 3 November 1976.

4. *Pravda*, 22 March 1977.

5. *A Chronicle of Current Events* (henceforth *Chronicle*), nos 1–51 (continuing), contains several hundred examples of this process. Nos 1–11 are contained in P. Reddaway, *Uncensored Russia: The Human Rights Movement in the Soviet Union* (London and New York, 1972), and nos 16–51 have been published by Amnesty International, London. Nos 1–15 are being made available by Routledge and Kegan Paul (London) on microfiches.

6. See for example L. Kvachevsky's conversation with KGB officers in *Chronicle* 34 (Russian edn by Khronika Press, New York).

7. See Michael Browne, *Ferment in the Ukraine* (London, 1971) pp. 231–3. A possible exception is R. Duzhyns'ky.

8. A marginal exception was Aida Skripnikova, against whom a 1962 sentence of banishment was enforced at the end of 1965. See M. Bourdeaux and X. Howard-Johnston, *Aida of Leningrad* (Reading, U.K., 1972) pp. 23–5.

9. Small exceptions here were three Tatars given one-year sentences for 'hooliganism' after being arrested in September 1965: E. Dzhemilev, R. Seidametov and Khairetdinova. See P. Dornan, *Reestr osuzhdyonnykh v bor'be za prava cheloveka v SSSR*, Spravochnik no. 78 (Research Dept, Radio Liberty, Munich, 1971) (covers 1953–71).

10. A samizdat list of Baptist prisoners dated June 1964 lists 174 then in prison. The sentences (given for 146 of them) indicate that about 100 of these 146 should still have been in captivity in December 1966, the date of the next available list. However, as only five in fact were, at least around 95 (and probably considerably more) must have been released early. The 1964 list appears in *Communist Exploitation of Religion, Hearing before the Subcommittee to Investigate the Administration of the Internal Security Act of the Committee on the Judiciary, U.S. Senate, 6 May 1966*, pp. 33–42, and in a modified form in M. Bourdeaux, *Religious Ferment in Russia* (London, 1968) pp. 211–29. The 1966 list is document AS 796 in *Sobranie dokumentov samizdata* (Radio Liberty, Munich, n.d.) vol. 14.

11. See Andrew Blane, 'A Year of Drift', *Religion in Communist Lands (RCL)*, 1974, no. 3, pp. 9–15.

12. Ann Sheehy, *The Crimean Tatars, Volga Germans and Meskhetians* (2nd edn, London, 1973) pp. 13–14.

13. M. Tatu, *Power in the Kremlin* (London, 1969) pp. 429–30.

14. A. Solzhenitsyn, *Bodalsya telyonok s dubom* (Paris, 1975) p. 112. This source

receives some confirmation from Roy Medvedev, *Politicheskii dnevnik* (Amsterdam, 1972) pp. 50–1, 244 (issues for June 1965 and June 1967).

15. The trial was widely reported each day in, especially, Soviet and British media.
16. Group of Ronkin and Khakhayev. See P. Reddaway, *Uncensored Russia: The Human Rights Movement in the Soviet Union* (London, 1972).
17. See V. Chornovil, *The Chornovil Papers* (Toronto, 1968).
18. See L. Labedz and M. Hayward (eds), *On Trial: The Case of Sinyavsky (Tertz) and Daniel (Arzhak)* (London, 1967).
19. See a vivid account in V. Bukovsky, *To Build a Castle* (London, 1978) pp. 198–204.
20. Tatu, op. cit., p. 487.
21. This concerned especially the writer V. Tarsis and his *Ward 7* (see Bukovsky, op. cit., pp. 192–5, and Bloch and Reddaway, *Russia's Political Hospitals: The Abuse of Psychiatry in the Soviet Union* (London, 1977) pp. 65–7); the student Evgeny Belov (ibid., pp. 68–70); and the literary scene as described in the Yugoslav press by M. Mihajlov in early 1965 (his articles appeared in book form in English as *Moscow Summer* (New York, 1965)).
22. Exceptions were six very young dissenters arrested in connection with the Moscow demonstration of 5 December 1965, four of whom were released after brief internments in mental hospitals (Yu. Vishnevskaya, O. Vorob'yov, L. Gubanov, S. Morozov); Bukovsky was held in mental institutions until July 1966, and V. Batshev was exiled for 5 years as a 'parasite'. In 1966 A. Dobrovolsky, Yu. Galanskov and V. Kuznetsov were briefly psychiatrically interned. V. Aidov and Ya. Berg were arrested in Moldavia in November 1966. Among Ukrainians the only exceptions were A. Shevchuk, S. Karavansky and N. Kachur (*Chronicle* 17). On these cases see Dornan, op. cit.
23. Solzhenitsyn, op. cit., p. 112. See also Bukovsky, op. cit., p. 182.
24. Tatu, op. cit., pp. 471–87.
25. Labedz and Hayward, op. cit.
26. See note 21.
27. See M. Bourdeaux and P. Reddaway, 'The Recent History of the Soviet Baptists', in M. Hayward and W. Fletcher (eds), *Religion and the Soviet State: a Dilemma of Power* (London, 1969) pp. 128–9; and M. Bourdeaux, *Faith on Trial in Russia* (London, 1971).
28. See the December 1966 list (note 10) and the August 1968 list in Rosemary Harris and Xenia Howard-Johnston, *Christian Appeals from Russia* (London, 1969) pp. 92–143.
29. See Trevor Beeson, *Discretion and Valour: Religious Conditions in Russia and Eastern Europe* (London, 1974) chs 2–4; and a relatively frank assessment of the religious situation by a leading state official, which leaked into samizdat in 1976, *Chronicle* 41, pp. 125–7.
30. See Pavel Litvinov (ed.), *A Demonstration in Pushkin Square* (London, 1969).
31. The volumes were *Phoenix '66*, ed. by Galanskov, and the *White Book* on the Sinyavsky–Daniel trial, ed. by Ginzburg. For bibliographical references, see Reddaway, op. cit., p. 443, note 7, and p. 441, note 2.
32. Twenty-one of these belonged to a revolutionary Christian underground group based in Leningrad (*Chronicle* 1), and eight to the underground Ukrainian National Front (*Chronicle* 17, pp. 64–6).

33. Very minor reprisals were taken in two cases. See Labedz and Hayward, op. cit., pp. 236–7, 303–4.

34. A. Bek in *Zhurnalist* (1967) no. 2, p. 15, as quoted in a little known, but very valuable book, Martin Dewhirst and Robert Farrell (eds), *The Soviet Censorship* (Metuchen, N.J., 1973) p. 6.

35. For a discussion of this episode see Alexander Yanov, *The Russian New Right: Right-Wing Ideologies in the Contemporary USSR* (Institute of International Studies, University of California, Berkeley, Calif., 1978) ch. 3.

36. See M. Dewhirst, 'Soviet Russian Literature and Literary Policy', in Archie Brown and Michael Kaser (eds), *The Soviet Union since the Fall of Khrushchev* (2nd edn, London, 1978) esp. pp. 182, 186.

37. Several of the chief censor's orders have leaked into samizdat. See, e.g., those concerning Solzhenitsyn (*Chronicle* 34, p. 91) and Galich and others (*Chronicle* 35, pp. 156–9).

38. See Dewhirst and Farrell, op. cit., pp. 107–20; *Politicheskii dnevnik*, 1, p. 253; *Chronicle* 19, pp. 196–7.

39. Solzhenitsyn, op. cit., pp. 154–83.

40. See ibid., pp. 184–246, and the section 'The Struggle Intensifies' in L. Labedz, *Solzhenitsyn: A Documentary Record* (Harmondsworth, 1972).

41. Solzhenitsyn, op. cit., p. 217.

42. See Litvinov, op. cit.

43. *Politicheskii dnevnik*, 1, p. 243.

44. Chornovil was arrested in August 1967, but as his book had not yet appeared (in the West) he was virtually unknown. He got only 3 years, and even this was halved, after his book came out, to eighteen months.

45. Reddaway, op. cit.

46. I. Burmistrovich in Moscow and O. Nazarenko and V. Karpenko in Ukraine were those arrested. On all this see ibid., pp. 67–70, 80–90, 288–90, and *Polit. dnevnik*, 1, pp. 303–6.

47. Ibid., pp. 300–4; Reddaway, op. cit., p. 76.

48. The appearance of Sakharov's essay may well have contributed to the relative moderation of a big attack in *Lit. gazeta*, 26 June 1968, on Solzhenitsyn two weeks later.

49. Reddaway, op. cit., pp. 191–2, 381.

50. Ibid., chs 4 and 5, and N. Gorbanevskaya, *Red Square at Noon* (London, 1972).

51. On the explosion of samizdat at this time, see Reddaway, op. cit., especially the Introduction and chs 17 and 18.

52. Ibid., chs 6, 7, 12 and 16.

53. See Solzhenitsyn, op. cit., pp. 279–309; Labedz, op. cit., pp. 205–31; Zhores Medvedev, *Ten Years after Ivan Denisovich* (New York, 1973) chs 17 and 19.

54. Solzhenitsyn, op. cit., pp. 319–21.

55. Ibid., pp. 313–35; Labedz, op. cit., pp. 235–59.

56. On the structure of this chief directorate and its relation to other parts of the KGB structure, see John Barron, *KGB: The Secret Work of Soviet Secret Agents* (New York, 1974) ch. 4.

57. But see Yanov, op. cit. A study of contemporary Russian nationalism, written from a more sympathetic standpoint by John Dunlop of Oberlin College, is nearing completion.

58. Reddaway in Brown and Kaser, op. cit., pp. 139–41, 148.
59. *Chronicle* 17; Leonard Schroeter, *The Last Exodus* (New York, 1974) chs 9–11.
60. Ibid., ch. 22.
61. This judgment about the West German and Israeli governments is based partly on my private talks with some of their official advisers, and partly on study of the public record. See also ibid., pp. 188–92, and passim.
62. See my article (mostly on official manipulation of the Georgian Church) in *RCL* (1975) no. 4–5, esp. p. 15.
63. See almost every issue of the *Chronicle* since no. 17. Two book-length studies of Lithuanian dissent have just appeared, by M. Bourdeaux and V. Stanley Vardys, but have not yet been available to me.
64. See *Chronicles* 24–28 and L. Plyushch, *History's Carnival: A Dissident's Autobiography* (New York and London, 1979) chs 17–18.
65. Solzhenitsyn, op. cit., pp. 371–406; A. D. Sakharov, *Sakharov Speaks* (London, 1974) pp. 165–230; Reddaway, in Brown and Kaser, op. cit., pp. 133–5, 148–50.
66. As note 65.
67. See, e.g., *Chronicle* 35 and *Chronicle* 44, pp. 197–98.
68. Solzhenitsyn, op. cit., pp. 411–80; *Chronicle* 32. It is possible that Sakharov is right in thinking that the Politburo has decided he cannot be deported because it thinks his knowledge of Soviet nuclear matters could still help the West. In this case, the strength of his foreign lobby is protecting him only from arrest. However, in early 1977 an official book *On the Deportation of A. D. Sakharov* was nearing completion. See *Chronicle* 44, p. 185.
69. Bloch and Reddaway, op. cit., esp. Ch. 10.
70. V. Bolshakov [as quoted in F. Barghoorn, *Détente and the Democratic Movement in the USSR* (New York, 1976) p. 184].
71. *Chronicle* 24.
72. *Chronicle* 32, pp. 115–16.
73. *Chronicle* 51, pp. 45–7, See also 14 other directives of 1968–77, almost all secret, summarised in *Chronicle* 46, pp. 57–9, and 48, pp. 44–5.
74. For the decree introducing it see *A Chronicle of Human Rights in the USSR (CHRU)*, (1973) no. 1, p. 74. For sharp samizdat responses see *Chronicle* 27, pp. 340–1.
75. *Chronicle* 32, pp. 64–7.
76. *Chronicle* 27, pp. 337–8.
77. *Chronicle* 34, pp. 92–3.
78. *Chronicle* 37, pp. 58–60, and 47, pp. 173–4.
79. See *Vedomosti Verkhovnogo Soveta i Pravitel'stva Estonskoy SSR* (1977) no. 37, resolution no. 436, and a commentary in *Radio Liberty Research Bulletin*, Munich, RL 8/78, 9 January 1978 (it is not clear if similar legislation has been introduced throughout the USSR); and *Vedomosti Verkhovnogo Soveta SSSR* (1978) no. 37, decree no. 587. More generally, see Dietrich Loeber's heavily documented paper, 'Samizdat under Soviet Law', in D. D. Barry, W. E. Butler and G. Ginsburgs, *Contemporary Soviet Law* (The Hague, 1976).
80. See the commentary on this law by G. Ginsburgs in *CHRU* (1979) no. 33.
81. For commentaries see W. Sawatsky, 'The New Soviet Law on Religion', *RCL* (1976) no. 2, pp. 4–10, and Patrick O'Brien, 'Constitutional Totalitarianism', *Survey* (1977–8) no. 104

82. See full text, printed as an appendix in A. Podrabinek, *Punitive Medicine* (Ann Arbor, Michigan, due to appear in late 1979). On the lack of effect see ibid. and Bloch and Reddaway, op. cit.

83. A possible exception is the dismantling of Khrushchev's anti-parasite legislation, but this was partially offset by the tightening of article 209. See note 78.

84. See *CHRU* (1973) no. 4–5.

85. Solzhenitsyn, op. cit., p. 381. This occurred on 13 September 1973.

86. See testimony of Robert Bernstein in *Basket III: Implementation of the Helsinki Accords, Hearings before the Commission on Security and Co-operation in Europe*, vol. III, 19, 24, and 25 May 1977, US Government Printing Office, no. 92–301, 1977, pp. 152–64; also references given in *Chronicle* 32, p. 181, note 44.

87. See J. S. Berliner and F. D. Holzman, 'The Soviet Economy: Domestic and International Issues', in William E. Griffith (ed.), *The Soviet Empire: Expansion and Détente* (Lexington, Mass., 1976) esp. pp. 134–8.

88. See *Chronicle* 38, pp. 70–8 (on Sakharov) and 78–91 (on Kovalyov).

89. *Chronicle* 38–40, and T. Khodorovich (ed.), *The Case of Leonid Plyushch* (London, 1976).

90. See *Chronicle* 40–1 (Moroz), 42–3 (Starchik), 43–4 (Borisov).

91. On all these developments, see *Chronicles* 32–47, passim.

92. *Chronicle* 43.

93. *Chronicle* 33.

94. *Chronicle* 44.

95. On all this see *CHRU* (1979) no. 34.

96. *Chronicle* 40.

97. *Chronicle* 44, p. 185.

98. *Chronicle* 43, pp. 52–3; 44, pp. 5–11, 76–7 (pp. 39–43 report the mysterious circumstances of a metro explosion on 8 January 1977 which many dissenters suspect may have been a specially-timed KGB provocation to assist the campaign against the Helsinki groups).

99. *Chronicle* 44–6. The Ukrainians Rudenko and Tikhy were quickly given severe sentences in June in an unsuccessful KGB attempt to intimidate the groups. These two were chosen as they were leading members of the Ukrainian group but not known abroad.

100. *Chronicle* 44, *CHRU* (1977) no. 25.

101. Volumes I–VII of the series of which details are given in note 86 covered the hearings up to 11 July 1978.

102. *Chronicle* 50, 51.

103. UPI report from Moscow, quoting published interview by Deputy Minister of Internal Affairs B. Shumilin, *International Herald Tribune*, 20 April 1979.

104. On Lithuania see *Chronicle* 27 and 47; on Georgia see *Chronicle* 49, pp. 85–7; on Novocherkassk see Plyushch, op. cit., pp. 58–60, and A. Boiter, 'When the Kettle Boils Over', *Problems of Communism* (1964) no. 1, pp. 33–42.

105. A case-study yet to be done in depth is the Soviet treatment (and often expulsion) of foreign journalists. David Bonavia, *Fat Sasha and the Urban Guerrilla* (New York, 1973) provides some perceptive first-hand insights.

106. See L. Alekseyeva's data in *CHRU* (1978) no. 29.

107. Listed in P. Reddaway's letter in *Index on Censorship* (1979) no. 5.

108. See for example Sakharov's reports in *Chronicle* 44, pp. 193–5.

109. Middle–level and ideological officials are regarded by Roy Medvedev as specially 'neo-Stalinist'. See his *Kniga o sotsialisticheskoi demokratii* (Amsterdam, 1972) p. 58.

10 Some Concluding Observations

T. H. Rigby

When the Bolsheviks took power in 1917 they did so with the goal of building a socialist and ultimately a communist society.[1] Seeing themselves as the agents of an inexorable world historical process, they felt authorised to establish a regime of unlimited power, which they termed 'the dictatorship of the proletariat'. The exercise of this power in pursuit of the goal which constituted its sole justification was not to be hampered by any laws or institutions, however useful or necessary such might prove as instruments of their mission. Although the policies they would adopt to further the goal of communism were seen as being in the ultimate interests of the people, the latter's inevitably faulty perception of their ultimate interests ruled out the acceptance of any machinery of government that would make 'temporary' majorities of popular representatives the arbiters of policy. The wielders of this revolutionary power, however, did not see this as implying arbitrary rule, possessing as they did a strong sense of their responsibility to history. It was precisely because of *this* concept of responsibility that they could not tolerate another which equated it with *responsiveness* to the current demands of popular majorities, which they saw as being in the profoundest sense irresponsible.

Since it was their mission totally to transform society, all spheres of life had to be brought under conscious direction and management, and the logic of this was the establishment of hierarchical structures of command answerable to the supreme leadership for each and every branch of social activity and bound together by the machinery of the party into a single 'mono-organisational system'.

The creation of such a system was not completed overnight, nor was its necessity clearly perceived when the Bolsheviks assumed power. As Neil Harding shows in this volume, Lenin (and Bukharin too) appeared to believe at first that a 'commune' form of society and polity, with centralised direction limited to setting the overall course, would emerge from the revolution, although the illusoriness of any such expectations became apparent to them both before the civil war was over. In practice, during these early years the infant revolutionary regime advanced with giant strides towards the creation of a mono-organisational society. The concessions to market forces under the New Economic Policy represented only a partial and temporary setback to this progress, which was resumed with a vengeance in the late 1920s, its consummation coinciding with the consolidation of Stalin's personal dictatorship. Not only in the economy, but in all areas of endeavour, including the arts and intellectual life generally, existing autonomies were eliminated bit by bit as service to programmes held to conduce to the ultimate goal of communism displaced other standards of value and their implementation was entrusted more and more exclusively to official hierarchies. Richard Taylor's chapter traces the early phases of this process in detail in one particular field of the arts, while Anthony Kemp-Welch has shown how the actual processes of *Gleichschaltung* in any particular field and the terms in which the latter was harnessed to the regime's purposes often depended largely on the initiatives of ambitious groups and individuals within it, who perceived the overall intent of Stalin and his entourage and rode to power through promoting acceptable formulas to implement it.

The socio-political system established in these years persists in its essentials to the present day. Power is heavily concentrated in the hands of a small self-perpetuating oligarchy managing all social activities through an elaborate complex of centralised bureaucratic organisations, and this determines the character of the policy-making process and of 'politics' understood as the competitive promotion of individual and group ends. Furthermore the authority of this system in its day-to-day operation is still principally legitimated on the same grounds as legitimated its creation: the achievement of communism. That is to say, what citizens are required to do by officials of the various organisations to which they are subject in different aspects of their lives is claimed to be incumbent on them *because* it conduces to communism. Whether it really does is not of course the point. Social activity focuses on the performance of *tasks* assigned by one's hierarchical superiors in pursuance of sub-goals held to contribute to the final goal of communism. The structure of authority, power and policy-making is thus analogous to that of an army at war or a firm whose survival depends on the production and marketing of its goods. It is intended to be a rationally devised and operating system but the predominant criterion of rationality is that of conformity not to the rules through which it operates but to the achievement of the sub-goals and tasks passed down from the supreme leadership. It is in this sense that I have defined it as a 'goal-rational' rather than a 'rational–legal' system of authority. This predominance of ends over means is no longer expressed through the doctrine of the 'dictatorship of the proletariat', but remains entrenched through the formulas and processes designed to ensure the 'leading role' of the party, in practice of the party leadership, which proclaims its intent to operate through the institutions and rules of the state and of 'voluntary' organisations, but retains a free hand in determining the shape of these rules and institutions and the content of their activity, even to the extent of abolishing or bypassing institutions or requiring or condoning departures from their rules where this is deemed necessary for the achievement of their assigned tasks.

The Soviet authority structure, however, like those of other complex societies, is not a 'pure' type, and its predominant goal-rational component is reinforced and permeated by other components of a rational–legal, traditional and charismatic character, which in certain spheres and certain times and circumstances have assumed considerable salience and efficacy. The case of one such component, the Stalin cult, has been closely examined by Graeme Gill in this volume. That the emergence of this cult and of the personal dictatorship to which it at first conduced and later reflected should have coincided in time with the full flowering of the mono-organisational system raises the question whether there is a causal connection between the two. Although some of the material in both Gill's and Kemp-Welch's chapters is suggestive in this connection, we have not directly confronted this question in the present volume. Certainly, as Archie Brown's chapter on the changing power of the General Secretary within the ruling oligarchy reminds us, a personal dictator is not essential to the *persistence* of the mono-organisational system.

What, then, are the minimal conditions for a radical modification of this system, and in what area of life might one expect such a radical modification to be initiated, if it is to be initiated at all? The regime's evident success in suppressing unorthodox opinions gives

little encouragement to believe that this will come from developments in the sphere of ideas and values, although such developments
could contribute to a climate in which change would be easier. One
does not need to take a Marxian view of the primacy of the
economic to suspect that the latter is likely to prove crucial in this
connection. Alec Nove's analysis in Chapter 5 makes it clear that no
radical modification of the mono-organisational system could
eventuate as long as the centrally planned and directed economy
remains. This was also understood by some of the Czechoslovak
Communist reformers of the 1960s, although they perceived the
connection, as it were, from the other end. That is to say, having
became convinced that their country's economic problems could
not be solved without shifting from Soviet-type central planning
and direction to a form of market socialism, they recognised that the
latter would not be free to operate without substantial comp-
lementary changes in other spheres, including the politico–
administrative and intellectual spheres. If their initiatives had been
permitted to reach full fruition, the indications are that the
predominantly goal-rational structure of authority would have
given way to a largely rational–legal one.

Can the 'Prague Spring' be seen as prefiguring some future
'Moscow Spring' – one which no external policeman would be
available to arrest? Certainly the signs have not been propitious
over the last decade. On the other hand, within the conservative
institutional and ideological shell of the Brezhnev regime evol-
utionary change has not stopped, and the resultant balance of
options and pressures that will be presented to future decision-
makers is impossible to predict. Reference has already been made to
the possible influence of unorthodox ideas and values, and we must
remember that open dissent is not the only channel through which
attitudinal changes may enter and take root in Soviet society. Socio-
economic developments, particularly continuing urbanisation,
rising educational levels, and the spread of more sophisticated
technology, are of obvious relevance, although we should beware of
the ethnocentric error of simply *assuming* that a 'pluralist' society
with a market economy can provide the *only* environment capable of
absorbing and adapting to such developments.

No less important are possible developments in the specifically
political realm. The changes at the top leadership level described by
Brown hold some prospect for the further institutionalisation of
patterns of oligarchical rule conducive to more 'pluralistic' modes of

decision-making, habituation to which could enable leaders to contemplate with greater equanimity such changes in the economic order as appear to be essential to any substantial modification of the mono-organisational system. Nevertheless, we should not under-estimate the inertia of established socio-political systems or the natural caution of entrenched elites in agreeing to changes which might carry incalculable consequences for their power and privi-leges. For the decisive steps to be taken which alone will make possible the shift from a mono-organisational system to one marked, in Leonard Schapiro's words, by 'the supremacy of law, civil liberties, the dignity of the individual and the liberty of the human spirit, unrestrained except by its own conscience and the minimal limits of a true legal order', qualities which 'make up the true heritage of European civilization, of which both the United States and Russia can justly claim to be the heirs',[2] we must perhaps wait upon acts of outstanding intelligence, courage and imagination on the part of some future and, alas, difficult-to-discern Soviet leadership.

NOTES

1. Of course in 1917 the Bolsheviks anticipated that their revolution would spark off 'proletarian' revolutions in industrially more advanced countries and that the transition to socialism in Russia would form part of an international process in which the initiative was likely to pass to the 'proletariat' of Western Europe. However the system of power and authority created to serve the tasks of 'building socialism' conceived as an international process proved equally appropriate to the tasks of building 'socialism in one country'.

2. Leonard Schapiro, 'Some Afterthoughts on Solzhenitsyn', *Russian Review*, 33 (1974) p. 421.

Index